Oct. 12, 1995

Dear Mom,

Happy Birthday!

We love you.

Love,
Gary + Amy

THE BEST BOOK OF
TRIVIA

THE
BEST BOOK OF
TRIVIA

By V. Schei and Jack Griffin

GALLERY BOOKS
An Imprint of W. H. Smith Publishers Inc.
112 Madison Avenue
New York City 10016

Published by Gallery Books
A Division of W. H. Smith Publishers Inc.
112 Madison Avenue
New York, New York 10016

Printed in the U.S.A.

1   2   3   4   5   6   7   8   9

ISBN: 0-8317-4920-2

Contents

To Dal Romano, Al Calmiere,
Pat Wait, and Karen Moore

There are many things of which
a wise man might wish to be ignorant.
—Ralph Waldo Emerson

To Spit Largely:
Ambition

Madame de Pompadour's microscope sold at auction in 1976 for $74,000.

Several celebrities have had flags flown over the Capitol Dome in their name. Among them are Frank Sinatra and Boy George.

George Bush was the youngest navy pilot during World War II. He was 18.

Edgar Allan Poe attended West Point Military Academy, but only for a few months. As the error of his decision became clear to him, Poe arranged to be court-martialed, compiling a list of infractions complete enough so as not to tempt the court to be merciful. The secretary of war approved his discharge on February 8, 1831.

When he was 15, Al Capone joined a New York street gang called the Five Pointers.

At the age of 12, future president Jimmy Carter read *War and Peace*.

Around 1790 Joseph Bramah introduced his patent padlock and posted a bounty of 200 guineas to the first person to pick it. The prize went untouched for forty years, when an American locksmith succeeded in a sixteen-day assault on the lock.

In 1848 Gail Borden heard about the terrible tragedy that had befallen the Donner party. At the time, he was living in Galveston, Texas, a town he had helped lay out. Borden was upset by the story of the Donners, and when he learned that some of his friends were planning to leave for California, he set about inventing some kind of portable food. In 1849 he devised a meat biscuit.

The biscuit was a success, and in 1851 Borden went with some samples of his meat biscuit to London for that city's Great Exhibition (his biscuit won the Great Council Gold Medal). During the return voyage, the ship Borden was on encountered heavy seas, the two cows in the ship's hold became too seasick to be milked, and an immigrant infant died. The hungry cries of the other babies aboard the ship convinced Borden that he had to find a way to condense milk. He succeeded in doing so in 1853.

The Civil War brought tragedy to Borden's family: one of his sons fought for the Union, one fought for the Confederacy. The war also brought fame and fortune to Borden: his condensed milk was used by the Union Army as field rations. Borden went on to patent processes for concentrating fruit juices and other beverages. As he once remarked, "I mean to put a potato into a pillbox, a pumpkin into a tablespoon, the biggest sort of watermelon into a saucer . . .The Turks made acres of roses into attar of roses . . . I intend to make attar of everything."

TWELVE LABORS OF HERCULES
1. Killing Nemean lion (a beast no weapons could wound)
2. Killing Hydra (nine-headed snake)
3. Capturing hind of Artemis
4. Capturing Erymanthian boar
5. Cleansing Augean stables in a day
6. Killing man-eating Stymphalian birds
7. Capturing Cretan wild bull
8. Capturing man-eating mares of Diomedes
9. Procuring girdle of Amazon Hippolyta
10. Procuring the cattle of the monster Geryon
11. Stealing the Golden Apples from garden of Hesperides
12. Bringing Cerberus up from Hades

Winston Churchill, Adolf Hitler, and Dwight D. Eisenhower were all painters. To Hitler goes a singular honor: his works are the only ones that have been subsequently faked.

One of Ronald Reagan's favorite sayings is "There's nothing so good for the inside of a man as an outside of a horse."

American author John Dos Passos was awarded a US patent for one of his inventions. In 1959 he was granted a patent for a "toy pistol that blows soap bubbles."

Henry Stanley, famous for the understated greeting he delivered in darkest Africa ("Dr. Livingstone, I presume?"), served on both sides of the American Civil War. He enlisted in the Dixie Greys, a Confederate unit attached to the 6th Arkansas, and was captured during the Battle of Shiloh. To get out of prison, he volunteered to join the Union Army. He never saw any action in his blue uniform, however, for he came down with dysentery and was discharged.

Time magazine was originally going to be called *Facts*. (The first edition of *Time* appeared in March 1923.)

The first edition of the *Guinness Book of World Records* was only 198 pages long.

If the elder Pliny is to be believed, at least one Roman had so developed the art of fattening snails for the table that their shells attained to a capacity of several quarts.

Between 1875 and 1882, the notorious outlaw Black Bart preyed on Wells Fargo stages in California. Successfully eluding the best men Wells Fargo and the California authorities could find, Black Bart made off with the cash boxes from twenty-seven stages. Black Bart (whose real name was Charles E. Boles) occasionally left something in return for the cash he stole: doggerel verse. His most well-known short poem reads:

> I've labored long and hard for bread
> for honor and for riches
> but on my corns too long you've tred
> you fine-haired sons of bitches.

He signed this, "Black Bart, the Po-8."

Black Bart was eventually captured and sent to prison. After about four years behind bars, he was released. He promised he would leave Wells Fargo stages alone. A reporter asked him if he intended to write more poetry. "Young man," replied Black Bart, "didn't you just hear me say I will commit no more crimes?" He lived out the last years of his life in New York City, where he moved easily, unknown and unrecognized, along the crowded avenues. He died in 1917.

When John F. Kennedy graduated from high school, he was ranked sixty-fourth out of a class of 112 students. Even so, his classmates voted him "the most likely to succeed."

John F. Kennedy's first book was *Why England Slept*. He donated all the money he made from the sale of the book in Great Britain to the city of Plymouth, which had been destroyed by German bombs. He used the royalties he earned from the sale of the book in the United States to buy his first car, a Buick.

Willie Sutton was perhaps America's most dedicated bankrobber. ("He worked so hard," his wife once said.) When police searched his residence in 1930, they found thirty-five assorted driver's licenses, about the same number of automobile license plates, a box of made-up employment references, catalogs of architectural floor plans, union cards, seaman's identification, gas masks, weapons, and three thousand rounds of ammunition.

Stephen Crane published his first book, *Maggie: A Girl of the Streets* (1893), under the pseudonym Johnston Smith, a name he made up from what were at that time the two most common names in the New York City phone book.

Thomas Gainsborough (1727–88), painter of the *Blue Boy,* had it in his mind to contradict Sir Joshua Reynolds, who had maintained that blues could not be concentrated in a painting.

Warren Harding was the first president to know how to drive an automobile.

Good guys and people pretending to be good guys have been wearing white for centuries. Roman politicians wore spotless white togas when they went around campaigning. The Latin word for a person wearing such a white garment is *candidatus;* we now call politicians on the stump *candidates.*

The first breath an infant takes really is the most difficult of a lifetime. Because a newborn's lungs are collapsed and surfaced with viscous fluids, the initial breath must be twice as forceful as the second and about four times as powerful as normal breathing.

In 1776, 95 percent of the population of the American colonies was involved in farming, producing the necessities of life both for themselves and for the nonfarming city dwellers; today, only 2 percent of the population of the United States is involved in farm work.

When he was 7, Heinrich Schliemann received from his father a very special Christmas present, an illustrated book in which there was a picture of the ancient city of Troy engulfed in flames. Enthralled by the picture, Schliemann became obsessed with the desire to find the remains of Troy. He accumulated a fortune in business and, at the age of 41, retired to devote himself to his dream. In 1871 he went to Hissarlik, in Asian Turkey, and began digging. He dug his way through nine successive cities and villages that had occupied the site. And he found Troy. He believed it was the last city, but it is more probable that the seventh city was the one that Homer made famous.

A six-week political convention of 1573 ushered in the modern age of electoral machination and media manipulation. The occasion was the election, by the entire assembled Polish nobility, some 38,000 strong, of a new king. (Sigismund II, last of the Jagiello dynasty, had just died.)

Candidates were backed by the individual resources of Denmark, Sweden, Prussia, France, Russia, the Pope, and innumerable smaller factions, each plumping for their man. But the French had the good fortune to be represented by a man of political genius, Montluc, Bishop of Valence.

A veteran diplomat, Montluc served Charles IX and his ambitious wife, Catherine de Medici, who was anxious to put their son Henry, Duke of Anjou, on the Polish throne.

It would be hard to fault Montluc's campaign, even by modern standards: he first defused the issue of the St. Bartholomew's Day Massacre (which his employer, Charles, had thoughtlessly ordered up eight months previously), letting slip a flurry of plausible, sometimes contradictory, explanations which permanently confused the issue and minimized political liability.

And he did what he could to spruce up the duke's image—the duke was known to all of Europe as a profligate and no-account prince. Next, he distributed money in adversary camps to gain key intelligence, at the same time cannily thwarting infiltration of his own staff. But his coup, his most enlightened tactic, was to have 1500 copies secretly *printed* of his client's election appeal. All the other parties had turned out, laboriously handwritten, only thirty-two manuscript copies each of their own statements.

No wonder then that the name of Anjou was on all lips. The duke was elected but had never really wanted a kingdom so far away from Paris and left it a year later to become Henry III of France.

Some credit Montluc also with political dirty tricks: a huge assembly tent fell during the Swedish ambassador's oration but, as with all the best dirty tricks, Montluc cannot be directly implicated in the collapse of Swedish dignity.

Al Jennings was one of the Old West's most inept outlaws. Although he sincerely yearned to be a notorious desperado, he just didn't have the requisite wherewithal. He attempted to begin his life of crime in 1885. Determined to stop—and rob—a train, he piled logs across the tracks and set himself up nearby in ambush. Poor Jennings was dismayed when the train didn't even slow down—it just smashed right through his barricade.

He next tried to stop a train by riding alongside it, blasting away with his Colt. The engineer misunderstood the would-be outlaw's antics and cheerily waved back at him. When Jennings finally managed to stop a train, he overestimated the amount of dynamite needed to open the safe and blew up the entire train car. At this point, Jennings became a moderately wanted man, and the famous lawman William ("Uncle Billy") Tilghman set out to arrest him. Before saddling up, Tilghman bet a friend he could capture Jennings without unholstering his revolver. Tilghman won the bet, and Jennings spent a few years in jail.

By the time he got out, those seeking western fame had been provided with a less perilous route: motion pictures had come into existence. Both Jennings and Tilghman recognized the financial potential of films, and the two men—outlaw and marshal—got together in 1908 in a small town in Oklahoma to make a film, which they called *The Bank Robbery*. Tilghman handled the camera; Jennings eagerly took the role of the bank robber. The novice filmmakers failed to give the locals advance notice, and there were a few awkward moments when the townspeople opened fire on the masked man trying to rob their bank.

Tilghman did not go on to become a famous movie director, although he did make another film, *The Passing of the Oklahoma Outlaws,* in 1915. Known for his honesty and courage, he continued to face actual bad men—including the Doolin gang—until late in life. As he explained to his friend Theodore Roosevelt, he owed his survival to being just "one-sixteenth of a second faster on the draw" than the men he faced. In 1924, at the age of 71, Tilghman was still a marshal in Oklahoma, but he was slowing down. He was shot dead one night that year by a drunken, trigger-happy bootlegger.

Al Jennings enjoyed a long life, and he spent most of it bragging about his outlaw career. He wrote an autobiography, *Beating Back,* and he hung around movie lots, sometimes being asked to serve as "technical adviser" on westerns. (Jennings performed this service for *The*

Oklahoma Kid, a 1939 western that is notable because it stars James Cagney and Humphrey Bogart.) Jennings, too, had famous friends, including William Sydney Porter. He had met Porter while the two were in prison. Porter, who was behind bars for embezzlement of bank funds, later took the name of one of the prison guards, Orrin Henry, and became famous as O. Henry. Jennings and O. Henry frequently got together for drinking sprees. Following one such outing—a night-long New Year's celebration in New York City—a very hung over O. Henry drew a humorous sketch of Jennings taking a temperance vow. Jennings died in 1962, aged 98.

Michelangelo once faked a classical Roman piece, a sleeping Cupid, and at his patron's prompting, sold it through an eager, if unscrupulous, dealer to a cardinal in Rome. The sculptor had been unwilling to chip away at the nose and other protuberances in the time-honored way of forgers of antiquities, and the pristine condition of the statue attracted suspicion. Neither could Michelangelo, when questioned, bring himself to deny authorship—it was after all a stylistic triumph.

The cardinal got most of his ducats back but sought the friendship of this virtuoso chiseler.

So liberal were the terms given in Washington to well-connected railroads and land speculation companies that very little of the best land west of the Mississippi was ever available for purchase by "sweat equity." Homesteaders, taking advantage of the Homesteading Act (1862), acquired less than 3 percent of western lands. Most pioneers and early settlers paid cash or took out mortgages for their plots.

Benjamin Thompson (1753–1814), Count Rumford, was a unique American. One-time prime minister of Bavaria, member of Britain's Royal Society, high-level spy for France, Britain, and Bavaria, Massachusetts-born Thompson revolutionized the science of artillery and invented the drip coffeepot.

He was to have been the first commandant of West Point, too, but embarrassing disclosures of his secret activities for the British during the Revolution caused the plan to be discreetly scrapped.

The first major engagement of the Civil War, First Bull Run (or First Manassas), ended in disaster for the Union: the headlong retreat of the Union troops became a rout and was matched only by that of the panicked civilians who had turned out in their Sunday finery to enjoy a picnic while witnessing the set-to. The nation became aware of the seriousness of the conflict, and President Lincoln began casting about for some sort of dramatic action that might help end the war. For that reason, Lincoln gave his consent to the men proposing one such move: enlisting the aid of Italian patriot Giuseppe Garibaldi.

Among those most enthusiastic about obtaining the services of Garibaldi was Lincoln's secretary of state, William Henry Seward (who had earlier proposed declaring war on most of Europe so as to unite the nation). Garibaldi was not such a strange choice: he was the world's most famous guerrilla fighter and was a symbol of national unification. He was known as the liberator of the enslaved and the oppressed. (He had also been born on July 4 and had spent time in the United States.) Through consuls in Europe, Garibaldi was offered a command in the Union Army.

Garibaldi, who at that time was in temporary retirement on the island of Caprera, north of Sardinia, was interested in the plan, but he made a few stipulations: he wanted to be commander-in-chief of the Union forces, and he wanted the power to abolish slavery. Garibaldi made it clear that he would fight for the Union only if the war was a war to free the slaves (some of his associates in Italy told him that the war was really being fought for economic reasons). The US consuls explained to Garibaldi that only the president could be the commander-in-chief and that the abolition of slavery was a touchy matter. They offered Garibaldi instead the rank of major general and an independent command. Victor Emmanuel (proclaimed king of Italy in 1861) gave Garibaldi permission to go to America, but Garibaldi never went. The issue of slavery was too important to him, and by the time Lincoln finally abolished slavery, in 1863, Garibaldi was involved in other affairs. The Civil War was fought without Garibaldi's aid, but he did not forget the matter entirely: he named one of his grandsons Lincoln.

If it is true that music "soothes the savage breast," it is also true that it may have an opposite effect. Wagner's *Lohengrin* made a deep impression on young listeners Adolf Hitler, aged 12, and Ludwig II of Bavaria, aged 15. Both found in the music an inspiration to megalomanic ambition, Hitler for the bloody domination of Europe and Ludwig for the squandering of Bavaria's wealth in constructing a string of fairyland castles.

The longest absence from the planet is a record currently held by three Soviet cosmonauts. They left orbit and returned to Earth on October 2, 1984, after 237 days in space.

Or esorjie de or narsichisle sin chismar lachinguel. "The utmost of the dwarf is to spit largely."

—Gypsy proverb

Elephants Jumping:
Animals and Plants

In a genuine flea circus only females are used; males are too small and relatively weaker. The tugging, tossing, and dancing routines of "trained" fleas are merely a result of restraining these natural jumpers with invisibly fine gold wires. Level of activity is controlled by temperature.

The more robust human flea, an increasingly rare species, is preferred over dog or cat fleas. Thus the ringmaster provides the flea meals, sometimes twice a day.

The cheetah's rate of acceleration is formidable: it can go from a standing start to 45 miles per hour in two seconds.

The humps that give camels their distinctive outline are composed for the most part of fat. The camel accumulates this fat when both food and water are available; during long treks across desert wastes, the animal can draw on this fat, the hydrogen molecules of which combine with inhaled oxygen to form water. Thanks to their humps, camels can go without water for as long as eight days during the summer and eight weeks during the winter.

Giraffes cannot swim at all.

State Birds and Flowers

State	State Bird	State Flower
Alabama	Yellowhammer	Camelia
Alaska	Willow ptarmigan	Forget-me-not
Arizona	Cactus wren	Saguaro
Arkansas	Mockingbird	Apple blossom
California	California valley quail	Golden poppy
Colorado	Lark bunting	Rocky Mountain columbine
Connecticut	Robin	Mountain laurel
Delaware	Blue hen chicken	Peach blossom
Florida	Mockingbird	Orange blossom
Georgia	Brown thrasher	Cherokee rose
Hawaii	Hawaiian goose	Hibiscus
Idaho	Mountain bluebird	Syringa
Illinois	Cardinal	Native violet
Indiana	Cardinal	Peony
Iowa	Eastern goldfinch	Wild rose

Kansas	Western meadow lark	Sunflower
Kentucky	Kentucky cardinal	Goldenrod
Louisiana	Brown pelican	Magnolia
Maine	Chickadee	White pine cone and tassel
Maryland	Baltimore oriole	Black-eyed Susan
Massachusetts	Chickadee	Mayflower
Michigan	Robin	Apple blossom
Minnesota	Common loon	Pink and white lady's-slipper
Mississippi	Mockingbird	Magnolia
Missouri	Bluebird	Hawthorn
Montana	Western meadow lark	Bitterroot
Nebraska	Western meadow lark	Goldenrod
Nevada	Mountain bluebird	Sagebrush
New Hampshire	Purple finch	Purple lilac
New Jersey	Eastern goldfinch	Purple violet
New Mexico	Roadrunner	Yucca
New York	Bluebird	Rose
North Carolina	Cardinal	Flowering dogwood
North Dakota	Western meadow lark	Wild prairie rose
Ohio	Cardinal	Scarlet carnation
Oklahoma	Scissor-tailed flycatcher	Mistletoe
Oregon	Western meadow lark	Oregon grape
Pennsylvania	Ruffed grouse	Mountain laurel
Rhode Island	Rhode Island Red	Violet
South Carolina	Carolina wren	Carolina jessamine
South Dakota	Ring-necked pheasant	Pasqueflower
Tennessee	Mockingbird	Iris
Texas	Mockingbird	Bluebonnet
Utah	Sea gull	Sego lily
Vermont	Hermit thrush	Red clover
Virginia	Cardinal	Flowering dogwood
Washington	Willow goldfinch	Coast rhododendron
West Virginia	Cardinal	Rhododendron
Wisconsin	Robin	Wood violet
Wyoming	Meadow lark	Indian paintbrush

Bats are the only mammals that fly.

Elephants walk at a pace of about four miles per hour; they can charge at speeds up to 25 miles per hour.

As far as is known, only one oceangoing insect exists, a water strider of the genus *Halobates*. It lays eggs on drifting seaweed or on the backs of snails.

There is no single most poisonous snake. The effects of snake venom greatly depend on the method of injection, whether into the bloodstream, into muscle, or just under the skin, and different species of victim react differently.

Toxicity tests against several species and with a range of injection routes do show that sea snakes as a group are deadliest for the amount of venom administered. The most potent, perhaps, is the beaked sea snake, *Enhydrina schistosa*.

Almost as deadly, among land snakes, is the African boomslang, *Dispholidus typus,* but honorable mention must be given to the cascabels of South America, *Crotalus durissus horridus* and *terrificus*. Bites from these last two are somewhat toxicologically bizarre and required development of new types of antivenin. The taipan of Australia and kraits of Asia round out the list.

No doubt cobras cause more human deaths each year than any other variety, but this is due to their numbers and wide distribution as well as to their highly effective toxin.

Bamboo has reliably recorded growths of up to four feet in a twenty-four-hour period.

Because it has only been seen four times the golden carpet is thought to be the rarest plant in North America. Found only in Death Valley, it requires an inundation to blossom, a very rare event in the California desert.

ANIMALS: LONGEVITY AND SPECIALIZED NAMES

	Avg. Life span (years)	Male	Female	Young	Group
Antelope	10	buck	doe	fawn	herd
Bear	15–50	boar	sow	cub	sleuth
Cat	15	tom	queen	kitten	cluster
Cattle	20	bull	cow	calf	herd
Deer	10–20	buck, hart, stag	doe, hind	fawn	herd
Dog	12–15	dog	bitch	puppy	kennel
Donkey	20	jack	jenny	foal	herd
Duck	10	drake	duck	duckling	team
Elephant	60	bull	cow	calf	herd
Fox	10	dog-fox	vixen	cub	skulk
Giraffe	10–25	bull	cow	calf	herd
Goat	10	billy-goat	nanny-goat	kid	herd
Goose	25	gander	goose	gosling	skein, gaggle
Hippopotamus	30–40	bull	cow	calf	herd
Horse	20–30	stallion	mare	foal	herd
Kangaroo	10–20	buck	doe	joey	mob
Lion	25	lion	lioness	cub	pride
Ostrich	50	cock	hen	chick	flock
Pig	10–15	boar	sow	piglet	drove
Rabbit	5–8	buck	doe	kit	warren
Rhinoceros	25–50	bull	cow	calf	crash
Sheep	10–15	ram	ewe	lamb	flock
Tiger	10–25	tiger	tigress	cub	
Whale	20	bull	cow	calf	school, pod
Zebra	20–25	stallion	mare	foal	herd

There are earthworms in Australia that measure two yards in length when contracted and as much as ten feet when extended.

A *bête noire* ("black beast") was originally—in the elaborate French hunting codes of the fourteenth century—a boar, sow, wolf, fox, or otter. These troublesome animals might be hunted by common folk but not the nobler *bêtes rouges* ("red beasts"), most of which were varieties of deer. Hunting them was reserved to aristocrats.

Though *bug* is not correctly used to mean any insect indiscriminately, it is correct when referring to a member of the order *Hemiptera*—also called "true bugs."

The cheetah is the most easily tamed of the big cats.

During his travels in China, Marco Polo heard stories about the island of Madagascar. According to the traders and travelers he met, the island was the home of a giant bird, a bird so large and powerful that its favorite food was elephant. The bird would grab an elephant with its talons, lift it high in the air, and then drop it, killing it. This monster bird also appears in the mythology of medieval Arabs, where it is called the roc, or rukh. The bird is mentioned in *The Thousand and One Nights,* particularly in the stories of Sindbad the Sailor.

The fabulous roc of the *Arabian Nights,* the bird Polo heard about, was probably the so-called elephant bird, an extinct species once native to Madagascar. These monster birds may have survived until as late as 1649. Today, they are known only from bone fragments and a few eggs.

The birds stood more than ten feet high and weighed 1000 pounds. Their eggs, the largest single cells in the animal kingdom, measured up to 13 inches and held about two gallons of liquid. It is unlikely that these birds dined on elephants, and if they did, they must have killed the elephants in some unimagined way, for like their relatives—the rheas, ostriches, kiwis, and moas—the elephant birds were absolutely flightless.

Bacteria may hit speeds up to 30 miles per hour moving short distances in their fluid milieu.

Turkeys are good fliers. They do not, however, migrate.

Giraffes have been known to kill lions with a kick.

St. Bernards employed in traditional rescue work never carried a cask of brandy around the neck. This image is owed to the imagination of Sir Edwin Landser, who painted the accessory into his *Alpine Mastiffs Reanimating a Traveller* (1820).

Guano is the excrement of seafowl. Over the centuries it has been used as both a potent fertilizer and as a source of explosives (it contains nitrogen, phosphate, and potash). The ancient Incas executed anyone who dared to disturb their guano-producing birds; at one time guano exports made up 80 percent of the gross national product of Peru.

Guano created something of an agricultural revolution during the early nineteenth century. It was such a success that President Millard Fillmore demanded that Congress "employ all the means properly in its power" to assure the importation of guano. In 1856 Congress complied, passing the Guano Act, which gave the United States claim to any guano islands discovered by Americans. Today, guano is again popular, particularly among those people who grow marijuana. Some of the guano used today comes from the excrement of bats.

All the evidence points to the fact that mitochondria, the energy-producing organelles in human and other animal cells, were at first an independent life form. Their DNA is not animallike, their membranes are peculiar, and a cell cannot manufacture one: they reproduce independently. Evidently, they moved in with animals very early in the evolutionary process and, in consequence, higher life forms cannot exist without them.

Cats have six major blood groups, A–F; dogs have five, A–E; and humans four, A, B, AB, and O.

Only the labels are similar: transfusions among the species are emphatically ruled out.

The neck of a giraffe has only seven vertebrae, the usual number in mammals—even man. Those in a giraffe are elongated, of course.

Body lice much prefer to reside in clothing, sallying forth at mealtimes. Among essentially nude populations of Africa the louse, with little other choice, will infest strands of glass beads.

The elephant is the only animal with four knees.

Earthworms live from five to ten years.

Spider farms have been a subject of newspaper hoaxing ever since the 1890s, when the Philadelphia *Press* first ran the story of a Pennsylvania farmer allegedly supplying webs to prettify the cellars of wine merchants.

Reporters missed the real story, which is the expensive trade in spider silk in the optics industry. Quality crosshairs for gunsights and surveying instruments have for several centuries been made from lengths of spider silk, obtained in small reels from, yes, spider farmers.

Pigeons have responded to the sound of C eleven octaves below middle C, a tone detected by no other species. Because such sounds have great range, zoologists theorize that some birds may navigate from a thousand miles away or more by the sounds of ocean surf.

The jackrabbit is not a rabbit: it's a hare.

Calculation shows that a 130-ton (90-foot) blue whale must develop at least 520 horsepower to move itself in the water.

The heart of a giraffe weighs 25 pounds.

The ginkgo, or maidenhair, tree is a "living fossil"; there were gingko trees during the Triassic period—while there were dinosaurs roaming around. The gingko tree is indeed a hardy survivor, and for that reason it is valued today both in Europe and the United States for use along urban streets and avenues. The gingko is able to survive the smoke, pollution, and low temperatures of the big cities.

Catgut, used in the centuries before nylon to string lutes, guitars, vihuelas, and such, is made from sheep intestine. The need for this subterfuge has not been explained.

Even when they are deep in the deepest ocean depths, in the dark abysses never reached by even the faintest sunlight, most fish swim right-side up. They know they're right-side up because they have small organs of equilibrium called statocysts. The inner cavities of statocysts are lined with delicate hairs and usually contain a few loose objects like grains of sand.

There were no English, or house, sparrows in the United States until Thomas Woodcock, president of the Brooklyn Natural History Society, decided to introduce them. Sometime around 1847 he let loose several pairs. None of them survived, so he tried again in 1852. This time he was successful: the birds thrived. We call the little birds English sparrows only because that is where Woodcock got his samples: the birds are not native to England and are actually close relatives of the African weaverbird.

All polar bears are left-handed.

Cockroaches can move at speeds up to 29 centimeters per second (nearly 14.5 miles per hour), but they have no endurance. And though they seem very quick, they are not in the same class with a truly fast insect, the centipede; some species attain 50 centimeters per second (about 24 miles per hour).

Electric eels in the eighteenth century were called cramp-fish or torpedoes.

The mythological Greek Hydra, a nine-headed serpent, probably originates in the not infrequent observation of genuine two-headed snakes. In such specimens, seen in captivity, the two heads may compete for food, attack and even attempt to swallow one another.

Grizzly bears are not grisly—according to their name, they're gray. Although they're usually a brownish yellow, their name comes from *gris* ("gray").

The common urban cockroach, native to Europe but thriving inhabitant of the northeastern United States, is known as the German cockroach *(Blattella germanica)*. That is what it is known as everywhere but in Germany. In its homeland, it is called by several names, according to locale: in the north, it is called the Swabian roach; in the south, it is the Prussian roach; in the east, it is the Russian roach; and in the west, it is the French roach.

Until recently it was thought koalas had a common and fragile diet, eating in seasonal rotation up to six varieties of eucalyptus leaf, seeking always the variety least toxic in each season. Improbable and untrue.

The koala, research has discovered, is able to digest eucalyptus—as almost no other animal is able to do—but lives in constant danger, in its arid Australian habitat, of finding insufficient water in these leaves. (Koalas do not drink: their name, in fact, comes from an aborigine word meaning "no drink.") Though appearing well nourished, the koala may die of dehydration but not from selecting the wrong eucalyptus.

Thanks to its long neck, the giraffe is the tallest of living quadrupeds (some male giraffes are eighteen feet tall, from hoof to crown). The giraffe's Latin name is *Giraffa camelopardalis,* and, in fact, giraffes were once called camelopards—"camel leopards." The name refers to the fact that the animal's head looks like that of a camel, and it has spots like those on a leopard.

Praying mantises ignore anything that doesn't move.

The camel originated in North America. One group of these North American animals migrated to Asia, becoming the single-humped Arabian camel, or dromedary, used in Arabia and North Africa; another went to South America, becoming the guanaco, alpaca, llama, and vicuna. Both groups became extinct in North America after a glacial period.

Turkeys don't come from Turkey; they're native to North America. European visitors to the New World confused the native wild fowl with a bird with which they were familiar, the guinea fowl. The Europeans believed the guinea fowl came from Turkey—it didn't, of course, it came from Guinea, West Africa, but it was imported to Europe by way of Turkey. In the midst of all this confusion, the American bird got stuck with the erroneous provenance of the European bird. (There are those who contend that the bird's name is nothing more than an imitation of its "turk-turk" call.)

Quite understandably—given their pillarlike legs and their massive bodies—elephants cannot jump. They therefore cannot pass barriers too wide or too high to step over.

Decimals Forever: Anxiety

Ostriches do not bury their heads in the ground. They do, however, sometimes lower their heads to the ground—to rest their long necks.

The American bombers of World War II, among them the B–17, B–24, B–25, and B–29, are well known, but one plane, the B–2, has been forgotten. The B–2 never flew; it existed only in the standard GI phrase for unidentified approaching aircraft: "Be too bad if they're not friendly."

When Hitler assumed power in Germany in 1933, he set about ridding his Reich of "dangerous" foreigners, including Mickey Mouse. In 1936 the Soviet Union, too, banned Mickey Mouse. Not to be outdone, Mussolini banned Mickey Mouse from Italy in 1938. In 1954 Mickey Mouse was banned in East Germany. The irrepressible rodent was evidently displaying anti-Communist behavior.

Little boys were dressed in blue long before little girls were dressed in pink. In ancient times, male babies were dressed in blue because blue was believed to ward off evil spirits; girls got whatever was handy. Only much later were little girls given a color of their own.

O. Henry's last words were "Turn up the lights. I don't want to go home in the dark."

Elizabeth Barrett Browning's tombstone reads, "Be not afraid; it is I."

Elephants are not at all afraid of mice but do exhibit fear, it has been observed, in the presence of rabbits and dachshunds.

While he was president, Franklin Roosevelt always slept with a gun under his pillow.

During the war in Vietnam, the Pentagon asked an American playing card manufacturer to ship 3 million aces of spades to the US troops in Vietnam. The GIs had discovered that the Vietcong had a morbid fear of the ace of spades (it is considered a "death card" by several cultures). The Vietcong tended to avoid tanks, buildings, and anything else adorned with the card.

At the time coffee was introduced into England—about the mid-seventeenth century—it was widely believed to cause sterility and congenital deformity.

Among the *caboclos,* peasants of Brazil, there is a frightening beast of legend, the *curupira*. One who spots the tracks of this monster and flees will only come to grief, since the curupira's feet are put on backward to deceive its quarry.

Istanbul's Topkapi Museum (former palace of the Turkish sultans) contains a vast collection of unbroken celadon—Chinese porcelain of a celebrated light green hue. The pristine condition of the china is highly unusual, but at the Turkish court dropping a royal dish was punished by death.

Celadon was generally popular among potentates as it was reported to neutralize poisoned food served in it.

Whenever the president of the United States takes an airplane trip over ocean waters, rescue vessels are stationed at intervals of 250 miles all along the route.

The first cooking stove was installed in the White House in 1850, during the term of Millard Fillmore. The cooks took one look at the contraption and quit (they were used to cooking the presidential meals in the fireplace). The stove was a novelty to everyone: an expert in the use of the newfangled device had to come from the Patent Office and explain its use to the exasperated cooks.

Plato supposedly rewrote the first sentence of *The Republic* fifty times.

Among the anachronistic offices of Great Britain is that of Raven Master at the Tower of London. It is his job to clip the wings of the Tower's raven population every three months, lest they fly away—and bring an ancient doom upon the kingdom.

"America is a mistake; a gigantic mistake, it is true, but none the less a mistake."

—Sigmund Freud

When Albert Einstein left Germany in 1933 the Nazis put a price of 20,000 marks on his head.

As Jean Auguste Ingres led his students through the Louvre he would bid them close their eyes when passing by any work of his archrival, Eugène Delacroix.

Though faith in an afterlife has declined among Americans generally to the 25–30 percent level, about 80 percent of those dying profess a belief in it.

The collected tales of the brothers Grimm when first published in 1812 were banned in Vienna as a work of superstition.

J. Edgar Hoover would not allow anyone to walk on his shadow.

". . . write me what your way is of hiring a new servant. Do you send to the police? or how else?"
—Ludwig von Beethoven

The British have now put into use a decimal coinage, but the idea had long been debated. From a humorous speech of Robert Lowe in Commons, 1855:

"If the proposed system were adopted, they would all be compelled to live in decimals forever; if a man dined at a public house he would have to pay for his dinner in decimal fractions. He objected to that, for he thought that a man ought to be able to pay for his dinner in integers."

In a more serious vein, such math must have been especially frightening to the House, of whom it was alleged at the time that, factually, only four members had a tolerable understanding of fractions.

Strains of the Jumping Flea: Art and Music

Apropos of their first meeting (in Rome, 1915) Igor Stravinsky returned to Switzerland with a sketch of himself by Pablo Picasso. At the border, Swiss authorities impounded the drawing as a probable war map.

The most famous picture of George Washington crossing the Delaware is by Emanuel Leutze. Leutze painted the picture in Düsseldorf, Germany. He wanted Washington's soldiers to look American, so he habitually grabbed American tourists who happened by his studio and made them pose. For the head of Washington, he copied the bust by the Frenchman Jean Antoine Houdon. The river he used as a model for the Delaware was the Rhine.

Samuel F. B. Morse supported himself in his true profession—portrait painting—while working on his inventions.

The tromba marina (sea horn) is not a horn but a single, long, resonating string played only in its harmonics. Medieval nuns used it—they were forbidden to play horns—to fill in brass parts.

OPERAS AND THEIR COMPOSERS

Georges Bizet
Carmen

Gaetano Donizetti
Lucia di Lammermoor

Charles Gounod
Faust

Ruggiero Leoncavallo
Pagliacci

Jules Massenet
Manon

Wolfgang Amadeus Mozart
Don Giovanni
The Marriage of Figaro
The Magic Flute

Modest Mussorgsky
Boris Godunov

Jacques Offenbach
The Tales of Hoffman

Giacomo Puccini
La Boheme
Madame Butterfly
Tosca

Gioacchino Rossini
The Barber of Seville

Richard Strauss
Der Rosenkavalier
Salome

Giuseppe Verdi
Aïda
Un Ballo in Maschera
Otello
Rigoletto
La Traviata
Il Travatore

Richard Wagner
Lohengrin
Die Meistersinger von Nürnberg
Parsifal
The Ring of the Nibelung
  Das Rheingold (The Rinegold)
  Die Walküre (The Valkyrie)
  Siegfried
  Die Götterdämmerung (Twilight of the Gods)
Tannhäuser
Tristan und Isolde

Tail fins, the exuberant hallmark of 1950 American automobiles, were inspired by the twin vertical stabilizers of the P–38 fighter plane. Harley Earl, a General Motors designer, first incorporated his new concept in the 1948 Cadillac.

In Chinese painting there is only one manifesto, and it was set down fifteen centuries ago by Hsieh Ho. It consists of six guiding principles that have unified Chinese artists and their work ever since.

The six canons are: (1) imbue the work with life and spirit; (2) handle the brush with vigor, give inner strength to each line; (3) be truthful in depicting objects; (4) use color as it appears in nature; (5) attend to harmony in composition, arrangement of the picture; and (6) endlessly copy and transcribe masters of the past.

Verdi wrote his *Requiem* (1874) in honor of the death of novelist Alessandro Manzoni.

The Comma of Pythagoras is not a punctuation mark but the excruciating margin by which the last note in a scale is mistuned when each note in the progression has been derived by tuning a perfect fifth above its predecessor. Even the ratio of the resultant tone to its theoretical value is an ugly one: its simplest form is 531441/524288. By practical musicians this sound was called the "wolf."

If a similar curdling disagreement is produced by tuning through the notes in an octave by a progression of major thirds the result is the Comma of Didymus or Ptolemy, by either name just as sour, but the error is slightly less, 81/80 out of tune.

Because it is not possible, mathematically, to tune by any true interval and still arrive at true octaves, the history of tunings, or "temperaments," is a history of compromises. J. S. Bach's *Well-Tempered Clavier,* with pieces written in every major and minor key, was a brilliant argument for spreading the tonal discrepancies evenly around the scale; no wolf-producing notes would have to be avoided.

The "cattle call" that made country singer Eddie Arnold famous did not work as spectacularly for earlier composers. A melody played on the seven-foot alphorn, whose range is restricted to no more than six notes even for barrel-chested virtuosi, is called a "ranz de vache," or cattle song.

Rossini, Wagner, Schumann, Strauss, and even Beethoven (opening of last movement of his Sixth Symphony) were struck by these simple melodies and used them, but they lie buried in larger works.

Musical themes can be looked up just like words, alphabetically. A large sourcebook might start with A A A A A A A A (from Stravinsky's *Petrouchka*) and A A A A A A A G (from Ivanovici's *Danube Waves*), running through 10,000 or more permutations of the musical notes A through G.

The last entry, the musical equivalent of *zyzzogeton,* is G♯ F♯ E D C C, from a Debussy prelude.

In using such a compendium there is one technical wrangle, i.e., all themes must be transcribed into the key of C before looking them up. Thus, one of the world's most repetitious motifs, a string of fifteen E♭'s in Beethoven's Sonata No. 12 (key of A♭), appears in a dictionary as fifteen Gs (key of C).

But even musicians are seldom able to hum themes from avant-garde pieces, and you won't find many in the dictionary.

Renoir employed himself from the age of 13 to 21 first in painting porcelain and later window blinds.

The method once used to begin work on a Renaissance fresco is nearly identical to that used in preparing a modern billboard.

In fresco, a full-size drawing, called the cartoon, was perforated along its lines, held against fresh plaster, and dusted with charcoal or another powder. The line drawing thus transferred to a wall was used as a guide for painting. Billboards are generally prepared by tamping a chalk or charcoal bag over the wheel-cut perforations of a large stencil.

Controversy surrounds the *Madonna of the Rocks* by Leonardo da Vinci. Any reference to the work must mention the city in which it hangs, London or Paris. There are two, stylistically identical.

One hangs in the Louvre, the other in Britain's National Gallery. Art historians and connoisseurs dismiss neither painting, as both are masterful. Attribution to Leonardo seems probable for either or both, so that neither group of partisans desists in referring to the works by only one title.

Fra Lippo Lippi (1406–69) admitted to charges of cheating his apprentice of payment, but only after torture had been applied. The parsimonious painter, haggling with a Medici patron, once claimed, "God has left me with six nieces to find husbands for, all sickly and useless."

The Bayeux Tapestry, 230 feet long, 20 inches wide, and reputedly worked on by Mathilde, wife of William the Conqueror, is no tapestry but an embroidery.

A "consort" is a Renaissance musical group consisting of one type or family of instrument, e.g., all recorders, all viols, etc. When an unrelated instrument joins, the result is a "broken consort."

Georges Seurat (1859–91) never referred to his technique as pointillism—a term coined by critics—but as luminism.

Chinese aristocrats made a pastime of drawing up lists of the greatest painters in order of greatness and comparing them with those of other Chinese aristocrats. Here is a ranked listing of the most eminent composers, all-time, as elicited from the participants at a 1964 American musicological congress. You are invited to disagree.

1. Bach, J. S.	34. Gluck	67. Landini
2. Beethoven	35. Puccini	68. MacDowell
3. Mozart	36. Franck	69. Bach, J. C.
4. Haydn, F. J.	37. Dvorak	70. Leoninus
5. Brahms	38. Buxtehude	71. Gabrieli, A.
6. Handel	39. Bruckner	72.5. Carissimi
7. Debussy	40. Sibelius	72.5. Pergolesi
8. Schubert	41. Rameau	74. Marenzio
9. Wagner	42. Frescobaldi	75. Smetana
10. Chopin	43. Ockeghem	77. Praetorius
11. Monteverdi	44. Stravinsky	77. Borodin
12. Palestrina	45. Scarlatti, A.	77. Gounod
13. Verdi	46. Dunstable	79. Haydn, J. M.
14. Schumann	47. Bizet	80.5. Sousa
15. Des Prez	48. Gesualdo	80.5. Sullivan
16. di Lasso	49. Rossini	82.5. Bellini
17.5. Purcell	50.5. da Vittoria	82.5. Janacek
17.5. Berlioz	50.5. Fauré	85. Donizetti
19. Strauss, R.	52. Dowland	85. Webern
20. Mendelssohn	53. Bach, K. P. E.	85. Willaert
21. Tchaikovsky	54. Rimsky-Korsakov	87. Offenbach
22. Vivaldi	55. Perotinus	88.5. Ravel
23. Mahler	56. Wolf	88.5. Delius
24. Byrd	57. Bartok	91. Elgar
25. Dufay	58. Grieg	91. Hindemith
26. Machaut	59. von Weber	91. Satie
27. Schutz	60. Gibbons	93.5. Cherubini
28. Liszt	61. Sweelinck	93.5. Foster
29. Mussorgsky	62. Schönberg	95. de Rore
30. Corelli	63. Strauss, J., Jr.	96.5. Boccherini
31. Scarlatti, G. D.	64. Saint-Saens	98.5. Franco of
32. Gabrieli, G.	65.5. Telemann	Cologne
33. Couperin	65.5. Lully	98.5. Clementi
		98.5. Tartini

Casting around for someone to do some painting in St. Peters, Pope Benedict IX asked for designs and examples from many artists. Vasari, biographer of Renaissance artists, claims that Giotto drew an exact circle with one motion of his brush and sent only this to the Pope, who "instantly perceived that Giotto surpassed all other painters of his time."

A great mural, *Aviation,* by Arshile Gorky, lay under successively applied coats of wallpaint at the Newark, New Jersey, airport until restoration began in the late 1970s. The work, commissioned in the WPA era, was for years listed in art texts as lost.

Our humble 4/4 time (four beats to the bar) was in the medieval musical scheme of things known as the "imperfect time of the lesser prolation in diminution."

And the fact that this meter is often denoted in musical score by a capital letter C has nothing to do with "common time," as it is usually called. Rather, early musicians broke the symbol for perfect time, a circle, in half to signify imperfect time.

To supervise the perfection of music the Mandarin bureaucracy of China created a special office and a code (of right and wrong musical theory) both called *huang jong,* or yellow bell.

The musical signs (♯ ♮ ♭) for sharp, natural, and flat, strangely enough, are all derived from the Gothic script form of the letter *b*. It all stems from the novelty of adding a seventh note, in the High Middle Ages, to the perfectly adequate six then contained in scale modes. But where to put it?

There are two semitones between A and C, where the seventh will fall in the key of C. The problem of designating which was the required B became the more general problem of designating any sharping or flatting, not just of B itself. (Not a problem for the Germans, of course, who then and now clearheadedly call B flat just plain B, and just plain B, H.)

Through time, and much misunderstanding, everyone came to writing their bs in systematically deformed ways.

Michelangelo was left-handed. So was Leonardo da Vinci (and so was Jack the Ripper).

Medieval and Renaissance contracts with artists quite often mentioned, to the exclusion of other colors, that the blues must be ultramarine and of highest quality. Contractors were trying to assure that ground lapis lazuli and no less durable and intense pigment would be employed. Blues made from ammoniated copper were a great deal cheaper but changed color fairly soon after the last brushstroke was slapped on.

One afternoon during the late 1820s, the lawyer-turned-portraitist George Catlin happened to be present at Charles Wilson Peale's Philadelphia museum of natural history when it was visited by a group of western chieftains. Catlin was deeply impressed by the Indians and decided to dedicate his life to the portrayal of what he felt to be a vanishing race of men. Around 1832 he made his first trip west and went on to become one of the greatest painters of American Indians.

To run the "gamma-ut" is to run the musical scale beginning at its first note, "ut," on a musical staff with its stylized G clef sign. The G was called by its Greek name, gamma, by the musical staff's medieval originators.

Of course "ut" has long since been replaced by "do," an easier syllable to sing. And gamma-ut has been shortened to gamut.

As to "ut" and the rest of the solfege syllables, Guido of Arezzo (ca. 990–1050) is responsible. The intonations in his novel system of vocal training employed the initial syllables of a Latin hymn for St. John's Day in which successive phrases happen to fall on the rising pitches of a major scale: "*Ut* queant laxis/ *re*sonare fibris/*mi*ra gestorum/ *fa*muli tuorum/ *so*lve polluti/ *la*bii reatum/ . . ." "Ti", the seventh note, was not then a part of the scale and was added later.

The Hawaiian ukulele originated in Portugal, where it was called the machete. One man, a British army officer named Edward Putvis, was responsible for making the instrument popular in Hawaii. Putvis, an avid and adept machete player, was in Hawaii during the late 1800s. He was a small man and was evidently very active—he jumped around while playing his machete. His antics earned him the nickname *ukulele* (from *uku*, "small person" or "flea," and *lele*, "jumping"). When Hawaiians began constructing the four-stringed guitars themselves, they called them ukuleles in honor of Putvis.

Up the Hill . . . Oh, About Half a League: Authors

When American poet William Carlos Williams was in medical school, his schoolmates devised a nickname for him based on his initials: they called him "Water Closet."

Edmond Rostand based the hero of his play *Cyrano de Bergerac* on Savinien Cyrano de Bergerac, a seventeenth-century swordsman, ardent lover, and author who had an unusually large nose. The real Cyrano fought many duels over insults to his nose. He also wrote novels, including two romances about visits to the sun and the moon.

Washington Irving wrote under several pen names, including Geoffrey Crayon and Jonathan Oldstyle (his friend James K. Paulding joined him as Oliver Oldstyle). The name of Irving's fictional Dutch historian, chronicler of his *History of New York* (1809), Diedrich Knickerbocker, gave us *knickerbocker,* a nickname for a descendant of the early Dutch settlers of New York and, indeed, a nickname for a native or resident of New York.

French novelist Stendahl served as a dragoon in Napoleon's army and was present in 1812 at the burning of Moscow.

Herman Melville dedicated *Moby-Dick* (1851) to his neighbor and friend Nathaniel Hawthorne.

Some pen names are famous: Mark Twain (Samuel Langhorne Clemens), Lewis Carroll (Charles Lutwidge Dodgson), George Orwell (Eric Blair), O. Henry (William Sydney Porter), Ned Buntline (Edward Z. C. Judson), Stendahl (Henry Beyle; he is reported to have written under 170 other pen names), Maxim Gorky (Alexei Peshkov; "Maxim Gorky" means "Maxim the Bitter"), Molière (Jean Baptiste Poquelin), George Sand (Armandine Aurore Lucile Dupin), Voltaire (Francois Marie Arouet), Mary Renault (Mary Challans), John Le Carré (David Cornwell), and George Eliot (Mary Ann Cross). Some pen names are not so well known: Ben Franklin wrote under the name Richard Saunders; the Brontë sisters, Charlotte, Emily, and Anne, wrote as the Bell brothers—Currer, Ellis, and Acton; Charles Dickens used the name Boz; the poet Edna St. Vincent Millay wrote prose under the name Nancy Boyd.

Stephen Crane had had no direct experience of war when he wrote *The Red Badge of Courage* (1859). His only knowledge of battle was what he had gleaned from Tolstoy and *Battles and Leaders of the Civil War*. His achievement is thus all the more remarkable (Erich Maria Remarque, author of *All Quiet on the Western Front,* considered Crane's work the greatest antiwar novel ever written). Because of Crane's successful treatment of war in *The Red Badge of Courage,* he was thrust into the role of war correspondent.

Charles Lutwidge Dodgson took his first two names, latinized them, reversed them, and came up with Lewis Carroll.

THE PLAYS OF WILLIAM SHAKESPEARE

Histories
Henry VI, Part I
Henry VI, Part II
Henry VI, Part III
Richard II
Richard III
King John
Henry IV, Part I
Henry IV, Part II
Henry V
Henry VIII

Tragedies
Titus Andronicus
Romeo and Juliet
Julius Caesar
Hamlet
Othello
King Lear
Macbeth
Antony and Cleopatra
Coriolanus·
Timon of Athens

Comedies
The Comedy of Errors
The Taming of the Shrew

The Two Gentlemen of Verona
Love's Labour's Lost
A Midsummer Night's Dream
The Merchant of Venice
Much Ado About Nothing
As You Like It
Twelfth Night
The Merry Wives of Windsor
Troilus and Cressida
All's Well That Ends Well
Measure for Measure

Tragicomedies
Pericles
Cymbeline
The Winter's Tale
The Tempest

Harriet Beecher Stowe based the character of Uncle Tom in *Uncle Tom's Cabin* on Josiah Henson, a slave who escaped from Maryland to Canada, where he became a Methodist preacher, opened a sawmill, and helped more than one hundred other slaves escape to Canada. Henson wrote his autobiography, *The Life of Josiah Henson,* in 1849.

Stephen Crane died in Germany, where he had gone to seek a cure for his tuberculosis. He was 28 years old.

The Rover Boys, the Bobbsey Twins, and Tom Swift were all created by Edward Stratemeyer. Stratemeyer began his career editing stories written by Horatio Alger. When Alger died, Stratemeyer was chosen to assume his identity and wrote eleven posthumous books for the "Rise in Life" series. Stratemeyer created Tom Swift in 1910; the first Tom Swift book was *Tom Swift and His Motor-Cycle.* Swift was always involved with the creation of new and exciting machines, such as airplanes, cars, tanks, and ships. Stratemeyer based the character of Tom Swift on his personal idol, Henry Ford. In 1906, he founded the Stratemeyer Syndicate; by the time of his death, in 1930, he had written, conceived, or directed more than 800 juvenile books, using his own name and sixty-two pseudonyms.

Robert Louis Stevenson, James M. Barrie, and Arthur Conan Doyle all studied at Edinburgh University, and they all attended classes given by Dr. Joseph Bell. The eminent surgeon was an impressive man: he could deduce the nationality, livelihood, habits, and personal history of a man just by looking at him. He was fascinated, he said, by "the endless significance of trifles." It was Doyle who was most impressed by Dr. Bell. When he graduated from the university in 1881, Doyle went into business as an oculist. When his business did not prosper, he decided to try writing. Impressed by the works of Edgar Allan Poe, he wrote a detective story. The detective he invented was a very clever man. Doyle named his character Sherlock (after a cricketer he had once played against) Holmes (after American jurist Oliver Wendell Holmes), but all the rest of Sherlock Holmes is pure Dr. Bell.

Benjamin Franklin wrote under seven pen names; Washington Irving used five.

There are only seven known signatures of William Shakespeare in existence. Because of his poor handwriting, it is not clear how Shakespeare spelled his name.

Lewis Carroll based the Alice of *Alice in Wonderland* and *Through the Looking Glass* on Alice Liddell, daughter of Henry George Liddell, dean of Christ Church College. Alice was a very lucky girl. Aside from the attentions of Carroll, she was given drawing lessons by John Ruskin.

Lillian Hellman died in 1984. She left part of her $4 million estate for the creation of a fund for Marxist writers to be named after her lover, mystery writer Dashiell Hammett.

Nikos Kazantzakis based *Zorba the Greek* (1946) on George Zorbas, a man with whom Kazantzakis became involved in a mining venture.

e.e. cummings had his own special way of writing, and his poems are noted for their peculiarities of typography, language, and punctuation. cummings was particularly adverse to capital letters. His eccentric use of language got him in trouble during World War I, while he was serving as an ambulance driver. Military censors reading his letters home were not pleased by his codelike grammar, and cummings was tossed in a French prison, accused of treasonable correspondence. The experience gave him material for his first book, *The Enormous Room*.

A writer who works mainly for hire is called a hack writer. The word comes from *hackney*, a carriage kept for hire, and is also used for taxicab drivers: hacks.

Niccoló Machiavelli based his best-known work, *The Prince*, on Cesare Borgia. Borgia was the ideal Renaissance prince—intelligent, cruel, treacherous, and ruthlessly opportunistic.

The 1957 film *The Bridge on the River Kwai* was based on a book by Pierre Boulle. The screenplay for the film was written by Carl Foreman and Michael Wilson, but they were not given credit, for both men were at that time blacklisted. The screenplay was credited to Boulle—who spoke no English.

Louisa May Alcott, author of *Little Women*, detested little girls and wrote the book only for money.

Don Quixote de La Mancha, by Cervantes, has been reprinted more often than any other volume except the Bible.

George Orwell was born Eric Blair. In creating his pseudonym, he took George from the patron saint of England; Orwell was the name of a river that he had known as a boy.

None of Andrew Marvell's "serious" poetry was published during his lifetime. His housekeeper (claiming to be his widow) had some of his poems printed three years after his death, but he did not become famous for another 250 years (when he was discovered by the likes of T. S. Eliot).

Abraham Lincoln referred to Harriet Beecher Stowe, author of *Uncle Tom's Cabin,* as "The little lady who made this big war."

Author Kurt Vonnegut, Jr., was captured in Luxembourg during the Battle of the Bulge and was held in a German POW camp until the end of the war.

Omar Khayyam (ca. 1044–1123), author of the *Rubaiyat,* also wrote an algebra textbook still in use during the mid-twentieth century in remote regions of Iran. The poet begins: "By the help of God and His precious assistance, I say that algebra is a scientific art . . ."

F. Scott Fitzgerald died before finishing *The Last Tycoon* (1941). He based the character of the "tycoon" on Irving Thalberg, production executive of Metro-Goldwyn-Mayer.

Joseph Heller wanted to call his first novel *Catch–18,* but just before the book was due to be printed he was warned that Leon Uris was about to come out with a book with the same number in the title. It was an editor who finally came up with the new number, making the book *Catch–22.*

In 1957 Nikos Kazantzakis became ill as the result of a smallpox vaccination given him in Canton during a visit to China. He spent his last days in a hospital in Germany. Among those who visited him was his friend Albert Schweitzer.

Heinrich Heine's last words were "God will pardon me, it's his trade."

Louisa May Alcott served as a nurse in a Union hospital during the Civil War.

George Orwell's *Animal Farm* (1954) was rejected by twenty-three publishing houses before finally being accepted. One of the houses to turn down the manuscript was Faber and Faber; the editor who rejected it was T. S. Eliot.

Evan Hunter, Richard Marsten, Hunt Collins, and Ed McBain are all pseudonyms for the same writer, who was born Salvatore Lombino in 1926. He is best known as Evan Hunter, a name that he made up from Evan, the name of an impressive man he met in a literary agency, and hunter, which seemed to him like a good name for a young man on the make.

The Mystery Writers of America give an annual award for the best mystery. The award is called the Edgar; it is named for Edgar Allan Poe.

Lytton Strachey's last words were "If this is dying, then I don't think much of it."

Alexandre Dumas père based *The Three Musketeers* (1844) on the memoirs of Charles de Batz-Castelmore d'Artagnan, a French soldier under King Louis XIV.

Oscar Wilde died in a Paris hotelroom. Among his final statements was "This wallpaper is killing me; one of us has got to go."

James M. Barrie based the characters in his play *Peter Pan* on a friend's children.

George Orwell wanted to call his last novel *The Last Man in Europe*. He was ultimately persuaded to choose a new title and selected *1984*—there was no significance to the choice, and other dates were considered.

Samuel Langhorne Clemens planned to seek his fortune in South America but gave up the idea to become a steamboat pilot on the Mississippi River. It was there that he encountered the phrase "mark twain," meaning "two fathoms deep," but that was not the inspiration for his famous pseudonym, Mark Twain. The pseudonym Mark Twain had already been adopted by an older riverboat pilot named Isaiah Sellers, who used it to sign his pompous articles in the New Orleans *Picayune*. Clemens burlesqued Sellers's articles in another New Orleans paper, the *True Delta*. Clemens's parodies were so biting that Sellers never wrote again. Clemens later adopted Sellers's pseudonym, perhaps as a form of reparation.

Louisa May Alcott wrote under the pseudonym A. M. Barnard.

> Up the hill, up the hill, up the hill
> out of the field,
> And over the brow and away.

The rhythms are somehow familiar. Alfred Tennyson (1809–92) wrote the lines in 1882 in belated commemoration of the *other* British cavalry charge at Balaklava on October 25, 1854. For these lines are from *The Charge of the Heavy Brigade* ("the gallant three hundred . . ."), an event of which Tennyson felt it necessary to take poetic note in his capacity as Poet Laureate of England.
The Charge of the Light Brigade:

> Half a league, half a league, half a league onward,
> All in the valley of Death rode the six hundred.

had been penned in a patriotic fervor in December 1854 when news of the battle reached England. Tennyson, in fact, had a thousand copies of the poem printed at his own expense for distribution to survivors of the suicidal charge.

As Tennyson's initial excitement over the skirmish waned, he thought it more fitting that posterity not read the line:

> Not tho' the soldier knew someone had blundered.

He attempted to delete this truthful reference to military incompetence from the second printing. Popular protest kept the line in.

For the record, the Light Brigade numbered exactly 607 men. That any of them got back alive is largely owed to the French Chasseurs d'Afrique, who staged a supporting charge to extricate the British light cavalry.

Three Days in an Idaho Bordello: Bad Advice

Sea doctors of the eighteenth century mention that sailors were frequently struck by lightning. While recognizing that masthead conductors might help, they recommend, unhelpfully, that in thunderstorms deckhands quickly get into wet clothing.

During the fierce Battle of Spotsylvania (May 8–19, 1864), Major General John ("Uncle John") Sedgwick, commander of the Union VI Corps, found a group of his men reluctant to advance on the Confederate lines. Urging them forward, he reassured them, "They couldn't hit an elephant at this distance." At that instant he was shot and killed by a Rebel sharpshooter.

"Gaiety is the most outstanding feature of the Soviet Union."
—Joseph Stalin, 1935

The Greeks believed that certain stones had special powers. Amethyst, for instance, was believed to prevent drunkenness. The name of the stone comes from the Greek words *a* ("not") and *methystos* ("drunken"). Medieval Europeans inherited the Greek notions; Middle Ages tosspots were quite fond of the stone.

In 1937, 220 experts in world affairs were invited to rate the possibility, within ten years, of war between 88 pairings of world nations. The pair least likely to open hostilities in their estimation was Denmark and the United States, with only a 6 percent probability. Japan and China were 94 percent favorites to go to war (but Japan and China were already at war, so the probability is actually too low, or the panel of experts had missed a few headlines).

At 89 percent was reckoned Japan and the USSR, a war that never really got underway, though serious border incidents occurred.

The worst guess was a low probability, 38 percent, of war between the United States and Italy.

Lansford Warren Hastings was one of the guides of the first planned overland wagon migration to Oregon, in 1842. In 1845 he wrote a guidebook called *Emigrant's Guide to Oregon and California.* Hastings's book was based more on his fertile imagination than on actual topography. He paid no mind to broad desert wastes or to impassable mountains. One copy got into the hands of two wealthy brothers, Jacob and George Donner. They accepted as gospel Hastings's advice and were particularly impressed by his suggestions for shortening the trip.

Hastings claimed to have discovered a new, shorter route. He named this route the Hastings Cutoff. Two groups had already traveled this route when the Donners set out; it is unfortunate that the Donners did not have the opportunity to ask them about the veracity of Hastings's book. Of the eighty-nine members of the ill-fated expedition, only forty-five survived the ordeals of the journey, which has become famous for its instances of cannibalism.

The fate of the Donners did nothing to tarnish Hastings's reputation. During the Civil War he sided with the South and devised a plan to capture southern California, Arizona, and New Mexico for the Confederacy. Nothing came of it, and when the war ended he went to Brazil, where he got permission to colonize the Amazon River with Americans. He returned to the United States and published another guide, the *Emigrant's Guide to South America*. He managed to find a home on the banks of the Amazon River for a bunch of unreconstructed Confederates and their families. He died in 1868 while returning to Alabama for more emigrants.

The Italian dictator Benito Mussolini was born in 1883. His father, a blacksmith and an ardent Socialist, named him after the Mexican statesman and national hero Benito Juarez.

To prove that the water of Paris was perfectly safe to drink, English novelist Arnold Bennett drank a few slugs of it from a carafe. He died three months later of typhoid fever.

Medieval physicians believed jade cured ailments of the urinary tract and broke up kidney stones. The name of the stone comes from the Spanish *(piedra de) ijada* ("loin stone").

According to one study, Americans are bombarded by 1600 commercial messages every day; only eighty of these are consciously noted, and fewer than fifteen evoke some response.

Trying to anticipate the future, W. F. Ogburn in 1934 published 150 ways in which radio, then a novelty, would affect the nation. He predicted that politicians would have to keep more of their campaign promises.

Winston Churchill believed that alcoholic beverages were "one of the distinguishing marks of the higher types and races of humanity."

In March 1616, the English philosopher Francis Bacon and a Scottish physician named Witherborne took a carriage ride through the snowy streets of London. The two learned men discussed a novel idea of Bacon's, the possibility of using snow rather than salt to preserve meat. They stopped at a grocer's, bought a chicken, and, scooping up handfuls of snow, stuffed the bird. The experiments proved fatal to Bacon: he took ill with bronchitis and pneumonia and died within a month.

The noisy flocks of starlings that often make a nuisance of themselves are the result of one man's whimsy. Eugene Schieffelin, German immigrant and prosperous businessman, was a devoted admirer of the works of William Shakespeare. In honor of the great dramatist—and as a gift to his new homeland—Schieffelin decided to introduce to America all of the species of birds mentioned in Shakespeare's plays. Countless pairs of unfortunate birds—song thrushes, skylarks, nightingales—met only doom when he released them into the skies of New York. In March of 1890, Schieffelin got around to *Henry IV, Part I*— and the starling *(Sturnis vulgaris)*. He released forty pairs in Central Park. Within a few years the hardy birds with their iridescent plumage were darkening the skies of numerous states.

Historians ascribe James Madison's defeat in his 1777 reelection bid (to the Virginia legislature) to his refusal to distribute free whiskey to the voters, as was then customary.

When Christopher Columbus left Spain in 1492, he was convinced that he was sailing toward China and Japan. He therefore took along a translator who spoke Arabic—Columbus thought he might prove useful.

The Wright brothers believed that the airplane would bring about world peace: with airplanes, nations could keep a close watch on one another and thus prevent surprise attacks.

It was always inadvisable in the ancient world to block a sage's sunlight. This lesson was learned by Alexander the Great when he visited the Greek philosopher Diogenes, known as "the Cynic."

Disdaining all conventional comforts, Diogenes lived in a large earthenware tub. He is said to have chucked his last remnant of easy living—a cup—when he saw a poor man drinking from cupped hands.

Full of praise for the wise man, Alexander asked him if there was anything he might do for him. "Only step out of my sunlight," snapped the cynic. (This evidently did nothing to diminish Alexander's esteem of Diogenes, for he was quoted as saying, "If I were not Alexander, I would be Diogenes.")

Nazi leaders of the mid 1930s expressed gratitude to the Americans for their pioneering lead in compulsory sterilization of "socially undesirable" types—the feebleminded, mentally defective, epileptic, and so forth. (Twenty-eight states had enacted some form of sterilization law by 1935; annual totals ran between twenty and thirty thousand operations.)

Of course, the Germans went to work with a will, sterilizing several hundred thousand people in the first years of their program. Noting the German achievement, Virginia eugenicist Dr. Joseph S. DeJarnette advised the state legislature to enlarge the program, warning that "the Germans are beating us at our own game."

Pentagon planners searched frantically in the years 1982–84 for places to put their proposed MX missile. Ideas rejected because of strategic vulnerability, expense, or general silliness included guessing-game silos (many silos, fewer missiles shuttled randomly among them), railroad racetrack launchers, cruising truck carriers, and underwater and airborne systems.

The climactic 1984 proposal would put missiles and launch crews under western mountain ranges at a depth of 3500 feet. Buried with the military hardware would be tunneling machinery to dig out after an attack and deliver a nuclear counterpunch months or perhaps years behind schedule.

Hiram Stevens Maxim was born in Maine in 1840. He invented several useful items during the course of his life, and some of his creations helped make the 20th century forever distinct from the 19th. His first patent was for an improved curling iron. He then invented a locomotive headlight and an automatic sprinkler fire extinguisher. His next invention was an electrical pressure regulator. When it was shown at the Paris Exhibition of 1881, the regulator won Maxim the Legion of Honor from the French government. Following this great achievement, Maxim spent a few years traveling through Europe. In Vienna he met an acquaintance, another American tourist. When Maxim mentioned his recent glory to this old friend, the man was unimpressed. "Hang your

57

chemistry and electricity!" he declared. "If you want to make a pile of money, invent something that will enable these Europeans to cut each other's throats with greater facility."

Maxim did just that. He went to London and, in 1884, perfected the machine gun. In 1901 he was knighted for his efforts by an appreciative Britain. Sir Hiram lived until 1916, long enough to see his most famous invention put to use on the battlefields of World War I.

From 1931 to 1941, all graduating cadets at Japan's Naval Academy had to answer the same question: "How would you carry out a surprise attack on Pearl Harbor?"

"Not worth a continental" was popular wisdom after the Revolutionary War. It describes things of doubtful value generally and government scrip (denominated in "continentals" during the war) particularly. But a number of senators and a few representatives had greater vision than the public: they bought up the depreciated currency through the 1790s and then enacted legislation redeeming it in full on the US Treasury.

In order to prepare herself for her role as a prostitute in the 1980 film *Heaven's Gate,* Isabelle Huppert spent three days in a bordello in Idaho.

Got to Eat Somewhere: Bad Manners

A close friend of Edouard Manet was Theodore Duret, a Parisian journalist. Their first meeting was not a sociable occasion:

In the year 1865 Manet was notorious; the scandal of his *Dejeuner sur l'herbe* had not died, the more recent *Olympia* had merely enlarged his leering public. He fled in high temper to Madrid.

Nothing agreed with him. At one restaurant he sent dish after dish back to the kitchen. But each was intercepted by a seemingly famished stranger at the next table—this was Duret, en route from Portugal to Paris, genuinely famished, and unaware of his glowering compatriot's identity. Manet believed he had been recognized and cruelly mocked by this cretin, whom he assailed for "pretending to relish this disgusting cooking." Their taste in art, however, proved to be much closer.

The emperor Nero enjoyed shoving drunken companions into open sewer holes. The emperor Heliogabalus liked to serve his dinner guests artificial food made of glass or marble: they were compelled to eat it.

After the Battle of Waterloo, the Duke of York had a hallway in his home lined with teeth from horses killed in the battle.

Cheating at dice in the seventeenth century was little different, except in its professional argot, than more recent methods:

Topping a die was to hold one, with a deft finger, against the lip of the dice cup, while rattling the other as if to make a fair throw.

Slurring was only possible when the dice were shaken by hand; it is the art of the flat, sliding throw. As a rule only one die could be satisfactorily controlled.

Knapping was a throw against some seemingly innocent obstacle, bringing a die suddenly to rest at a desired orientation.

Stabbing required a deceptively constructed cup or box, a narrow one that prevented the dice from shifting faces during the shake. It was only necessary then to release the dice flatly, spinning but not tumbling.

And *palming* the dice meant the same thing in 1684 as it does in 1984.

What was brand new to sharps of 1684 was bristle-dice: improved fullams, or loaded dice. Time honored practice for making high fullams (4,5,6) and low fullams (1,2,3) had always involved drilling and filling with mercury or lead, rounding selected corners, or, the crudest expedient, introducing dice with a redundacy of certain number faces and lacking others. But the bristle-die was fitted with a tiny hog bristle on corners that favored its landing on chosen faces. With elementary sleight of hand the short filaments could be instantly removed if the lucky dice attracted a challenge.

"When I hear anyone talk of culture, I reach for my revolver.".

—Hermann Goering (1893–1946)

Ethelred the Unready (978–1016) urinated in his baptismal font.

The Sicilian city of Syracuse was of central importance to both the Romans and the Carthaginians during their frequent wars. The Romans finally took the city in 212 BC, during the Second Punic War. It was a hard fight: the city was protected by ingenious defenses (including short-range catapults) devised by the famous Greek mathematician, physicist, and inventor Archimedes.

Archimedes was well known to the Romans, and the commander of the conquering force, Marcus Claudius Marcellus, ordered that Archimedes be spared. While the great city was being sacked, a Roman soldier came upon the 75-year-old Archimedes intent on drawing geometric diagrams in the sand. The soldier asked Archimedes what he was doing. The disgruntled old man curtly told the soldier to go away and stop blocking his light. At this, the soldier ran Archimedes through with his sword.

In the course of the clean-up after Three Mile Island's radiation accident, monitoring equipment detected radioactive cat feces at some distance from the site. It appears that cats found contaminated mice still palatable and in the natural course of things were spreading "hot" debris.

"I represent a woman, and I ought to represent her as faithfully as I can." So spoke Edward Hyde, Viscount Cornbury and governor of New York and New Jersey from 1702 to 1708. And, indeed, Cornbury took extraordinary measures to faithfully represent his cousin, Queen Anne, whose representative he was in the colonies. Although unmistakably male, Cornbury dressed as a female. He wore gowns and hoop skirts (most of which he selected from his wife's closet).

The citizens of New York first became aware of Cornbury's taste in fashion when a night watchman spotted what he believed to be a drunken prostitute wandering around outside the governor's mansion. Approaching the large "female," the watchman was shocked to recognize the English governor. He was further shocked when, shrieking with joy, the governor lunged at him and gave his ears some none-too-gentle tugs.

These were hard times for the colonists of New York and New Jersey: they had an unusually zany governor. Some people accepted the governor's explanation—they agreed that he was just taking his role as representative of the queen in a particularly literal manner. Others thought he dressed as he did to better show off his facial resemblance to the queen. No one in those straitlaced days mused on the more intimate implications of Cornbury's proclivities. Furthermore, Cornbury's dressing up as a woman was not his solitary flaw. He was an ear fetishist. At a banquet given in his honor, Cornbury delivered a lengthy and detailed panegyric on his wife's ears. He declared them to be the most exquisite ears he had ever seen, and he called on all the men present to line up and, one at a time, feel for themselves those marvels of auricular design. Nor were his wife's the only ears to delight Cornbury. Taking a nocturnal stroll through the city's streets became a dangerous undertaking, for Cornbury had the habit of hiding behind trees and then pouncing on passersby. Giggling hysterically, he would reach with sure aim for the unfortunate citizen's ears, which he would then give hard, unwanted pulls (he had powerful paws).

The real problem with Cornbury, however, was that he was a thief. He had accepted his post in the "dreary" colonies only to flee his creditors, and he used the colonies' money as he saw fit. He built himself a nice, big home and kept up his wardrobe. (His wife, suffering her husband's depredations, took to borrowing clothes from local women—she never returned a stitch.) In the end, Cornbury was tossed in debtor's prison. He was freed when his father died, and he inherited his family's estate. He paid off his debts and returned to Britain. The empty pockets and sore ears of New York and New Jersey were not soon forgotten; Cornbury did his part in sowing the seeds of rebellion.

It does occasionally happen that members of the electoral college—that small body which officially elects the American president—vote contrary to the ticket on which they are pledged. Most recently, Democratic electors of Alabama cast ballots in 1960 for Harry Byrd and Strom Thurmond instead of Kennedy and Johnson as they had promised.

T. S. Eliot was a practical joker. He liked to give exploding cigars to critics.

Llamas are infamous for their bad breath.

When eating: "Let thy hands be clean. Thou must not put either thy fingers into thine ears, or thy hands to thy head."

—Fra Bonvirino da Riva, 1290

The French prelate and statesman Cardinal Richelieu spent most of his time and energies in European politics. He also found the time to be a patron of the arts and to found the French Academy. And he invented the table knife. Richelieu was distressed by the messy and dangerous habit of using sharp daggers for carving food. He was particularly upset when his courtiers used their daggers as toothpicks. The cardinal ordered that knives be made with rounded ends.

Marcel Duchamp (1887–1968), the only major artist to be reckoned also a great chess player, spent his honeymoon (in 1927) contemplating chess problems. One night his bride glued the chess pieces to the board. They were divorced three weeks later.

On his deathbed, British statesman Benjamin Disraeli was asked if he wished to be visited by Queen Victoria. "Why should I see her?" he responded. "She will only want to give a message to Albert." Those were his last words.

In 1973 Marlon Brando refused to accept his Academy Award for his role in *The Godfather,* declaring that the motion picture industry had done great·damage to the identity of the American Indian. He sent an Indian woman in his place. Her name was Satcheen Littlefeather (she was actually an actress named Maria Cruz).

"To wipe the nose on the cap or sleeve belongs to rustics; to wipe the nose on the arm or elbow to pastry cooks; and to wipe the nose with the hand, if by chance at the same instant you hold it to your gown, is not much more civil. But to receive the excreta of the nose with a handkerchief turning slightly away from noble people is an honest thing."

—Erasmus (1469–1536), *Civility*

Jean Anthelme Brillat-Savarin (1755–1826), a great chef and gastronome, was for a time appointed to France's highest court, the Court of Cassation. His habit of carrying dead game in his pockets, to ripen, put him in a bad odor with his fellow judges.

In 1871, during the brief German military exercise known as the Franco-Prussian War, Prussian troops turned the house of Camille Pissaro at Louviciennes into a butcher shop. They shipped some of his work to Prussia—souvenirs—and constructed walkways through the spring muds with finished canvases. Over 1400 pictures vanished.

For three years following Napoleon's defeat at Waterloo in 1815, France was occupied by soldiers—British, Prussian, Austrian, and Russian—from the victorious allied armies. The brief presence of Russian soldiers in Paris is recorded in the word *bistro,* used for wineshops and small restaurants. Either impatient or eager to get out of such establishments (many were off limits to the troops), the Russians habitually yelled *bystra!* ("quickly") at the scurrying Parisian waiters. The word somehow caught on.

In writing his great dictionary Samuel Johnson filled eighty notebooks with the copyings of his clerical staff, who gathered up Johnson's inked annotations from the chosen sources. Johnson defaced, thus, enough of the books he borrowed from his friends to account for around 240,000 quotations. And yet he defined a lexicographer as: "A writer of dictionaries, a harmless drudge . . ."

Maurice Utrillo had the compulsive and unpleasant habit of attacking pregnant women. During his resultant sojourns in the local jails, he would often paint, making gifts of the work to his jailers. As Utrillos fetched a reasonable price, he was not unpopular with the authorities.

When he was 10, David Niven was expelled from boarding school. He had sent a sick chum a very special get-well gift, a matchbox full of dog excrement.

In 1901 J. P. Morgan went on a trip through Europe. An important man, he was invited to dinner by several notable personages, including the King of England. While dining alone with Kaiser Wilhelm II, the American financier was disturbed to hear the German leader mention the subject of socialism. Glaring at the kaiser, Morgan declared, "I pay no attention to such theories."

The Hanover dadaist Kurt Schwitters went out of his way to look up the Berlin dadaist George Groscz while in that city. The ill-tempered Groscz, an ex-boxer who sometimes greeted callers with his fists, opened the door and announced that he was *not* George Groscz. Schwitters, on his way back down the stairs, turned suddenly, knocked again at the door and averred categorically he was *not* Kurt Schwitters. This was, as far as is known, the only time these two artists never met.

Cary Grant was expelled from school at the age of 14 for attempting to sneak into the girls' bathroom. He then ran away to join a troupe of traveling acrobats. He performed as a song-and-dance man and did occasional juggling.

The original Peeping Tom was a tailor named Tom who plied his trade in Coventry around 1040. Like the other inhabitants of Coventry, Tom must have complained when the local earl, Leofric, imposed harsh taxes on the town. And Tom must have felt grateful praise for Leofric's wife when she beseeched him to remit the taxes. But Leofric jokingly told her he would decrease the taxes only if she would ride naked through the town's streets at noon. Lady Godiva took him at his word and issued a proclamation asking all Coventry's citizens to remain indoors with their windows shut at the appointed hour. She then took her famous ride, sitting on a white horse with only her long blond hair to hide her nakedness. But the tailor named Tom, unable to restrain himself, peeped through his shutters—and was instantly struck blind.

While he was president, the thrifty and taciturn Calvin Coolidge never turned down an invitation to a social gathering, even though he didn't seem to enjoy himself (too many people trying to get him to talk) and he always left punctually at ten o'clock. When someone finally asked him why he went to the parties, he replied, "Got to eat somewhere."

Range...About
Thirty Yards: Bliss

For her eighth birthday, Shirley Temple received 135,000 presents.

Although he never graduated from Princeton (he left in 1917 to join the army), F. Scott Fitzgerald always remembered his days there fondly. Indeed, he used Princeton as the setting for his first novel, *This Side of Paradise*. He died while eating a Hershey chocolate bar and reading a football article in the *Princeton Alumni Weekly*.

George Armstrong Custer was the proud owner of the table on which U. S. Grant had written the surrender terms that ended the Civil War.

In order to keep the wife of Francesco del Giocondo happy while he painted her portrait, Leonardo da Vinci hired people to play, sing, and jest. He achieved his end: *Mona Lisa's* smile has become famous.

When the famous canine hero Rin Tin Tin died, in 1932, he was being held by Jean Harlow.

French novelist Honoré de Balzac drank fifty cups of coffee each day. (He died at the age of 51.)

The late 1800s were the heyday of patent medicines, many of which derived their kick from cocaine. One of the most popular of these remedies for myriad ailments was Vin Mariani, a "French tonic wine" composed of two ounces of fresh coca leaves to each pint of Bordeaux wine. Among the notables who gushed praise for the potent beverage were Thomas Edison, Sarah Bernhardt, Emile Zola (who called it "the Elixir of Life"), John Philip Sousa, and Jules Verne.

"God rejoices in odd numbers."
—Virgil (70–19 BC), *Eclogue 8:77*

Katharine Lee Bates, an English professor at Wellesley, wrote the words to "America the Beautiful" after being inspired during a climb to the top of Pikes Peak in 1893.

The first people to witness a striptease were Parisian students who gleefully watched an artist's model disrobe at the Bal des Quatre Arts on February 9, 1893. The seductive dancing didn't please everyone, however, and gendarmes soon arrived and carted off the girl.

When a court fined her 100 francs, the students went crazy and began tearing apart the Latin Quarter; the army had to be called out to quell the riot.

Marie Taglioni was the first ballerina to dance on her toes. (She was also the first première ballerina to wear a tutu.)

Florence Nightingale never traveled without her pet owl. She kept it in a pocket.

Fra Angelico (1387–1455) wept uncontrollably whenever he painted a Crucifixion.

The gripping strength of infants is 30–40 percent greater when they are nude than when fully clothed or merely diapered.

BOOKS OF THE OLD TESTAMENT

ROMAN CATHOLIC CANON	PROTESTANT CANON	ROMAN CATHOLIC CANON	PROTESTANT CANON
Genesis	Genesis	Wisdom	
Exodus	Exodus	Ecclesiasticus	
Leviticus	Leviticus	Isaias	Isaiah
Numbers	Numbers	Jeremias	Jeremiah
Deuteronomy	Deuteronomy	Lamentations	Lamentations
Josue	Joshua	Baruch	
Judges	Judges	Ezechiel	Ezekiel
Ruth	Ruth	Daniel	Daniel
1 & 2 Kings	1 & 2 Samuel	Osee	Hosea
3 & 4 Kings	1 & 2 Kings	Joel	Joel
1 & 2 Paralipom- enon	1 & 2 Chronicles	Amos	Amos
		Abdias	Obadiah
1 Esdras	Ezra	Jonas	Jonah
2 Esdras	Nehemiah	Micheas	Micah
Tobias		Nahum	Nahum
Judith		Habacuc	Habakkuk
Esther	Esther	Sophonias	Zephaniah
Job	Job	Aggeus	Haggai
Psalms	Psalms	Zacharas	Zechariah
Proverbs	Proverbs	Malachias	Malachi
Ecclesiastes	Ecclesiastes	1 & 2 Machabees	
Canticle of Canticles	Song of Solomon		

JEWISH SCRIPTURE

Law
- Genesis
- Exodus
- Leviticus
- Numbers
- Deuteronomy

Prophets
- Joshua
- Judges
- 1 & 2 Samuel

1 & 2 Kings
Isaiah
Jeremiah
Ezekel
Hosea
Joel
Amos
Obadiah
Jonah
Micah

Nahum
Habakkuk
Zephariah
Haggai
Zechariah
Malachi

Hagiographa
Psalms
Proverbs
Job

Song of Songs
Ruth
Lamentations
Ecclesiastes
Esther
Daniel
Ezra
Nehemiah
1 & 2 Chronicles

PROTESTANT APOCRYPHA

1 & 2 Esdras
Tobit
Judith
Additions to
   Esther

Wisdom of
   Solomon
Ecclesiasticus
   or the Wisdom
   of Jesus Son
   of Sirach

Baruch
Prayer of Azariah
   and the Song
   of the Three
   Holy Children

Susanna
Bel and the
   Dragon
The Prayer of
   Manasses
1 & 2 Maccabees

BOOKS OF THE NEW TESTAMENT

Matthew
Mark
Luke
John
Acts of the
   Apostles

Romans
1 & 2 Corinthians
Galatians
Ephesians
Philippians
Colossians

1 & 2 Thess-
   alonians
1 & 2 Timothy
Titus
Philemon
Hebrews
James

1 & 2 Peter
1, 2, 3 John
Jude
Revelation (Ro-
   man Catholic
   canon;
   Apocalypse)

Marie Antoinette adored Pouilly-Fumé, a golden, fruity wine of the Loire Valley. She was so enamored of the wine's bouquet that she had the fragrant blossoms of the Pouilly vines distilled to make perfume.

Franz Liszt gave his second concert at the age of 11. He did so well that one of the delighted listeners, Beethoven, gave him a kiss.

Washington Irving was named for George Washington. When he was 6, he was taken to see Washington. According to tradition, Washington gave his namesake a few friendly pats on the head.

Saint Joseph of Copertine (1603–63), a Franciscan monk, was reputed (by Pope Urban VIII, among others) to become airborne in his meditative raptures. His range was about thirty yards.

Bean Soup and Pancakes:
Boredom

The chalkboards American schoolchildren spend so much time scrutinizing were introduced to America in 1714 by a German immigrant named Christopher Dock. Dock set up the first such teaching aid in Skippack, Pennsylvania.

While in the field, Union soldiers during the Civil War dined on Van Camp's Pork and Beans and Borden's condensed milk.

It takes forty minutes to hard-boil an ostrich egg.

The dot over an "i" is properly called its tittle.

The oldest of American college fraternities is Sigma Pi, founded at William and Mary in 1752. Phi Mu, established at Wesleyan College in 1852, is the oldest sorority.

Claude Monet and Auguste Renoir, toward the end of their careers, were occasionally unable to say which of them had painted particular canvases at Argenteuil (1873–74). They had **often** worked there side by side upon the same subjects.

Rutabagas were brought to the United States by Swedish immigrants.

Daniel Defoe based *Robinson Crusoe* (1719) on the actual story of Alexander Selkirk. The son of a shoemaker, Selkirk ran away from home and went to sea. In 1703 he joined a privateering expedition led by Captain William Dampier. In October 1704, off the coast of Chile, Selkirk became embroiled in an argument with the captain of the ship he was on, a man named Thomas Stradling, and—at his own request—he was put ashore on a nearby island, Mas a Tierra. He remained on the island until February 1709, when he was rescued by another privateer, Woodes Rogers, and brought to England, where he became something of a celebrity and caught the attention of Defoe. Selkirk had spent over four years on his island; Defoe increased this to twenty-four in his book.

At the age of 7, Orson Welles could recite from memory all of *King Lear*.

Ricky Nelson's real first name was Eric.

A googol—it was named by a 9-year-old—is the number one followed by a hundred zeros. A googolplex is a googol times itself a hundred times, a number larger than anything physically countable in the universe.

Italian troops in World War I spent most of the war fighting Austro-Hungarian forces in battles one through eleven of the Isonzo. Finally, in 1917, a German corps arrived on bicycles, and the front moved at last a few miles deeper into Italy.

The last passenger pigeon died at 1:00 PM, September 1, 1914, at the Cincinnati Zoological Park.

Franklin D. Roosevelt, the longest presidential incumbent, exercised the veto more often than any other, 631 times.

The science of ethnoconchology is the study of seashell use and patterns of trade among the world's peoples, ancient and modern.

Myra Belle Shirley became famous as Belle Starr, "the bandit queen." During her lifetime, she went through half a dozen husbands and as many lovers (most of whom died violent deaths). Before her death, she remarked, "I regard myself as a woman who has seen much of life."

The First Congress (1789–91) considered 268 bills and enacted 108. Recent Congresses process 30,000 or more bills, but enact only a few hundred.

K-rations, the field issue to World War II troops, were composed of such foods as pemmican, canned cheese, veal loaf, ham spread, malted milk tablets, candy bars, bouillon cubes, and instant coffee.

Leonardo da Vinci once suggested that an artist caught short of ideas might stare at a bare stucco wall; the textural irregularities would take on forms in the aritst's imagination, providing him with inexhaustible subjects. Solving the same problem Chinese artists had come up with something very similar in advice written some centuries before Leonardo's. Dampened ricepaper pasted on any surface would stimulate the artistic vision with its random veins and rifts.

Traditionally, the "von" in front of a German surname indicated noble degree. In the nineteenth century it became fashionable to use the longer "von und zu"—a bit of a snobbish way of saying: "Not only are we noble, we still own the family castle."

On all Swedish ships at sea, the Thursday evening meal is bean soup and pancakes.

Count Your Puffins:
Buying and Selling

Hector Berlioz was not the first, nor the last, composer to have been envious of the salaries of operatic performers, but Berlioz actually calculated the stars' vocal scale in a seven-month season at about one franc per syllable.

In 1700 the hanging of twenty-four pirates cost nearly £19. The marshal of the Admiralty High Court incurred expenses of £2/3/0 for gallows construction, £4 for burials, £11 in rope and executioner's fees, and shelled out £1/16/9 for entertainment—buying dinners for the London sheriff, various deputies, and other officials.

For a Philadelphia family of five in 1851 a week's groceries could be had for about $4.25. Meat cost only ten cents a pound but butter was thirty-one cents. Still, this was nearly twice the budget for the same average family of 1833.

The first coin-operated vending machine was in use at Alexandria in the third century BC. Five drachmas in the slot bought an automatic squirt of holy water.

The portrait of George Washington that appears on the one-dollar bill is that done by Gilbert Stuart.

To the ancient Romans, Juno, wife and sister of Jupiter, was the goddess of many things, including the heavens, the moon, war, women, virginity, childbirth, and marriage rites. She was also known as Juno Moneta (from the Latin *monere,* "to warn"), or "Juno of the Warnings," "Juno the Adviser." Romans prayed to her when they had some particularly difficult problem to solve. Her temple on the Capitoline Hill was known as Juno Moneta, or simply Moneta. In 269 BC, the first silver coins were produced in a mint set up in that temple. The coins made there were referred to as coming from Moneta. In Italian, *moneta* is still a word for "coin"; *moneta* exists in English, too: *money.*

It is not easy for foreign visitors to the United States to count their change. Unlike the coins of almost every other country in the world, US coins have no numerical markings.

The first written advertisement was found in the ruins of Thebes; it is probably more than 3000 years old.

In the Europe ruled by Charlemagne (742–814), no coin larger than one silver penny, the denier, was in circulation. Although the denarius was officially reckoned at twelve to the solidus and 240 to the libra, these denominations existed only as conveniences in ledgers and account books. Such coins were actually minted later by the English—shillings and pounds—and by the French—sous and livres.

The refrain to a child's ditty, "pop goes the weasel," originates in England at the beginning of the Industrial Revolution. In its many variants the lyrics tell of a factory worker obtaining his Saturday night drinking money by pawning ("popping") the family iron ("weasel").

Lord & Taylor, founded in 1826, is the oldest retail store in New York City.

The extent of International Telephone and Telegraph's (ITT) involvement in the 1972 overthrow of Salvador Allende of Chile will never be made fully known. Ironically, ITT participation in plots to prevent Allende's election invalidated its $92 million insurance claim against OPIC (Overseas Private Investment Corporation), an American government agency that insures corporations against the risks of doing business in foreign countries. OPIC doesn't insure against losses incurred through meddling in local politics.

Rights to the Comstock Lode were sold in 1859 by its discoverer, Henry Comstock, for $11,000. But $300,000,000 worth of gold and silver was pulled from this mine.

Nikolai Gogol (1809–52) plotted his greatest novel, *Dead Souls,* on a bit of flimflam involving a sharp trade in titles and mortgages to dead serfs. In fact, during Gogol's lifetime the number of mortgaged serf souls increased from 1.8 to 6.6 million (amounting to about 400 million rubles of debt). State credit institutions took a bath when Russian serfs were emancipated in 1861 by Czar Alexander II.

Monarchs often raised money by selling commissions in the armed forces. In the time of Louis XIV and XV of France, regiments might have several colonels, who took command by turns.

WORLD CURRENCIES

Country	Currency
Afghanistan	afghani (100 puls)
Albania	lek (100 qindarka)
Algeria	dinar (100 centimes)
Andorra	franc (fr) & peseta (SP)
Angola	kwanza (100 lweis)
Antigua	dollar (100 cents)
Argentina	peso (100 centavos)
Australia	dollar (100 cents)
Austria	schilling (100 groschen)
Bahamas	dollar (100 cents)
Bahrain	dinar (1,000 fils)
Bangladesh	taka (100 paise)
Barbados	dollar (100 cents)
Belgium	franc (100 centimes)
Belize	dollar (100 cents)
Benin	franc
Bermuda	dollar (100 cents)
Bhutan	ngultrum
Bolivia	peso (100 centavos)
Botswana	pula (100 thebe)
Brazil	cruzeiro (100 centavos)
Brunei	dollar (100 sen)
Bulgaria	lev (100 stotinki)
Burma	kyat (100 pyas)
Burundi	franc
Cameroon	franc
Canada	dollar (100 cents)
Central African Republic	franc
Chad	franc
Chile	new peso (100 old escudos)
China: People's Republic	yuan (10 chiao; 100 fen)
Colombia	peso (100 centavos)
Congo	franc
Costa Rica	colón (100 centimos)
Cuba	peso (100 centavos)
Cyprus	pound (1,000 mils)
Czechoslovakia	koruna (100 haleru)

78

Country	Currency
Denmark	krone (100 öre)
Dominica	dollar (100 cents)
Dominican Republic	peso (100 centavos)
Ecuador	sucre (100 centavos)
Egypt	pound (100 piastres; 1,000 millièmes)
El Salvador	colón (100 centavos)
Equatorial Guinea	ekuele
Ethiopia	dollar (100 cents)
Fiji	dollar (100 cents)
Finland	markka (100 penniä)
France	franc (100 centimes)
Gabon	franc
Gambia	dalasi (100 bututs)
Germany, East	mark (100 pfennings)
Germany, West	mark (100 pfennings)
Ghana	cedi (100 pesewas)
Gibraltar	pound (100 pence)
Greece	drachma (100 lepta)
Grenada	dollar (100 cents)
Guatemala	quetzal (100 centavos)
Guinea	syli
Guyana	dollar (100 cents)
Haiti	gourde (100 centimes)
Honduras	lempira (100 centavos)
Hungary	forint (100 fillér)
Iceland	krona (100 aurar)
India	rupee (100 paise)
Indonesia	rupiah (100 sen)
Iran	rial (100 dinars)
Iraq	dinar (1,000 fils)
Ireland, Rep. of	pound (100 pence)
Israel	pound (100 agorot)
Italy	lira
Ivory Coast	franc
Jamaica	dollar (100 cents)
Japan	yen
Jordan	dinar (1,000 fils)
Kampuchea	riel (100 sen)
Kenya	shilling (100 cents)
Korea, North	won (100 jun)
Korea, South	won (100 jun)

Country	Currency
Kuwait	dinar (1,000 fils)
Laos	kip (100 ats)
Lebanon	pound (100 piastres)
Lesotho	rand (100 cents) (SA)
Liberia	dollar (100 cents)
Libya	dinar (1,000 dirhams)
Liechtenstein	franc (Swiss)
Luxembourg	franc (100 centimes)
Macau (Port.)	pataca (100 avos)
Madagascar	franc
Malawi	kwacha (100 tambala)
Malaysia	dollar (100 cents)
Maldives, Rep. of	rupee (100 laris)
Mali	franc
Malta	pound (100 cents; 1,000 mils)
Mauritania	ouguiya (5 khoums)
Mauritius	rupee (100 cents)
Mexico	peso (100 centavos)
Monaco	franc (French)
Mongolian People's Republic	tugrik (100 möngö)
Morocco	dirham (100 centimes)
Nauru	dollar (100 cents) (SA)
Nepal	rupee (100 pice)
Netherlands	guilder (100 cents)
New Zealand	dollar (100 cents)
Nicaragua	córdoba (100 centavos)
Niger	franc
Nigeria	naira (100 kobo)
Norway	krone (100 öre)
Oman	rial (1,000 baiza)
Pakistan	rupee (100 paisas)
Panama	balboa (100 cents)
Paraguay	guarani (100 céntimos)
Peru	sol (100 centavos)
Philippines	peso (100 centavos)
Poland	zloty (100 groszy)
Portugal	escudo (100 centavos)
Qatar	riyal (100 dirhams)
Romania	leu (100 bani)
Rwanda	franc
St. Kitts-Nevis	dollar (100 cents)
St. Lucia	dollar (100 cents)

Country	Currency
St. Vincent	dollar (100 cents)
San Marino	lira (Italian)
Saudi Arabia	riyal (20 qursh)
Senegal	franc
Sierra Leone	leone (100 cents)
Singapore	dollar (100 cents)
Somali Republic	shilling (100 cents)
South Africa	rand (100 cents)
South-West Africa	rand (100 cents) (SA)
Spain	peseta (100 centimos)
Sri Lanka	rupee (100 cents)
Sudan	pound (100 piastres; 1,000 milliemes)
Surinam	guilder (100 cents)
Swaziland	lilangeni (pl. emalangeni) (100 cents)
Sweden	krona (100 öre)
Switzerland	franc (100 centimes)
Syria	pound (100 piastres)
Taiwan	dollar (100 cents)
Tanzania	shilling (100 cents)
Thailand	baht (100 satangs)
Togo	franc
Tonga	pa'anga (100 seniti)
Trinidad & Tobago	dollar (100 cents)
Tunisia	dinar (1,000 millimes)
Turkey	lira (100 kurus)
Uganda	shilling (100 cents)
United Arab Emirates	dirham (100 fils)
United Kingdom	pound (100 pence)
United States	dollar (100 cents)
Upper Volta	franc
Uruguay	peso (100 centésimos)
USSR	rouble (100 copecks)
Vatican City State	lira
Venezuela	bolivar (100 centimos)
Vietnam	dong (100 xu)
Western Samoa	tala (100 sene)
Yemen Arab Republic	riyal (40 bogaches)
Yemen PDR	dinar (1,000 fils)
Yugoslavia	dinar (100 paras)
Zaire	zaire (100 makuta [sing. likuta]; 1,000 sengi)
Zimbabwe	dollar (100 cents)

The indulgences that caused such a theological furor in the Middle Ages were available in two grades:

Plenary indulgences provided complete and whole remission of sins. Because this was a drain on the "treasury of merits," upon which forgiveness was theoretically drawn, no more than one of this kind could be issued in a day.

Partial indulgences knocked days or years of suffering off a sinner's future lot, but were not blue-chip because the Church never claimed officially to know how time is reckoned in purgatory.

Arthur Furguson made a very nice living selling things that didn't belong to him. His first recorded sale took place during the early 1920s in London: he sold Nelson's Column in Trafalgar Square to an Iowa tourist. Furguson found Americans pleasantly gullible. That same year he sold Big Ben and leased Buckingham Palace. Before Scotland Yard could catch up to him, he left Britain for the United States, homeland of his favorite dupes. There he managed to lease the White House to a cattle rancher ($100,000 a year for 99 years; the first year payable in advance).

In New York, he became involved in what would have been his greatest sale. He found an Australian and convinced him that the Statue of Liberty was on sale because New York Harbor was being expanded. It took a while for the Australian to raise the $100,000 deposit, and during the delay he became suspicious of Furguson. The Australian turned Furguson over to the police, who were delighted to finally meet him.

Southern commodity prices near the end of the Civil War reflected scarcity and the ballooning of Confederate currency. In March 1865, bacon stood at four dollars a pound, butter at six to eight; onions and apples sold at sixty to seventy dollars a bushel, Irish potatoes fetched ninety; whiskey might be had at from sixty-five to a hundred-fifty dollars a gallon, and morphine cost $350 an ounce.

(The open price of Southern whiskey was, thus, very close to the going bribe for Yankee whiskey in the army; the commissary officer of the Eighteenth Corps reported his staff was generally offered $25 a quart.)

George Washington was "land poor"; he owned a large estate, but he rarely had any available cash. Washington had to borrow money to travel to his first inauguration.

Ella Watson, better known as Cattle Kate, was a prostitute before she became an outlaw. She ran a brothel in Wyoming where cattle was the medium of exchange. Evidently her girls weren't bringing in enough steers, for she turned to rustling. She was caught and hanged.

"Hands up" was the trademark of train robber Bill Miner, who coined the phrase. His career spanned, off and on, the years 1869–1909.

Expenses for an aggressive business in the golden age of capitalists might include, as in these figures (ca. 1850) from the LaCrosse & Milwaukee Railroad:

one governor	$50,000
state comptroller	$10,000
thirteen head of Senators	$175,000
First Secretary, Upper House	$10,000
Ditto, Lower House	$5,000

Conrad Hilton, founder of the hotel chain, founded the Carte Blanche credit card company.

It is generally thought that Martin Luther's choice of ninety-five theses (nailed to the Wittenburg church door October 31, 1517—it was a Thursday) was to go Albert of Mainz one better. Albert had published ninety-four arguments in support of Leo X's *Bull of Indulgence* (1515).

Among Luther's ninety-five topics were:
(16) There seems to be the same difference between hell, purgatory, and heaven as between despair, uncertainty, and assurance.
(27) There is no divine authority for preaching that the soul flies out of purgatory immediately the money clinks in the bottom of the chest.
(29) Who knows whether all souls in purgatory wish to be redeemed in view of what is said of Saint Severinus and Saint Paschal. (Note: they wished to "serve time" for other souls.)
(82) Why does not the Pope empty purgatory out of charity?

Of curious pedigree is the word *dollar*: its ultimate origins are rooted in the monetary chaos and debased currencies of twelfth-century Germany. In that time the town of Halle minted a coin of uncompromised silver content. Called the heller or, later, thaler, its solid-sounding name was borrowed by many currencies within the patchwork fiefdoms of Germany and Austria. In English, it became dollar.

Americans don't always use the word *dollar:* there are several slang expressions for money, one of the oldest and most popular of which is *buck*. During the early eighteenth century, buckskins were used in barter on the American frontier. As early as 1720, hunters and traders were calling their buckskins *bucks,* using the word to mean a unit of trade. The word was later applied to money.

There are several slang expressions for money in Italy, too. There are also dialect words for money. In the Veneto, one of the several dialect words for money is *schei*. For part of its history, the Veneto was ruled by Austria, and the Austrians issued their own coins. Written on some of the smaller Austrian coins was the word *scheidemünze;* the Italians took the first five letters and came up with *schei*.

The Roman emperor Vespasian was a wise man. Faced with a bankrupt treasury, he cut expenses and instituted new taxes, including a tax on public urinals (he also sold the urine to tanners). When his son Titus reproached him for getting involved in such a "stinking" business, Vespasian took out a coin, held it under Titus's nose, and asked him if it smelled. Public urinals in Paris are still called *vespasiennes;* in Italy, they are *vespasiani*.

"They say that knowledge is power. I used to think so, but I now know that they meant money."

—George Gordon Byron (1788–1824)

On Lundy, a 1½-square-mile island eleven miles off England's southwest coast, the unit of currency is the puffin. About all that you can buy with your puffins, however, is the island's postage stamps.

Get a Younger Pig:
Celebrities

Gaspar, Melchior, and Balthazar—traditionally the Three Wise Men of the Nativity—are nowhere mentioned in the Bible.

Betty Crocker, symbol of wholesomeness for the General Mills Corporation, was concocted in the early 1930s. The recipe includes a surname from an ex-director of the company and a homey first name chosen at random.

A real cook was Fannie Merrit Farmer (1857–1915), author of *The Boston Cooking-School Cook Book* (1896). Through her book Farmer popularized the use of standard measures and measuring techniques in American home cooking.

"The Mad Hatter" who appears in Lewis Carroll's *Alice in Wonderland* was derived from a popular expression, "mad as a hatter." The phrase is derived from the fact that mercury is used in the production of felt hats. After years of working with the poisonous substance, many hatters were afflicted with uncontrollable twitching—they appeared "mad."

The lollipop was invented by George Smith during the early 1900s. Smith named his creation after Lolly Pop, a famous racehorse.

The Four Horsemen of the Apocalypse have mounts of different colors, white, red, black, and a "pale" one. They are released in the breaking of the first four seals of Heaven, at the end of the world.

Red, black, and pale horses betoken war, famine, and death respectively, but there is no general agreement in the symbolic interpretation of the white horse.

Tom Swift, courageous and ever-ready boy hero, lived in Shopton, New York. He had a sweetheart: Mary Nestor.

The name of the dog listening with rapt attention to "His Master's Voice" was Nipper.

A piebald horse is black and white, a skewbald brown and white. From this distinction comes the name of that famous horse of American folksong, "Stewball."

GODS AND GODDESSES

(Roman names are in parentheses)

Zeus (Jupiter): Supreme Ruler, Lord of the Sky

Poseidon (Neptune): Brother of Zeus, Ruler of the Sea

Hades, also called Pluto: Brother of Zeus, Ruler of the Underworld

Hera (Juno): Wife and sister of Zeus, Protector of Marriage

Ares (Mars): Son of Zeus and Hera, God of War

Athena (Minerva): Called "The Maiden." Sprang full-grown from Zeus's head. Goddess of the City; Protector of Civilized Life, Handicrafts, and Agriculture

Apollo: Son of Zeus and Leto. God of Light. Master musician and archer

Artemis (Diana): Twin sister of Apollo. Goddess of the Hunt, lover of wild things

Aphrodite (Venus): Daughter of Zeus and Dione. Goddess of Love and Beauty

Hermes (Mercury): Son of Zeus and Maia, who was daughter of Atlas. Zeus's messenger

Hephaestus (Vulcan): Son of Hera (sometimes said to be son of Zeus's son also). Keeper of the Forge of Olympus

Hestia (Vesta): Sister of Zeus, Goddess of the Hearth

Hebe: Goddess of Youth

Iris: Goddess of the Rainbow

Eros (Cupid): God of Love

Pan: The goatherds' and shepherds' god; a wonderful musician

Demeter (Ceres): Goddess of the Corn

Dionysus, also called Bacchus: God of the Vine

The Nine Muses (Inspirers of Man, companions to Apollo)
Clio: History
Urania: Astrology
Melpomene: Tragedy
Thalia: Comedy
Terpsichore: Dance
Calliope: Epic Poetry
Erato: Love Poetry
Polyhymnia: Songs to the gods
Euterpe: Lyric Poetry

The Three Graces (The incarnation of grace and beauty)
Aglaia: Splendor
Euphrosyne: Mirth
Thalia: Good Cheer

Herman Melville based *Moby-Dick* on a very real and very fierce white whale named Mocha Dick. Mocha Dick wrecked several ships and sank an Australian trader and a French merchantman. The mighty whale also overturned at least fourteen whaling boats and survived more than nineteen harpoons. Mocha Dick had his first encounter with whalers around 1819, the year Melville was born, and was still being hunted in 1851 when Melville wrote his famous novel. Mocha Dick was not named for his color but for the area of his first sighting, off the coast of Chile near Mocha Island.

Barry, Pluto, and Pallas (ca. 1800) are the progenitors of all modern St. Bernard dogs. The rest of the breed had perished in an epidemic at their Augustinian hospice atop the St. Bernard pass.

Benji, the small mutt catapulted to fame in the title role of the 1974 movie, broke into show business playing Higgins of "Petticoat Junction" for seven years.

The camel appearing on cigarette packages of the same name is drawn directly from a 1913 photograph, taken for the purpose, of Old Joe, a dromedary then featured in the Barnum and Bailey Circus.

The Barbie Doll was invented by Ruth Handler, cofounder, with her husband, of the Mattel Toy Company in 1945. She named the doll after her daughter, Barbie.

Erasmus, also known as Elmo, is a patron saint of sailors. Erasmus was a bishop in Syria during the reign of Diocletian. Persecuted for his Christian faith, he moved from place to place, finally meeting his doom in southern Italy. He was put to death by having his intestines wound out of his body on a windlass. Because a windlass looks something like a ship's capstan, he came to be honored as a patron saint of sailors. He is also remembered in "St. Elmo's fire," the flaming phenomenon sometimes seen in stormy weather at prominent points on ships or airplanes.

Another patron saint of sailors is better known today as Santa Claus. Santa Claus began as Nicholas, a fourth-century bishop of Myra in Asia Minor. In order to visit the various towns in his diocese, the bishop had to travel by boat, hence his role as a patron saint of sailors (Mediterranean fishermen still carry pictures of Nicholas, which they take out and parade around the deck during times of peril).

In 1087 Nicholas's relics were taken from Myra to Bari, Italy. Many miracles are attributed to Saint Nicholas. He is credited with restoring to life three boys who had been chopped up and pickled in salt by a butcher. He is also said to have given three bags of gold to the daughters of a poor man, thus saving the three girls from lives of prostitution. (Later tradition transformed the bags into three gold balls, which became the symbol of pawnbrokers.)

In the Netherlands and elsewhere, St. Nicholas's feast day (December 6) is a children's holiday and a time for gift giving. A carving of *Sinterklass* (Dutch for Saint Nicholas) adorned the prow of the first Dutch ship bringing settlers to New Amsterdam. The English in colonial New York adopted from the Dutch the by then unrecognizable saint, calling him Santa Claus (a contraction of *Sinterklaas*). They moved his feast day to the English gift-giving holiday, Christmas. Santa's sleigh, reindeer, North Pole abode, and jolly disposition are all later additions.

Babo's Law has nothing to do with bathtubs; it describes change in the volatility of mixtures. Similarly, Parseval's Identity (vectors) is not lost in the Crookes Dark Space or, for that matter, in the Hittorf or Farraday Dark Space (early electronics) either. Neither can Enke Roots (algebra) or Luder's Bands (crystallography) ever suffer Ruff Degradation (organic chemistry).

The voice of Charlie the Tuna in the Star-Kist Tuna advertisements is that of Hershel Bernardi. Bernardi provides the voices for other television-commercial characters, among them the Jolly Green Giant.

The ventriloquist actor Edgar Bergen got the idea for his dummy, Charlie McCarthy, while in high school. The dummy cost him $35, but his appearances with it helped pay for his education at Northwestern University. In 1937 Bergen was awarded a special Academy Award for his creation of Charlie: the Oscar he was given was made of wood, the only wooden Oscar ever made.

Some people claim that there was a particularly mischievous family of Irish folk living in the south of London during the 1890s. The members of this family were known for their wildness, and when the entire family got together their rowdy antics knew no bounds. They were the Houlihans, but as the stories about them spread through

Britain and across the seas, their name became Hooligan, giving us the word *hooligan,* used for any ruffian. Others claim the stories about the Houlihans are nothing but bunk. The word, they say, comes from a very ungentlemanly Irish hoodlum named Patrick Hooligan, who lived in Southwark, south of London, and performed most of his evil deeds around 1898. Both stories are probably spurious, but even if they don't explain the story of the word *hooligan,* they provide a notion of what the south part of London must have been like around the turn of the century.

Asta, wirehaired fox terrier playing a part written for schnauzer in the first few *Thin Man* movies, was played by Skippy.

The little boy pictured on boxes of Uneeda Biscuits is Gordon Stille, the 5-year-old nephew of Joseph J. Geisinger, the advertising copywriter who created the symbol. When the Uneeda Biscuit boy first appeared, in 1900, he was quite a hit. Children dressed up like him at masquerade parties, and the boxes showed up as props in popular movies.

Some famous horses of famous television and movie cowboys are:

Diablo—Cisco Kid
Loco—the horse of Pancho, Cisco's sidekick
Champion—Gene Autry
Trigger—Roy Rogers
Buttermilk—Dale Evans
Silver—Lone Ranger
Scout—Tonto
Tony—Tom Mix
Fritz—William S. Hart
Topper—Hopalong Cassidy
Phantom—white horse of Zorro
Tornado—black horse of Zorro

To Broadway actors are awarded Tonys, to movie stars Oscars, television players receive Emmys, but performing animals are recognized with the Patsy Award (Picture Animal Top Star of the Year), sponsored annually since 1951 by the American Humane Association.

First to receive this prestigious award was Francis, the Talking Mule. Checkers, Richard Nixon's political savior and arguably the most influential dog in American history, was passed up for the honor in 1952.

Names of the devil are many. In German legend he has been called *Krumnase* ("crooked nose"), *Raffenzahn* ("snaggletooth"), *Ziegenbart* ("goatbeard"), *Spiegelglanz* ("mirror-sight"), and *Schoppenstugk* ("pint") among innumerable others.

Calamity Jane's (1852–1903) real name was Martha Jane Canary. It is only a coincidence, however, that she began her career as the madam in a Blackfoot, Montana, whorehouse known as the Bird Cage.

About Mary and her lamb that went to school, it's all true. "Mary Had a Little Lamb" is one of the very few nursery rhymes with a single, documentable author. In this case, Sarah Josepha Hale (1788–1879) of Boston claimed her inspiration was from an actual school-days happening.

Hurricanes were not named after women until 1953. From 1979 (and 1978 in the Pacific) male and female names are used alternately.

There are five rosters of hurricane names presently in use, which are rotated from year to year in succession. Each roster contains twenty-one names. A name is struck, or retired, when it has become attached to a particularly famous storm, e.g., Betsy, Beulah, Camille, and Carla.

Best guesses as to the identity of the "Man in the Iron Mask" suggest he was Mattioli, state secretary to the Duke of Mantua and an active political enemy of Louis XIV. After his supposed kidnapping and imprisonment he was made to wear, in fact, a black velvet mask.

The constant companion of the redoubtable young sleuth of French comics, Tintin, is his dog Snowy. But Tintin has more in common with another dog, Rin Tin Tin (1916–32): both take their names from a popular French doll carried for luck by French soldiers throughout World War I.

The canine star was a German veteran of World War I. The courageous German shepherd was encountered in a German trench by an American infantry officer named Lee Duncan. Captain Duncan recognized the dog's potential and brought him back to Los Angeles to train him for a career in films.

The Smith brothers who appear on cough drop boxes, popularly identified as Trade and Mark, are really William and Andrew.

Maxwell's Demon is an imaginary beast that wishes to violate the laws of thermodynamics. He operates an imaginary shutter between chambers into which he tries to sort fast (hot) and slow (cool) molecules.

No one doubts that James Clerk Maxwell's accomplice could do this, but still there is no gain in useful energy. The law stands.

Our legal contests between fictitious persons—*John Doe v. Richard Roe*—are rooted in English property law, in which parties to some suits contended also as *Goodtitle v. Troublesome*. These legal aliases are thought up as a rule by the judge hearing the case.

Even Roman lawyers knew of this legal convenience and were especially fond of *Titius v. Seius*.

The most famous of American fictitious litigants is Jane Roe of *Roe v. Wade,* the controversial 1973 abortion-rights case. Roe, of course, will remain forever anonymous; Wade is Henry Wade, named to the suit in his capacity as city attorney for Dallas, Texas.

Cracker Jacks were developed in 1896 by F. W. Rueckheim and his brother Louis. The candy-coated popcorn got its name when an enthusiastic salesman declared it "crackerjack!" The Rueckheim brothers adopted the slogan "The More You Eat, the More You Want," and, in 1910, they began selling their Cracker Jacks in boxes containing coupons redeemable for prizes; in 1912 they began putting the prizes right in the boxes. In 1916 they began using the sailor boy Jack and his dog, Bingo, in their advertisements; in 1919 they put them on the box. The model for Jack was F. W.'s grandson, Robert. Robert did not live to enjoy his fame: he died of pneumonia at age 8.

H. G. Wells in *The Invisible Man* (1897) created a character with a nagging identity problem: not only does he fade from view, but he lacks a first name. Throughout the novel he is referred to only as Griffin, his last name.

In making the 1933 feature film based on this tale, screenwriters warmed up the title character a bit, christening him Jack Griffin. And producers gave the part to the highly personable Claude Rains—his first appearance in films. (Strictly speaking, this was a *non*-appearance, since Rains's face was swathed in bandages for the role.)

The aliases of Humpty Dumpty around the world include Hillerin-Lillerin, Annebadadeli, Wirgele-Wargele, Gigele-Gagele, Rüntzelken-Püntzelken, and Etje-Papetje.

Reproduced in its style from Saxony, the rhyme goes:
> Hümpelken-Pümpelken sat op de Bank
> Hümpelken-Pümpelken fêl von de Bank
> Do is Kên Dokter in Engelland
> De Hümpelken-Pümpelken kuräre kann.

And an old Danish version:
> Lille Trille
> Laae paa Hylde;
> Lille Trille
> Faldt ned of Hylde.
> Ingen mand
> I hele Land
> Lille Trille curere kan.

Pookas, of whom Harvey (six-foot invisible and magical rabbit of Mary Chase's 1944 play, *Harvey*) is the most noted, were more often encountered in the shape of an ass or mule. The ambition of these Celtic beasts is to lead travelers astray.

Producers of *Harvey* opened the play out of town with an inhabited $600 rabbit suit. It looked silly; the suit was written off after one performance.

Father Divine (d. 1965) was George Baker, diminutive four feet six inches but charismatic religious leader from Harlem. His temporal, as opposed to spiritual, empire was valued in excess of $10 million, consisting mostly of small businesses—barber shops, laundries, restaurants, and garages.

The most famous real live pig of recent history was Arnold Ziffel, a star of the television series "Green Acres." Arnold, of the Chester White breed, appeared only in 1968 and 1969 before his increasing girth caused his unpublicized replacement with a younger pig.

Out, Out, Brief Neanderthal: Death and Dying

"I'm shot if I don't believe I'm dying."

—Last words of Edward Thurlow (1731–1806)

Paraguay's male population has twice been nearly wiped out, in the War of the Triple Alliance (1870) and the Chaco War (1932), sinking in proportion to the female population to as low as one to five. By 1972, however, sexual parity had very nearly been reached.

At Shiloh—the second day, April 7, 1862—Confederate general Toutant Beauregard requested his medical officer, Dr. Brodie, to take the pulses of he and his staff "to ascertain the pulsations of the human system in the excitement of going into battle." They ranged from 90 to 130.

Napoleon was first buried, in May 1821, on St. Helena at Geranium Valley, a site for which the British government eventually paid £1200. Always cautious, they merely rented it for the first few years.

In 1840 the remains were exhumed and transported to Paris, where they were reinterred at Les Invalides.

James Madison's last words were "I always talk better lying down."

American industry produced mightily for military needs of World War II, but development was finished too late in the war for the bat bomb.

An idea introduced in 1942 with President Roosevelt's backing, the bat bomb was a one-ounce incendiary attached to a live bat. When released over Germany and Japan enemy forces would be diverted in large numbers to hunt down these reclusive firebugs.

A good idea on paper—America had a stategic reserve of bats in the Ney Caves of Texas exceeding 30 million, and the whole device required little more than a tiny string harness and a delay fuse. (Bats were to be given a sporting chance to chew through the harness before ignition took place.)

Unforeseen difficulties arose in the storage of bat munitions—bats chilled into sleep sometimes never woke up—and bat accidents led to the charring of some Allied real estate. Delivery of such a weapon also proved unexpectedly tricky. All the bugs were not worked out until mid–1945, just as the war came to an end.

William Cullen Bryant's last words were "Whose house is this? What street are we in? Why did you bring me here?"

Albrecht Durer, ever devoted to things scientific as well as artistic, died (1521) from pneumonia contracted when he traveled to Zeeland (northern Holland) to sketch a stranded whale.

Lord Byron's last words were "I must sleep now."

Actual hostilities with the British were not commenced by the Irish Republican Army until January 1919; they ceased December 6, 1921. In that time loss of life was about 750 on each side, but higher numbers of casualties were sustained within the IRA between December 1921 and April 1923, when bitter factions warred over terms of the new constitution.

Michael Collins, first commandant of the IRA, who eluded the British throughout that phase of the "troubles," was among the many IRA leaders killed in the subsequent internecine struggle.

Checkmate, the word that ends a game of chess, is from a Persian phrase *"Shah mat"* ("The king is dead"). Indeed, all our uses of the word *check* (and the British *cheque*) come from this Persian phrase.

Pierre Giraud, a noted architect of the French Revolutionary period, proposed in 1801 a scientific and space-saving solution to death and burial. In his perfected scheme, remains were made into a glass, which is molded into a bas-relief medallion of the deceased.

The idea, though technically feasible, never caught on. Instead, for the first time, the French were enabled by a decree of 1804 to own in perpetuity their own burial plots.

Any innovation was an improvement over the centuries-old custom of interrment beneath churches. Aside from contributing to poor public health, such practices were often condemned for leaving church floors treacherously uneven, as the slabs were so often moved and tilted by gravediggers.

The French revolutionary propagandist Jean Paul Marat was assassinated while taking a bath, but he wasn't sitting in his tub to get clean. Marat suffered from a skin disease, probably pruritus, and was tormented by constant itching. During 1790 and 1791 he had been outlawed for his inflammatory writings and had been forced to hide in the sewers of Paris. The dampness had exacerbated the disease. The only treatment that gave him any relief from the constant itching was soaking in a warm bath. On July 13, 1793, he was in his bath, writing an editorial. That is where Charlotte Corday found him—and stabbed him to death.

Presidents Lincoln, Andrew Jackson, Grant, and Garfield all died intestate—without leaving a valid will. (Lincoln and Garfield, of course, were assassinated.)

During the Spanish-American War, more US troops died from eating contaminated meat than from battle wounds.

Nearly everyone is agreed that Wild Bill Hickok held aces and eights (as reported by the undertaker, a Mr. Pierce) when he was murdered by Jack McCall. But confusion persists about the name of the saloon. It is variously reported by Hickok's contemporaries as "No. 6," "No. 66," and "No. 10" (but never reported as "No. 666," which is, of course, the "number of the beast").

As late as 1874 in Maine the practice of burying tuberculosis victims face down is reported. The superstitious purpose was to prevent consumption from afflicting the entire family. This practice is identical to that of Bulgaria for interring vampires.

The signers of the *Agreement on Ending the War and Restoring Peace in Viet Nam* were, for the United States, William P. Rogers (secretary of state) and, for North Viet Nam, Nguyen Duy Trinh (minister for foreign affairs).

The verbal formula which ended America's longest war, comprising Article 1 of both the bilateral and multilateral agreements, was: "The United States and all other countries respect the independence, sovereignty, unity, and territorial integrity of Viet-Nam as recognized by the 1954 Geneva Agreements on Viet-Nam."

America entered the Spanish-American War with gusto. When the first 16,000 US troops left Tampa, Florida, on their way to Cuba, on June 14, 1898, they sang rousing choruses of "There'll Be a Hot Time in the Old Town Tonight."

The fourteenth-century Black Death killed so many Europeans that the living had neither the time nor the room to bury the corpses. One way to get rid of the bodies was to dump them in a river, and the Rhone River in France was consecrated so that it could provide a suitable graveyard for the piles of victims.

David Livingston (1813–73), he whom Henry Stanley presumably found, is buried in two places. His heart and viscera were interred beneath a tree near Lake Bangweulu by his faithful servants Susi and Chuma. His crudely embalmed body, which they carried for nine months to the coast, was eventually buried beneath the floor of Westminster Abbey, though the first English officers encountered by Susi and Chuma were in favor of burying it on the spot.

Edgar Allan Poe based his detective story *The Mystery of Marie Roget* on an actual murder case, that of Mary Cecilia Rogers, who was murdered in New York City in 1841.

Rather than drink the coffee and wine that were offered him, Peter Ilyich Tchaikovsky decided to slake his lunchtime thirst with a glass of water. This was in St. Petersburg in 1893, during the month of November, the height of that city's annual cholera season. The water the great composer drank had not been boiled, but Tchaikovsky only shrugged his shoulders when his brother chastised him for his rash act. He then became violently ill. Five days later, he died of cholera.

Lyndon Johnson's favorite singer was Anita Bryant. He asked her to sing at his funeral, and she promised she would. She did, singing "The Battle Hymn of the Republic" at his funeral in 1973.

The only survivor of Custer's Last Stand was a horse named Comanche (the horse was wounded during the battle). When the horse died, its remains were shipped to the Smithsonian Institution and put on display.

Millard Fillmore spoke his last words to his doctor, who had just given him something to eat: "The nourishment is palatable," he said and then died.

The average Neanderthal man lived 29 years; the average Roman at the time of Caesar lived 36; during the eighteenth century, most men lived to be 45.

Virtue, Sloth, Beauty:
Entertainment

Rock star Boy George's real name is George O'Dowd.

Tokyo Rose, the Japanese radio propagandist of World War II, was actually seven women. Only Iva Toguri d'Aquino, a Japanese-American, was tried (and sentenced to ten years) after the war for her participation, which was construed as treasonous. Toguri was born in 1920 and received a degree in zoology from UCLA. She was released from custody in 1956 and was granted a pardon in 1977 by Gerald Ford, one of his last official acts.

For some reason the Nazi counterpart to Tokyo Rose, Axis Sally, never achieved the same notoriety. Mildred Gillars, a failed actress from Maine, was the only voice of Axis Sally.

New Hampshire was the first state in this century to authorize a state lottery, in 1964.

The legendary Sarah Bernhardt (1844–1923), French actress, gave her last performance (the play was *La Gloire*) in 1922, aged 78.

Merry-go-rounds made in England always move clockwise; when made elsewhere, counterclockwise rotation is the rule.

Pete Seeger wrote "Turn! Turn! Turn!" made famous by the Byrds.

Early in January 1914, the Mexican Revolutionary leader Pancho Villa decided to attack the city of Ojinaga, site of a federal garrison. He gathered his forces outside the city, organized them for the battle, and then sat down to wait. Villa had recently signed a contract with the Mutual Film Corporation, granting the American company the rights to all battle coverage of the war. He had promised the gringo filmmakers that he would schedule his battles during daylight hours whenever possible, and he was now postponing his attack until the camera operators could arrive. When the cameras were finally set up, the attack began.

The film has been lost, which is unfortunate, for it might have shed light on the mystery surrounding the disappearance of one of America's greatest satirists, Ambrose Bierce. In November 1913, Bierce was granted credentials as an observer with Villa's army. He went off to Mexico—and was never heard from again. He simply vanished. His last letter, however, reads, "Expect next day to go to Ojinaga." He is believed to have died during the fighting and to have been buried in an unmarked grave. Perhaps that long-lost movie contains his flickering image.

TV CLASSICS

ALL IN THE FAMILY
1971–
Archie Bunker: Carroll O'Connor
Edith Bunker (Dingbat):   Jean Stapleton
Gloria Bunker Stivic (1971–1978):   Sally Struthers
Mike Stivic (Meathead) (1971–1978):   Rob Reiner
Lionel Jefferson (1971–1975):   Mike Evans
Louise Jefferson (1971–1975):   Isabel Sanford
Henry Jefferson (1971–1973):   Mel Stewart
George Jefferson (1973–1975):   Sherman Hemsley
Irene Lorenzo (1973–1975):   Betty Garrett
Frank Lorenzo (1973–1974):   Vincent Gardenia

BEN CASEY
1961–1966
Dr. Ben Casey: Vince Edwards
Dr. David Zorba (1961–1965):   Sam Jaffe
Dr. Maggie Graham: Bettye Ackermann
Dr. Ted Hoffman: Harry Landers
Nick Kanavaras: Nick Dennis
Nurse Wills: Jeanne Bates
Jane Hancock (1965):   Stella Stevens
Dr. Mike Rogers (1965):   Ben Piazza
Dr. Daniel Niles Freeland (1965–1966):   Franchot Tone
Dr. Terry McDaniel (1965–1966):   Jim McMullan

BEVERLY HILLBILLIES, THE
1962–1971
Jed Clampett: Buddy Ebsen
Granny Clampett: Irene Ryan

Elly May Clampett: Donna Douglas
Jethro Bodine: Max Baer, Jr.
Milton Drysdale: Raymond Bailey
Jane Hathaway: Nancy Kulp
Cousin Pearl Bodine (1962–1963):   Bea Benadaret
Mrs. Drysdale: Harriet MacGibbon

BONANZA
1959–1973
Ben Cartwright: Lorne Greene
Little Joe Cartwright: Michael Landon
"Hoss" Cartwright (1959–1972):   Dan Blocker
Adam Cartwright (1959–1965):   Pernell Roberts
Hop Sing: Victor Sen Yung
Candy (1967–1970, 1972–1973):   David Canary
Dusty Rhoades (1970–1972):   Lou Frizzell
Jamie Hunter (1970–1973):   Mitch Vogel
Griff King (1972–1973):   Tim Matheson

COMBAT
1962–1967
Lt. Gil Hanley: Rick Jason
Sgt. Chip Saunders: Vic Morrow
Caje (Caddy Cadron):   Pierre Jalbert
Kirby (1963–1967):   Jack Hogan
Littlejohn (1963–1967):   Dick Peabody
Doc Walton (1962–1963):   Steven Rogers
Doc (1963–1965):   Conlon Carter
Pvt. Braddock (1962–1963):   Shecky Greene
Nelson (1963–1964):   Tom Lowell

DR. KILDARE
1961–1966
Dr. James Kildare: Richard Chamberlain
Dr. Leonard Gillespie: Raymond Massey
Dr. Simon Agurski (1961–1962):   Eddie Ryder
Dr. Thomas Gerson (1961–1962):   Jud Taylor
Receptionist Susan Deigh (1961–1962):   Joan Patrick
Nurse Zoe Lawton (1965–1966):   Lee Kurty

DRAGNET

1952–1970

Sgt. Joe Friday: Jack Webb
Sgt. Ben Romero (1951):   Barton Yarborough
Sgt. Ed Jacobs (1952):   Barney Phillips
Officer Frank Smith (1952):   Herb Ellis
Officer Frank Smith (1953–1959):   Ben Alexander
Officer Bill Gannin (1967–1970):   Harry Morgan

FATHER KNOWS BEST

1954–1963

Jim Anderson: Robert Young
Margaret Anderson: Jane Wyatt
Betty Anderson (Princess):   Elinor Donahue
James Anderson, Jr. (Bud):   Billy Gray
Kathy Anderson (Kitten):   Lauren Chapin
Miss Thomas: Sarah Selby
Ed Davis (1955–1959):   Robert Foulk
Myrtle Davis (1954–1959):   Vivi Jannis
Dotty Snow (1955–1957):   Yvonne Lime
Kippy Watkins (1954–1957):   Paul Wallace
Claude Messner (1954–1959):   Jimmy Bates
Doyle Hobbs (1957–1958):   Roger Smith
Ralph Little (1957–1958):   Robert Chapman
April Adams (1957–1958):   Sue George
Joyce Kendall (1958–1959):   Jymme (Roberta) Shore

THE HONEYMOONERS

1955–1971

Ralph Kramden: Jackie Gleason
Ed Norton: Art Carney
Alice Kramden: Audrey Meadows
Trixie Norton: Joyce Randolph
Alice (1971):   Sheila MacRae
Trixie (1971):   Jane Kean

I LOVE LUCY

1951–1961

Lucy Ricardo: Lucille Ball
Ricky Ricardo: Desi Arnaz
Ethel Mertz: Vivan Vance

Fred Mertz: William Frawley
Little Ricky Ricardo: Richard Keith

M*A*S*H
1972–1983
Capt. Benjamin Franklin Pierce (Hawkeye):   Alan Alda
Capt. John McIntyre (Trapper John) (1972–1975):
   Wayne Rogers
Maj. Margaret Houlihan (Hot Lips):   Loretta Swit
Maj. Frank Burns (1972–1977):   Larry Linville
Cpl. Radar O'Reilly: Gary Burghoff
Lt. Col. Henry Blake (1972–1975):   McLean Stevenson
Father John Mulcahy: William Christopher
Corp. Maxwell Klinger :   Jamie Farr
Col. Sherman Potter :   Harry Morgan
Capt. B. J. Hunnicut :   Mike Farrell
Maj. Charles Emerson Winchester (1977–   ):
   David Ogden Stiers
Lt. Maggie Dish (1972):   Karen Philipp
Spearchucker Jones (1972):   Timothy Brown
Ho–John (1972):   Patrick Adiarte
Ugly John (1972–1973):   John Orchard
Lt. Leslie Scorch (1972–1973):   Linda Meiklejohn
Gen. Brandon Clayton (1972–1973):   Herb Voland
Nurse Louise Anderson (1973):   Kelly Jean Peters
Lt. Nancy Griffin (1973):   Lynette Mettey
Various nurses (1973–1977):   Bobbie Mitchell
Gen. Mitchell (1973–1974):   Robert F. Simon
Nurse Kelly :   Kellye Nakahara
Various nurses :   Patricia Stevens
Various nurses :   Judy Farrell

THE MANY LOVES OF DOBIE GILLIS
1959–1963
Dobie Gillis: Dwayne Hickman
Maynard G. Krebs: Bob Denver
Herbert T. Gillis: Frank Faylen
Winifred (Winnie) Gillis: Florida Friebus
Zelda Bilroy: Sheila James
Thalia Menninger (1959–1960):   Tuesday Weld

Milton Armitage (1959–1960):   Warren Beatty
Riff Ryan (1959–1960):   Tommy Farrell
Melissa Frome (1959–1960):   Yvonne Lime
Davey Gillis (1959–1960):   Darryl Hickman
Mr. Pomfritt: William Schallert
Clarice Armitage (1959–1960):   Doris Packer
Mrs. Chatsworth Osborne Sr. (1960–1963):   Doris Packer
Chatsworth Osborne Jr. (1960–1963):   Stephen Franken
Mrs. Ruth Adams (1959–1960):   Jean Byron
Dr. Burkhart (1961–1963):   Jean Byron
Mrs. Blossom Kenney (1959–1961):   Marjorie Bennett
Lt. Merriweather (1961):   Richard Clair
Dean Magruder (1961–1963):   Raymond Bailey
Duncan Gillis (1962–1963):   Bobby Diamond

MISSION: IMPOSSIBLE
1966–1973
Daniel Briggs (1966–1967):   Steven Hill
Cinnamon Carter (1966–1969):   Barbara Bain
Rollin Hand (1966–1969):   Martin Landau
Barney Collier: Greg Morris
Willie Armitage: Peter Lupus
James Phelps (1967–1973):   Peter Graves
Paris (1967–1971):   Leonard Nimoy

STAR TREK
1966–1969
Capt. James T. Kirk: William Shatner
Mr. Spock: Leonard Nimoy
Dr. Leonard McCoy: DeForest Kelly
Yeoman Janice Rand (1966–1967):   Grace Lee Whitney
Sulu: George Takei
Uhura: Nichelle Nichols
Engineer Montgomery Scott: James Doohan
Nurse Christine Chapel: Majel Barrett
Ensign Chekov (1967–1969):   Walter Koenig

ZORRO
1957–1959
Don Diego de las Vega (Zorro):   Guy Williams
Don Alejandro: George J. Lewis
Bernardo: Gene Sheldon
Capt. Monastario: Britt Lamond
Sgt. Garcia: Henry Calvin

Elvis Presley had a middle name: Aron.

Kelly's goats, flying jinny, and carry-us-all are some early American expressions for the carousel.

Elton John's middle name is Hercules. (That is his legal name, but he was born Reginald Dwight.)

David Bowie named his son Zowie after "Zooey" in J. D. Salinger's *Franny and Zooey,* one of his favorite books.

The women chosen Miss America by the Miss America Beauty Pageant have not always enjoyed their role. Norma Smallwood of Oklahoma, Miss America 1926, refused to go to Atlantic City to crown her successor because the pageant officials refused to pay her the $600 she demanded for the trip. Bette Cooper, Miss America 1937, was shy. Only 17, she ran away the night she was crowned. The public attention was just too much for her, and she made very few public appearances. Also shy was BeBe Shopp of Minnesota, Miss America 1948. The reign of the 18-year-old farm girl was known as "Miss America's Moral Crusade" after the press misquoted her views on sex and alcohol. Because she had somewhat wide hips, she had to spend a lot of her time answering reporters' questions about what she planned to do about "that fat." Thus far only one Miss America has resigned her title, Vanessa Williams, Miss America 1984 and the first black Miss America. She resigned at the request of pageant officials when it became known that she had posed for nude photographs.

Redd Foxx's real name is John Elroy Sanford.

The citizens of the ancient Roman city of Pompeii enjoyed theater—open-air spectacles, Greek plays, farces, and burlesque mimes. Occasionally, a condemned criminal would be cast in the role of a doomed man and would be put to death on stage, the method of his execution fitting the plot requirements.

The first jazz record had *Livery Stable Blues* on one side and *Dixie Jass Band One Step* on the other. The performers were the Original Dixieland Jass Band, all of whom were white.

MOTION PICTURE ACADEMY AWARDS (OSCARS)

1927–28
Actor: Emil Jannings, *The Way of All Flesh*
Actress: Janet Gaynor, *Seventh Heaven*
Picture: *Wings*

1928–29
Actor: Warner Baxter, *In Old Arizona*
Actress: Mary Pickford, *Coquette.*
Picture: *Broadway Melody*

1929–30
Actor: George Arliss, *Disraeli*
Actress: Norma Shearer, *The Divorcee*
Picture: *All Quiet on the Western Front*

1930–31
Actor: Lionel Barrymore, *Free Soul*
Actress: Marie Dressler, *Min and Bill.*
Picture: *Cimarron*

1931–32
Actor: Fredric March, *Dr. Jekyll and Mr. Hyde:* Wallace
    Berry, *The Champ* (tie)
Actress: Helen Hayes, *Sin of Madelon Claudet*
Picture: *Grand Hotel*
Special: Walt Disney, *Mickey Mouse*

1932–33
Actor: Charles Laughton, *Private Life of Henry VIII*
Actress: Katharine Hepburn, *Morning Glory*
Picture: *Cavalcade*

1934
Actor: Clark Gable, *It Happened One Night*
Actress: Claudette Colbert, same
Picture: *It Happened One Night*

1935
Actor: Victor McLaglen, *The Informer*
Actress: Bette Davis, *Dangerous*
Picture: *Mutiny on the Bounty*

1936
Actor: Paul Muni, *Story of Louis Pasteur*
Actress: Luise Rainer, *The Great Ziegfeld*
Picture: *The Great Ziegfeld*

1937
Actor: Spencer Tracy, *Captains Courageous*
Actress: Luise Rainer, *The Good Earth*
Picture: *Life of Emile Zola*

1938
Actor: Spencer Tracy, *Boys Town*
Actress: Bette Davis, *Jezebel*
Picture: *You Can't Take It With You*

1939
Actor: Robert Donat, *Goodbye, Mr. Chips*
Actress: Vivien Leigh, *Gone With the Wind*
Picture: *Gone With the Wind*

1940
Actor: James Stewart, *The Philadelphia Story*
Actress: Ginger Rogers, *Kitty Foyle*
Picture: *Rebecca*

1941
Actor: Gary Cooper, *Sergeant York*
Actress: Joan Fontaine, *Suspicion*
Picture: *How Green Was My Valley*

1942
Actor: James Cagney, *Yankee Doodle Dandy*
Actress: Greer Garson, *Mrs. Miniver*
Picture: *Mrs. Miniver*

1943
Actor: Paul Lukas, *Watch on the Rhine*
Actress: Jennifer Jones, *The Song of Bernadette*
Picture: *Casablanca*

1944
Actor: Bing Crosby, *Going My Way*
Actress: Ingrid Bergman, *Gaslight*
Picture: *Going My Way*

1945
Actor: Ray Milland, *The Lost Weekend*
Actress: Joan Crawford, *Mildred Pierce*
Picture: *The Lost Weekend*

1946
Actor: Fredric March, *Best Years of Our Lives*
Actress: Olivia de Havilland, *To Each His Own*
Picture: *The Best Years of Our Lives*

1947
Actor: Ronald Colman, *A Double Life*
Actress: Loretta Young, *The Farmer's Daughter.*
Picture: *Gentleman's Agreement*

1948
Actor: Laurence Olivier, *Hamlet*
Actress: Jane Wyman, *Johnny Belinda*
Picture: *Hamlet*

1949
Actor: Broderick Crawford, *All the King's Men*
Actress: Olivia de Havilland, *The Heiress*
Picture: *All the King's Men*

1950
Actor: Jose Ferrer, *Cyrano de Bergerac*
Actress: Judy Holliday, *Born Yesterday*
Picture: *All About Eve*

1951
Actor: Humphrey Bogart, *The African Queen*
Actress: Vivien Leigh, *A Streetcar Named Desire*
Picture: *An American in Paris*

1952
Actor: Gary Cooper, *High Noon.*
Actress: Shirley Booth, *Come Back, Little Sheba*
Picture: *Greatest Show on Earth*

1953
Actor: William Holden, *Stalag 17*
Actress: Audrey Hepburn, *Roman Holiday*
Picture: *From Here to Eternity.*

1954
Actor: Marlon Brando, *On the Waterfront*
Actress: Grace Kelly. *The Country Girl*
Picture: *On the Waterfront*

1955
Actor: Ernest Borgnine, *Marty*
Actress: Anna Magnani, *The Rose Tattoo*
Picture: *Marty*

1956
Actor: Yul Brynner, *The King and I*
Actress: Ingrid Bergman, *Anastasia*
Picture: *Around the World in 80 Days*

1957
Actor: Alec Guinness, *The Bridge on the River Kwai*
Actress: Joanne Woodward, *The Three Faces of Eve*
Picture: *The Bridge on the River Kwai*

1958
Actor: David Niven, *Separate Tables*
Actress: Susan Hayward, *I Want to Live*
Picture: *Gigi*

1959
Actor: Charlton Heston, *Ben-Hur*
Actress: Simone Signoret, *Room at the Top*
Picture: *Ben-Hur*

1960
Actor: Burt Lancaster, *Elmer Gantry*
Actress: Elizabeth Taylor, *Butterfield 8*
Picture: *The Apartment*

1961
Actor: Maximillan Schell, *Judgment at Nuremberg*
Actress: Sophia Loren, *Two Women*
Picture: *West Side Story*

1962
Actor: Gregory Peck, *To Kill a Mockingbird*
Actress: Anne Bancroft, *The Miracle Worker*
Picture: *Lawrence of Arabia*

1963
Actor: Sidney Poitier, *Lilies of the Field*
Actress: Patricia Neal, *Hud*
Picture: *Tom Jones*

1964
Actor: Rex Harrison, *My Fair Lady*
Actress: Julie Andrews, *Mary Poppins*
Picture: *My Fair Lady*

1965
Actor: Lee Marvin, *Cat Ballou*
Actress: Julie Christie, *Darling*
Picture: *The Sound of Music*

1966
Actor: Paul Scofield, *A Man for All Seasons*
Actress: Elizabeth Taylor, *Who's Afraid of Virginia Woolf?*
Picture: *A Man for All Seasons*

1967
Actor: Rod Steiger, *In the Heat of the Night*
Actress: Katharine Hepburn, *Guess Who's Coming to Dinner*
Picture: *In the Heat of the Night*

1968
Actor: Cliff Robertson, *Charly*
Actress: Katharine Hepburn, *The Lion in Winter,*
     Barbra Streisand, *Funny Girl* (tie)
Picture: *Oliver*

1969
Actor: John Wayne, *TrueGrit*
Actress: Maggie Smith, *The Prime of Miss Jean Brodie*
Picture: *Midnight Cowboy*

1970
Actor: George C. Scott, *Patton* (refused)
Actress: Glenda Jackson, *Women in Love*
Picture: *Patton*

1971
Actor: Gene Hackman, *The French Connection*
Actress: Jane Fonda, *Klute*
Picture: *The French Connection*

1972
Actor: Marlon Brando, *The Godfather* (refused)
Actress: Liza Minnelli, *Cabaret*
Picture: *The Godfather*

1973
Actor: Jack Lemmon, *Save the Tiger*
Actress: Glenda Jackson, *A Touch of Class*
Picture: *The Sting*

1974
Actor: Art Carney, *Harry and Tonto*
Actress: Ellen Burstyn, *Alice Doesn't Live Here Anymore*
Picture: *The Godfather, Part II*

1975
Actor: Jack Nicholson, *One Flew Over the Cuckoo's Nest*
Actress: Louise Fletcher, same
Picture: *One Flew Over the Cuckoo's Nest*

1976
Actor: Peter Finch, *Network*
Actress: Faye Dunaway, same
Picture: *Rocky*

1977
Actor: Richard Dreyfuss, *The Goodbye Girl*
Actress: Diane Keaton, *Annie Hall*
Picture: *Annie Hall*

1978
Actor: Jon Voight, *Coming Home*
Actress: Jane Fonda, *Coming Home*
Picture: *The Deer Hunter*

1979
Actor: Dustin Hoffman, *Kramer vs. Kramer*
Actress: Sally Field, *Norma Rae*
Picture: *Kramer vs. Kramer*

1980
Actor: Robert De Niro, *Raging Bull*
Actress: Sissy Spacek, *Coal Miner's Daughter*
Picture: *Ordinary People*

1981
Actor: Henry Fonda, *On Golden Pond*
Actress: Katherine Hepburn, *On Golden Pond*
Picture: *Chariots of Fire*

1982
Actor: Ben Kingsley, *Gandhi*
Actress: Meryl Streep, *Sophie's Choice*
Picture: *Gandhi*

1983
Actor: Robert Duvall, *Tender Mercies*
Actress: Shirley Maclaine, *Terms of Endearment*
Picture: *Terms of Endearment*

To prepare himself for the role of a paralyzed war veteran in the 1950 film *The Men*, Marlon Brando lived in a veterans' hospital with actual paraplegics.

Hattie McDaniel was the first black to win an Academy Award. She was awarded an Oscar as best supporting actress for her role in *Gone with the Wind* (1939).

Scott Joplin's "Maple Leaf Rag," published in 1899, was the first instrumental piece to top the million mark in sales of sheet music. Joplin named the song after the Maple Leaf Club in Sedalia, Missouri.

Paul Anka composed "Here's Johnny," the theme song of Johnny Carson's "Tonight Show."

Rock star David Bowie was born David Hayward Jones. He changed his name to avoid confusion with David Jones of the Monkees; he took Bowie from the famous knife.

The house depicted in the 1945 film *The House on 92nd Street* was actually located on 93rd Street, between Park and Madison avenues.

Will Rogers's full name was William Penn Adair Rogers. He was born in 1879. In 1902 he joined Texas Jack's Wild West show in South Africa. He was billed as "The Cherokee Kid."

The first actor to play James Bond was Barry Nelson, who took the role in a live television version of *Casino Royale* in 1954. Since then, three actors have assayed the role of James Bond: Sean Connery, Roger Moore, and—in *On Her Majesty's Secret Service* (1969)—George Lazenby.

Billy Joel's middle name is Martin.

Neil Diamond wrote "I'm a Believer," the song made famous by the Monkees.

In 1951 Bing Crosby Enterprises became the first to successfully demonstrate black-and-white video recording on magnetic tape.

SOAP OPERA CHARACTERS

All My Children
Dr. Charles Tyler
Phoebe Tyler
Lincoln ("Linc") Tyler
Kitty Carpenter Tyler
Dr. Chuck Tyler
Kate Martin
Paul Martin
Anne Tyler Martin
Dr. Joe Martin
Nurse Ruth Martin
Dr. Jeff Martin
Tara Martin Brent
Phil Brent
(Little) Phil Tyler
Erica Kane Brent
Mona Kane
Nick Davis
Clem Wason
Dr. Frank Grant
Nurse Caroline Murray
Dr. David Thornton
Dr. Christina Karras
Danny Kennicott
Brooke English
Benny Sago
Tad Gardner
Donna Beck
Mrs. Lum

Another World
Jim Matthews
Liz Matthews
Alica Matthews Frame
Dr. Russ Matthews
Sharlene Frame Matthews
Pat Randolph
John Randolph
Michael Randolph
Marianne Randolph
Darryl Stevens
MacKenzie ("Mac") Cory

As The World Turns
Chris Hughes
Nancy Hughes
Dr. Bob Hughes
Donald Hughes
Tom Hughes
Natalie Bannon Hughes
Franny Hughes
Dr. David Stewart
Ellen Stewart
Dr. Dan Stewart
Valerie Conway Stewart
Dr. Susan Stewart
Judge Lowell
Emmy Stewart
Betsy Stewart
Annie Stewart
Dawn ("Dee") Stewart
Beau Spencer
Dr. John Dixon
Kim Dixon
Dr. Jim Strasfield
Grant Colman
Lisa Shea Colman
Alma Miller
Jay Stallings
Carol Stallings
Laurie Keaton
Mary Ellison
Teddy Ellison
Joyce Colman
Sandy Garrison
Kevin Thompson
Dick Martin
Nurse Marion Connelly
Nurse Pat Holland

Days Of Our Lives
Dr. Tom Horton, Sr.
Alice Horton
Mickey Horton
Maggie "Hansen" Horton

Rachel Cory
Jamie Frame
Ada McGowan
Gil McGowan
Tim McGowan
Iris Cory Carrington
Dennis Carrington
Louise Goddard
Rocky Olsen
Ken Palmer
Beatrice Gordon
Raymond Gordon
Olive Gordon
Sally Frame
Willis Frame
Bert Ordway
Emma Ordway
Molly Ordway Randolph
Clarice Hobson
Angela ("Angie") Perrini
Dr. David Gilchrist
Keith Morrison
Dr. Frank Prescott
Brian Bancroft
Scott Bradley
Jeff Stone
Evan Webster
Dr. Bill Horton
Dr. Laura Horton
Michael Horton, Jr.
Jennifer Rose Horton
Dr. Tom Horton, Jr.
Julie Anderson Williams
Doug Williams
David Banning
Hope Williams
Kim Williams
Robert LeClare
Rebecca North LeClare
Johnny Collins
Bob Anderson
Mary Anderson
Phyllis Anderson Curtis
Dr. Neil Curtis
Amanda Howard Peters

Dr. Greg Peters
Susan Peters
Eric Peters
Paul Grant
Helen Grant
Danny Grant
Valerie Grant
Don Craig
Linda Patterson Phillips
Jeri Clayton
Jack Clayton
Trish Clayton
Brooke Hamilton
Dr. Marlene Evans
Karl Duval
Sharon Duval
Hank
Rosie
Nathan Curtis

The Doctors
Dr. Matt Powers
Dr. Maggie Powers
Dr. Mike Powers
Toni Powers
Greta Powers
Dr. Althea Davis
Penny Davis
Mona Aldrich Croft
Dr. Steve Aldrich
Nurse Carolee Aldrich
Stephanie Aldrich
Erich Aldrich
Billy Allison
Jason Aldrich
Stacy Wells Summers
Dr. Paul Summers
Eleanor Conrad
Virginia Dancy
Lew Dancy
Sarah Dancy
Sarah Dancy
Nola Dancy
Jerry Dancy
Dr. Ann Larimer

Martha Allen
Ernie Cadman
Dr. Hank Iverson
Nurse Mary Jane Match

The Edge Of Night
Mike Karr
Nancy Karr
Laurie Karr Dallas
Johnny Dallas
Tracy Micelli
Danny Micelli
Bill Marceau
Lt. Luke Chandler
Kevin Jamison
Geraldine Whitney
John
Trudy
Adam Drake
Nicole Travis Drake
Olivia Brandeis ("Brandy") Henderson
Dr. Chris Neely
Dr. Clay Gordon
Draper Scott
Ansel Scott
Nadine Alexander
Raven Alexander
Steve Guthrie
Tony Saxon
Deborah Saxon
Molly O'Conner

General Hospital
Dr. Steve Hardy
Nurse Jessie Brewer
Dr. Peter Taylor
Nurse Diana Taylor
Martha Taylor
Mike
Dr. Lesley Faulkner
Dr. Adam Streeter
Terri Arnett
Dr. Rick Webber
Dr. Jeff Webber
Dr. Monica Webber
Audrey Hobart

Tommy Hobart
Dr. Tom Baldwin
Heather Grant
Dr. Mark Dante
Mary Ellen Dante
Dr. Gina Dante
Jill Streeter
Laura Vining
Dr. Gail Adamson
Lee Baldwin

Guiding Light
Bert Bauer
Mike Bauer
Hope Bauer
Dr. Ed Bauer
Freddie Bauer
Holly Norris Bauer
Christina Bauer
Barbara Thorpe
Adam Thorpe
Roger Thorpe
Nurse Peggy Fletcher Thorpe
Billy Fletcher
Dr. Sarah McIntyre (Werner)
T. J. Werner
Nurse Rita Stapleton
Eve Stapleton
Viola Stapleton
Ann Jeffers
Dr. Stephen Jackson
Ben McFarren
Jerry McFarren
Raymond Shafer
Dr. Justin Marler
Jacqueline Marler

Love Of Life
Mayor Bruce Sterling
Vanessa Sterling
Meg Dale Hart
Sarah Caldwell
Caroline ("Cal") Aleata Latimer
Rick Latimer
Hank Latimer
Ben Harper

Betsy Crawford
Dr. Tom Crawford
Arlene Lovett
Carrie Lovett
Ray Slater
Edouard Aleata
Charles Lamont
Felicia Flemming Lamont
Johnny Prentiss
Dr. Joe Cusak
Lynn Henderson
Ian Russell
Vivian Carlson

One Life To Live
Joe Riley
Victoria ("Vicky") Lord Riley
Cathy Craig Lord
Tony Lord
Dr. Jim Craig
Anna Wolek Craig
Vince ("Vinnie") Wolek
Wanda Webb Wolek
Nurse Jenny Wolek Siegel
Dr. Larry Wolek
Karen Wolek
Danny Wolek
Dr. Dorian Cramer Lord
Dr. Peter Janssen
Lt. Ed Hall
Carla Hall
Patricia Kendall
Brian Kendall
Dr. Will Vernon
Naomi Vernon
Brad Vernon
Samantha Vernon
Matt McAllister
Lana McLain

Ryan's Hope
Johnny Ryan
Maeve Ryan
Frank Ryan
Delia Reid Ryan
Bob Reid

Mary Ryan Fenelli
Jack Fenelli
Dr. Pat Ryan
Jillian ("Jill") Coleridge
Dr. Roger Coleridge
Dr. Faith Coleridge
Dr. Clem Moultrie
Dr. Seneca Beaulac
Dr. Bucky Carter
Dr. Alex McLean

Search for Tomorrow
Jo Vincente
Bruce Carson
Dr. Amy Kaslo Carson
Steve Kaslo
Liza Walton Kaslo
Dr. Gary Walton
Janet Collins
Wade Collins
Danny Walton
John Wyatt
Jennifer Pace
Walter Pace
Stephanie Collins Pace
Wendy Wilkins
Patti Whiting
Dr. Len Whiting
Scott Phillips
Kathy Phillips
Eric Leshinsky
Stu Bergman
Elly Harper Bergman
Dr. Bob Rogers
David Sutton
Woody Reed
Gail Caldwell

The Young and The Restless
Stuart Brooks
Jennifer Brooks
Lauralee ("Laurie") Brooks Prentice
Lance Prentiss
Lucas Prentiss
Vanessa Prentiss
Leslie Brooks Eliot

Brad Eliot	Kay Chancellor
Chris Brooks Foster	Liz Foster
Dr. Snapper Foster	Greg Foster
Peggy Brooks	Jill Foster
Jack Curtin (Curtzynski)	Ron Becker
Joann Curtzynski	Nancy Becker
Brock Reynolds	Karen Becker

When he was 14, Donald Sutherland got a job as a disc jockey at a Nova Scotia radio station, becoming Canada's youngest radio announcer.

Most of the laughter used on "laugh tracks" for television comedies is quite old—it was originally made for use on radio programs. The people one hears laughing at today's pratfalls are all quite dead.

Some distinctly non-Euclidean "theorems" are stenciled paintings of early nineteenth-century America. These works were generally of stylized flower or fruit arrangements assembled by home craftswomen into individual designs from an array of patterns.

Carole King and her husband Gerry Goffin were very impressed by one of their baby-sitters, Eva Boyd. Under the name Little Eva she recorded one of their songs, "Locomotion." The song and Little Eva became hits. (The name Little Eva was taken from a character in *Uncle Tom's Cabin*—an angelic white girl named little Eva who has a "delicate constitution.")

Glen Campbell played lead guitar on the Beach Boys' song "Good Vibrations."

Red Buttons was born Aaron Chwatt. At the age of 16, he got a job in a Bronx tavern as a bellboy-singer. He got his nickname from his red hair and the many buttons on his bellboy jacket.

The Poles did not invent the polka; the dance is from Bohemia.

Ray Charles was born Ray Charles Robinson. He dropped his last name to avoid being confused with the fighter Sugar Ray Robinson.

The first roller coasters were ice slides built in St. Petersburg, Russia, during the late 1600s. The French took the Russian idea and put wheels on the sleds.

Before the modern era the most spectacular lottery was sanctioned by the state of Louisiana (1868–90). It continued in business under private control in New Orleans until 1895 and at armslength, in Honduras, until 1906.

Chad and Jeremy once appeared on "The Dick Van Dyke Show"; they played a group called the Redcoats.

The famous "Spanish" dancer Jose Greco was born Costanzo Greco, in Italy.

When the reputedly unsinkable *Titanic* crashed into an iceberg and began sinking, Margaret ("Molly") Tobin Brown found herself in a lifeboat with some very downhearted fellow passengers. To raise their spirits, she sang songs and told jokes. When she was later asked about the experience, she quipped, "I'm unsinkable," becoming, of course, the "Unsinkable" Molly Brown.

Johnny Cash sang the theme song for the television series "The Rebel," starring Nick Adams.

To make his performance as a blinded war veteran in *Bright Victory* (1951) more convincing, Arthur Kennedy wore opaque contact lenses that rendered him completely sightless.

Alan Arkin began his performing career as a member of a folk-music group called the Tarriers. Arkin sang and wrote music. One of the songs he wrote was "The Banana Boat Song," which Harry Belafonte later made famous.

Though often used vaguely to signify the state of medieval theater, there are differences of subject matter among mystery, miracle, and morality plays. Mystery plays draw plot material from the Bible, miracle plays are devoted to the achievements of saints (hence lacking scriptural authority), and morality plays are populated by abstract personalities, e.g., Virtue, Sloth, Beauty, Gluttony, etc.

Little Sure Shot:
Etcetera

The White House was originally light gray; it was built of gray Virginia freestone. It was painted white after the British burned it in 1814.

Dark adaptation in human beings slows to a halt after eight minutes and then rapidly proceeds again for another thirty to forty minutes.

When Lifebuoy soap was first introduced, in 1897, it was called Lifebudy soap.

Before glass was affordable, window coverings used in Europe were made from panes of parchment, turpentine-treated cloth, oiled paper, or crystalline gypsum (selenite).

The Lear Jet Corporation was founded in 1962 by William P. Lear, who also invented the automatic pilot for jets and the eight-track stereo cartridge.

The first newspaper was the *Acta diurna,* instituted by Julius Caesar and posted daily in public places.

The first enemy flag captured by an American military unit was the King's Color of the 7th Royal Fusiliers, taken in 1775.

The name of the Indian leader Crazy Horse was Tashunca-uitco, a name which can also—and perhaps more accurately—be translated as "His Horse Is Crazy."

Brooklyn's first Italian resident was probably a certain Peter Caesar Alberto. When the Dutch took a survey of New Amsterdam in 1639, they listed Alberto as "the Italian" of Kings County.

Tom Carvel, the ice-cream manufacturer, was born Athanassos Carvelas in Greece.

Wyatt Earp's full name was Wyatt Berry Stapp Earp.

There are eleven stripes on the flag of Liberia, one for each of the men who signed the Liberian Declaration of Independence. The flag was designed by a group of seven women and is the only national flag that was designed by women.

Amerigo Vespucci, the man after whom America is named, grew up in Florence. Among his nextdoor neighbors was Sandro Botticelli.

In 1478 Isabella of Castille launched an inquisition against Spain's so-called Marranos, converted Jews who secretly practiced Judaism (*marrano* originally meant "pig"). In 1492, still busy expelling Jews and Moors from Spain, Isabella financed Columbus's voyage. One of Columbus's crewmen was Luis de Torres, a Marrano and therefore the first Jewish visitor to the New World.

The oldest Russian newspaper in the world is *Novoye Russkoye Slovo* ("New Russian Word"), a Russian-language daily published in New York City. It was founded in 1910. All of the Russian newspapers that existed in Russia in 1917 were abolished during the revolution and replaced by new ones.

The first non-Indian child born in North Dakota was born to black parents, in 1802.

The oldest national flag in the world is that of Denmark, the Dannebrog.

The first black man in the New World was Pedro Alonso Niño, a navigator and member of Columbus's crew in 1492.

Christopher Columbus was born in Genoa. He saw his beloved home city for the last time when he was about 27, but although he spent his life sailing under the flags of Portugal and Spain, he never relinquished his Genovese citizenship or became the naturalized citizen of any other country.

In 1912 John Wanamaker set up a wireless telegraph station in the window of his New York department store. Ostensibly, the station was there to keep in touch with the Philadelphia Wanamaker's, but it was actually a publicity stunt. On the evening of April 14, the station was being manned by 20-year-old Russian-American David Sarnoff. Sarnoff accidentally picked up the message "SS *Titanic* ran into iceberg. Sinking fast." He relayed the message to another steamer. As news of the disaster spread, President Taft ordered other stations to remain silent, and Sarnoff remained at his post for seventy-two hours, taking the names of survivors and directing other ships to the area.

Annie Oakley was born Phoebe Ann Moses. It was the great chief Sitting Bull who gave her her famous nickname. He called her *Watanya cicilia*—"little sure shot."

Last of the Blue Stockings: Fashion

J. Edgar Hoover got the idea for his "Ten Most Wanted Criminals" list from a friend, a fashion designer who had invented the survey called "Ten Best Dressed Women."

Though Raleigh brought tobacco and potatoes to the English, and Lord Arlington brought tea (1666), and Mrs. Dinghen Van den Plasse gave (1564) to the English their starch, literally, it was Jonas Hanway (1712–86) who conveyed to the island nation the umbrella.

The Stetson hat was devised by a Philadelphia hatmaker named John Batterson Stetson. Stetson went West seeking a cure for tuberculosis, and when he returned to Philadelphia he began manufacturing hats suited to the needs of the western cowboy.

In 1886 the tobacco magnate Pierre Lorillard IV, bored with the tailcoats usually worn at social affairs, had his tailor make a new, tailless coat in bright scarlet satin. Although the elder Lorillard refused to wear the new coat in public, his son, Griswald, wore one on the evening of October 10, 1886, to the Autumn Ball of the Tuxedo Park Country club at Tuxedo, New York. The coat is now known as the tuxedo.

French author Gérard de Nerval (1808–55) hanged himself by a corset string he had told his friends belonged to the famous Madame Maintenon.

Investigating the mechanics of fashion, one researcher (J. E. Janney, 1941) found in the case of 67 clothing fads at a women's college that six groups are distinguishable: (1) distingué faddists, nearly always successful in starting fads; (2) bizarre faddists, attract imitators but not for social occasions; (3) oscillating faddists, change styles quickly; (4) egregious faddists, never successful in establishing a trend (they attempted fifteen in the two-year course of the survey) and should they adopt a current fad, its popularity immediately expires among other groups; (5) conforming faddists, the 80–85 percent of the population who follow, usually weeks later, the fashion lead of other groups; and (6) obsolescents, impervious to fads, observing no special care or selection in dress.

With the exception of the heedless obsolescents, groups appear to work individually at a rate of about eight fads per annum.

Many denture wearers in nineteenth-century Britain were proud of their "Waterloo teeth," teeth that had been extracted from the dead of the great battle. Teeth from the dead of the American Civil War were also shipped to Britain, where they were put into dentures.

The cardigan sweater is named for the Earl of Cardigan, the British general who led the famous "Charge of the Light Brigade." Cardigans sometimes have raglan sleeves, which are named for Lord Raglan, the commander of the British forces in the Crimea and one of the men who witnessed Cardigan's cavalry attack.

The blue blazer is named for a British naval ship, the HMS *Blazer*. Weary of seeing his crewmen shabbily dressed, the captain had them all dress in identical blue jackets. The jackets soon became a fad.

The first button factory in the United States was established in 1800 in Waterbury, Connecticut.

Panama hats come from Ecuador. Although woven in Ecuador, they were for many years shipped to the world's markets by way of Panama—hence the name.

What is now known as a paisley design (after a Scottish town of textile eminence in the early eighteenth century) was known in its native India as *kairi,* a representation of the *triratna,* or three jewels of Buddha.

Among the finest cloths are the *pashmina* shawls of Kashmir, made from the wispy chin and belly hair of Himalayan goats. As the goats themselves are inaccessible, the hair is gathered in strands and tufts from bushes in which it has become caught.
Often called ring shawls—because the best material can be drawn easily through a woman's wedding band—such textiles are now exceedingly rare, fetching prices of $1000 and up.

Spats, whether built into a shoe or detachable, is short for spatterdashes, describing their original, protective purpose.

Women's clothes have the buttons on the left side and men's clothes have the buttons on the right side, a custom that supposedly dates to the Middle Ages: the buttons on men's garments were placed on the right to make it easier for men to undo their coats with their left hands while reaching for their swords with their right.

A rather specialized unit of measure is the clo. It quantifies the insulation value of clothing. Technically one clo equals 0.648 degrees C sec m^2/cal, which means that one clo worth of apparel will keep you comfortable in a ventilated room at 70 degrees Fahrenheit and less than 50 percent humidity.

Clo values for an ensemble range generally from about 5 in winter to 0.5 in summer. In Russia the year-long average clo value is 3.4, in the United States 2.9.

Although the scale may seem somewhat fanciful, it does permit a direct comparison between food costs (measured also by calories) and clothing costs. The cost, for example, of staying warm through buying clothes can be three to six times less than burning extra food calories for the same purpose.

The first instance of nudity in a modern Hollywood movie occurred in 1961's *Splendor in the Grass:* director Elia Kazan induced Natalie Wood to leap from a bathtub and, her back to the camera, run down a hallway.

Cupids and cherubs, which begin to proliferate in the art of the late Renaissance, are thought to have originated in the wealth and decadence of Alexandria during the waning of the Roman empire. There it was the custom to purchase children in large lots to decorate and enliven important entertainments. These party accessories found their way into Roman art and thence into the works of classical revivalists of the fifteenth century.

Correct terms for the fashionable bodice of 1890–1910 are monobosom and pouter pigeon.

When Clark Gable took off his shirt in a scene of 1934's *It Happened One Night,* audiences were startled to see that the popular star was not wearing an undershirt. Retail sales of undershirts immediately plummeted.

The double-breasted jacket was made popular by Edward VII.

Edward also began the custom of leaving the bottom button of a vest unbuttoned. He probably did so because he was fat.

Some Irish revolutionaries of the 1850s favored women's dress; they were called Lady Rocks and Lady Clares. And their mythical leader, Molly Maguire, seems to have crossed the Atlantic and settled in the coalfields of Pennsylvania.

William Hogarth (1697–1764) engraved a scene of the imagined funeral of one Joseph Vanaken (d. 1749), his casket attended by the despairing portrait painters of England. They were distressed because Vanaken had drawn and dressed ("heavenly velvets, satins") so many of the figures to which foremost portraitists attached only the necessary aristocratic faces.

The first US Marines, the Continental Marines organized during the American Revolution, wore a bit of vestigial body armor, black leather collars that served to protect their necks from saber slashes and powder burns. The stiff collars also kept the men's heads erect and were unanimously loathed by the marines. Although no longer forced to wear the irritating collars, marines are still known as leathernecks.

When news of George Washington's death reached France in 1799, Napoleon decreed ten days of official mourning. The ambitious young ruler was eager to identify himself with the American republicanism then popular. Napoleon also commissioned a bust of Washington to be made and placed in the Tuileries. Sculptor Giuseppe Ceracchi fashioned a bust of Washington clothed in a Roman toga.

In 1802, when Napoleon no longer felt compelled to feign republicanism, he ordered Ceracchi's head removed with the ever-popular guillotine.

The Roman emperor Nero never wore the same clothes twice.

John and William have always been the two most popular first names for American males. Forty percent of the men in colonial New England answered to one of the two. (The most popular women's names are Mary and Elizabeth.)

Miss Moncton, the Countess of Cork (d. 1840), was the last of the blue stockings. That is to say, she was the last of the society of women scholars descended from the original fifteenth-century Venetian organization.

Singing Cheese:
Food and Drink

Eskimos often buy refrigerators. They use them to keep food from freezing.

The official distinction between jellies and jams (or preserves) is that jellies are made of fruit juices, jams of the fruit itself. Neither meets standards if it falls below a ratio of 45 parts fruit ingredients to 55 parts sugar ingredients.
Marmalade is a preserve containing fruit peel.

Red wine contains larger trace amounts of gold than white wine—the scale runs from about 0.030 to 0.076 micrograms per liter.

Jerusalem artichokes don't come from Jerusalem, and they're not artichokes; they're sunflowers, and they're native to North America. Spanish explorers recognized them as sunflowers and called them *girasol* ("sunflower"); *girasol* eventually became Americanized to Jerusalem; no one knows where the "artichoke" part of the name comes from. In some areas, the sunflowers were originally called Canadian potatoes.

The first pizzeria in the United States was opened in New York City in 1895 at 53½ Spring Street.

Vichyssoise was first concocted in the United States. In 1910, while working at the Ritz-Carlton Hotel, French chef Louis Diat took the leek-and-potato soup that he recalled from his childhood, chilled and dressed it, and named it for a famous spa close to his native village.

A famous whiskey bottle in the shape of a log cabin figured in the 1840 presidential campaign of William Henry Harrison. Serendipitously, the Philadelphia distiller who supplied the booze was E. G. Booz. But Mr. Booz did not give us this national pastime. Booze, meaning tipple, has an ancient pedigree, running through the French and Germanic languages.

The chuck wagon was invented by Charles Goodnight.

The only place you can find sardines is in tin cans labeled "sardines." There is no specific fish called *sardine:* the word is used for several small fish, such as herring and pilchard. Calling the fish sardines is a reference to the plentitude of such fish near the island of Sardinia.

Champagne is classified for dryness, from driest to sweetest, *nature, brut, extra sec,* and *sec.*

The "Italian" specialty spaghetti and meatballs was invented in Brooklyn, New York.

That Americans would become a nation of coffee drinkers was in large degree a reflection of relations between Great Britain and her rebellious colonies. Tea tax discouraged consumption in the colonies and scarcity during the War of 1812 drove prices to over four times that of coffee. Also American-procured supplies were not nearly so fine as British; tea bulked by Chinese shippers with iron filings and dark sand badly hurt the market.

Tea is not only a beverage and a medium of exchange (it was minted into intaglioed ingots in Russia, Mongolia, and China) but an hors d'oeuvre—a pickled delicacy in Thailand and a special salad in Burma.

Pumpernickel, the dark bread made from whole, coarsely ground rye, gets its name from its supposed effect on those who eat it. *Pumpernickel* is composed of two German words: *Pumpen,* "to fart," and *Nickel,* "devil."

Jordan almonds don't come from Jordan; they come from Malaga, Spain. *Jordan* is an anglicized form of the Old French *jardin* ("garden")—they're garden almonds.

The Sumerians brewed nineteen different varieties of beer.

It was Julius Caesar who, in 48 BC, introduced to Rome the Gallic art of making pork sausages.

The first American restaurant to use printed menus was Delmonico's in New York City. It issued the first printed menus in 1836. One of the most expensive dishes listed was called Hamburg Steaks.

Maria Ann Smith was born in England and went to Australia in 1839. There, Ms. Smith experimented with apples. The apple she perfected still bears her name, the Granny Smith.

The celebrated French chef Marie Antoine Careme cooked for the mouths of several notable men, including Talleyrand, Czar Alexander I, George IV, and Baron Rothschild. It was while he was preparing meals for Alexander I that Careme invented beef stroganoff (named for a count named Paul Stroganoff). When not busy in the kitchen, Careme sent items of secret information home to France (and the waiting Talleyrand).

"The dumb, the deaf, the lame, such as had lost a member, pygmies, and mechanics were all fed according to what work they were able to do."

—From the *Li Chi,* ca. 400 BC

Honey can be quite bitter: that sometimes produced by Ceylonese bees from the flowers of a rubber plant is unpalatable. But it is not toxic, as is honey produced from rhododendron, azalea, henbane, and yellow jessamine.

Henri Perdeux, a French Huguenot, came to America in 1657 to escape religious persecution. One of his descendants is Frank Perdue, the poultry magnate.

Cantaloupe melons are named for Cantalupo, a papal villa near Rome where they were first cultivated.

The first US food trademark was the red devil granted in 1870 to Boston's William Underwood Company for its "deviled entremets."

The rich chocolate cake known as the sachertorte was devised in Vienna in 1832 by Franz Sacher. The 16-year-old kitchen apprentice came up with the specialty in honor of Prince von Metternich.

The Hudson River was once famous for its fish. So much sturgeon was fished out of the river during the prepollution days of the 1890s that it was nicknamed "Albany beef."

The red-and-white labels of Campbell soup cans were suggested by the Cornell college football team uniforms.

Tangerines get their name from Tangier, Morocco. They first arrived in Europe in 1805.

Welsh rarebit is just an alternate name for Welsh rabbit, and there's no reason to look for a rabbit in Welsh rabbit—the dish is made of melted cheese served over hot toast or crackers. The origin of the dish reflects English animosity toward their Welsh neighbors— the implication is that the Welsh are so poor that they could not afford even rabbit (the English countryside, evidently, swarms with rabbits).

Michelob beer was introduced in 1896 by Adolphus Busch, already famous for Budweiser. Until 1961, Michelob was sold only on draft.

All foods and even pure water are deadly when consumed in large enough quantities. For pure water fifteen gallons may cause death, for caffeine the lethal one-time dose is about 14 milligrams per kilogram of body weight. An average cup of coffee contains four milligrams of caffeine.

Proper preparation of the vanilla bean after harvest may take up to a year. Following a hot water bath the beans begin a gradual concentrating of their unique aroma and flavor. During the process they are protected by wool blankets, bathed in sunlight, and oiled to prevent chapping.

Marie Antoinette introduced the croissant to the French. The tasty pastries were invented in Vienna in 1683, and Marie, daughter of Maria Theresa of Austria, brought them with her when she married Louis XVI.

Kosher, when it appears on prepared food, means that certain standards and practices are adhered to in processing; glatt kosher means the very strictest standards have been met.

Brazil nuts come from Bolivia. They got their name because although they are picked in Bolivia, it is easier to export them from Brazil.

Lemonade was invented in Paris, France, in 1630.

The wines of Tuscany have delighted many generations. Even Michelangelo, who spent some happy time there, fell in love with the products of Tuscany's vines. "I'd rather have two flagons of Trebbiano," he wrote a nephew, "than eight shirts."

Liederkranz, the soft cheese that resembles a mild Limburger, was invented in 1892 by a Swiss-American cheesemaker named Emil Frey, in Monroe, New York. Frey tested his first batch of cheese on a German choral group, the Liederkranz ("garland of song"). They loved it; he named it after them.

Haste, Post:
Futility

The very first Indian treaty signed by the brand-new American government was in 1778 with the Delaware tribe. This treaty's most curious provision is an agreement "should it for the future be found conducive for the mutual interest of both parties to invite any other tribe who have been friends to the interest of the United States to join the present confederation and to form a state whereof the Delaware nation shall be the head, and have a representation in Congress . . ."

In other words, framers of this treaty envisioned Indian statehood and representation in Congress. No further mention of this notion occurs in any later dealings with any Indian tribe.

Lightning strikes the Empire State Building an average of twenty-three times a year.

The Boers, people of Dutch and French Huguenot descent living in South Africa, were devoutly fundamentalist. As late as 1886, the great Boer statesman Paul Kruger fiercely maintained that the earth was flat.

Heavy work meant that the Royal Navy faced a continuing crisis in hernias. At the time of its Napoleonic engagements the fleet requirement averaged 2873 single trusses and 743 double trusses per year.

A Dutch door is a door divided in half horizontally so that either part may be left open or closed. A Dutch oven is a large, heavy pot or kettle. We also have Dutch treat, the agreement that each person pays his or her own expenses. This last is one of several derogatory "Dutch" references that reflect English animosity toward the Dutch (born of their wars during the seventeenth century). Among the others are:

Dutch bargain: a transaction settled while both parties are inebriated

Dutch auction: an auction in which the auctioneer opens with a high price and lowers it until a buyer is found

Dutch courage: courage from drinking alcohol

Dutch defense: surrender

Dutch medley: the din that results from several musicians each playing a different tune

Dutch nightingale: a frog

Dutch uncle: a stern critic or adviser

Dutch widow: a prostitute

Dutch wife: a pillow used in the tropics to keep the legs clear of the bed linens and each other—a cooler sleeping arrangement

The first university course offered in the United States dealing with the American Revolution was at Harvard in 1839. Even at that time, sixty years after the event, the best text available, and the one adopted for the course, was an account written in Italian by Carlo Botta in 1809. Students used an English translation.

The first permanent colony in South Carolina was established in 1670 at Albemarle Point under William Sayle. The great English philosopher John Locke was asked to write a constitution for this new colony. Called the Fundamental Constitutions, Locke's work granted some popular rights but retained feudal privileges. The settlers refused to ratify it.

Controversy still surrounds America's first national flag, the Great Union or Cambridge flag, hoisted over Washington's headquarters January 1, 1776. With seven red and six white stripes and a Union Jack in the upper left quadrant, it was identical to the flag of Britain's East India Company.

That the colonists wished to fly the flag of the well-known importers of taxed tea is incomprehensible.

Robert E. Lee surrendered the Army of Northern Virginia to U. S. Grant at Appomattox Court House on April 9, 1865. The last battle of the Civil War took place more than one month later, on May 13, at Palmito Hill, near Brownsville, Texas. The last Confederate general to surrender was Edmund Kirby Smith, who surrendered to Edward R. S. Canby on May 26.

On June 2, 1924, an act of Congress declared all American Indians born in the United States to be US citizens. Before this, the native Americans were referred to as members of "domestic independent nations."

When Christopher Columbus returned from his second voyage to the New World, he brought back with him, among other items, 500 Carib Indians. He thought Queen Isabella would want to sell them as slaves. Isabella wasn't certain that it was lawful to capture peaceful people and sell them as slaves. She asked her religious advisers for their opinion. When the theologians couldn't make up their minds, she ordered Columbus to take the natives back to where they belonged.

MAJOR WARS

Name	Date	Winners	Losers
Abyssinian War	1935–1936	Italy	Abyssinia (Ethiopia)
American War of Independence	1775–1783	Thirteen Colonies	Britain
Austrian Succession, war of the	1740–1748	Austria, Hungary, Britain, Holland	Bavaria, France, Poland Prussia, Sardinia, Saxony, Spain
Boer (South African) War	1899–1902	Britain	Boer Republics
Chinese-Japanese Wars	1894–1895	Japan	China
	1931–1933	Japan	China
	1937–1945	China	Japan
Civil War, American	1861–1865	23 Northern States (the Union)	11 Southern States (the Confederacy)
Civil War, English	1642–1646	Parliament	Charles I
Civil War, Nigerian	1967–1970	Federal government	Biafra
Civil War, Pakistani	1971	East Pakistan (Bangladesh) and India	West Pakistan
Civil War, Spanish	1936–1939	Junta de Defensa Nacional (Fascists)	Republican government
Crimean War	1853–1856	Britain, France, Sardinia, Turkey	Russia
Franco-Prussian War	1870–1871	Prussia and other German states	France
Hundred Years War	1337–1453	France	England
Korean War	1950–1953	South Korea and United Nations forces	North Korea and Chinese forces
Mexican-American War	1846–1848	United States	Mexico
Napoleonic Wars	1792–1815	Austria, Britain, Prussia, Russia, Spain, Sweden	France
October War	1973	Ceasefire arranged by UN: fought by Israel against Egypt, Syria, Iraq, Sudan, Saudi Arabia, Lebanon, and Jordan	
Peloponnesian War	431–404 BC	Peloponnesian League, led by Sparta, Corinth	Delian League, led by Athens
Punic Wars	264–146 BC	Rome	Carthage
Russo-Japanese War	1904–1905	Japan	Russia
Seven Years War	1756–1763	Britain, Prussia, Hanover	Austria, France, Russia, Sweden
Six-Day War	1967	Israel	Egypt, Syria, Jordan, Iraq
Spanish-American War	1898	United States	Spain
Spanish Succession, War of the	1701–1713	England, Austria, Prussia, the Netherlands	France, Bavaria, Cologne Mantua, Savoy
Thirty Years War	1618–1648	France, Sweden, the German Protestant states	The Holy Roman Empire Spain

Vietnam War	1957–1975	North Vietnam	South Vietnam, United States
War of 1812	1812–1814	United States	Britain
Wars of the Roses	1455–1485	House of Lancaster	House of York
World War I	1914–1918	Belgium, Britain and Empire, France, Italy, Japan, Russia, Serbia, United States	Austria-Hungary Bulgaria, Germany, Ottoman Empire
World War II	1939–1945	Australia, Belgium, Britain, Canada, China, Denmark, France, Greece, Netherlands, New Zealand, Norway, Poland, Russia, South Africa, United States, Yugoslavia	Bulgaria, Finland, Germany, Hungary, Italy, Japan, Romania

Napoleon was not the first person to refer to England as "a nation of shopkeepers." Adam Smith used the phrase in his *Wealth of Nations* (1776), and it was used in other, even earlier, works. Napoleon picked up the phrase and used it contemptuously of his English foes; the English are said to have accepted it with pride.

Lyndon Johnson died one mile from the house in which he was born.

England's King George III never got over the—to him—disaster of the American Revolution. More than once, he vowed, "I shall never rest my head on my pillow in peace and quiet as long as I remember the loss of my American colonies."

The lobsters we eat in restaurants, which usually weigh about one and one-half pounds, are about 8 years old.

The most bizarre cure for hiccups was devised by John (Jack) Mytton, a noted English foxhunter of the early nineteenth century. Mytton was forever drunk and in debt—disguised as a highwayman he once robbed his own butler. While seeking refuge from creditors in Calais in 1822 he attempted to frighten his hiccups away by setting fire to his nightshirt. He survived; the fate of his hiccups is not recorded.

Of the fifty-six signers of the Declaration of Independence, one is not listed in the first records of this event. A number of delegates missed the activities of July 4, 1776, being absent or needing further authority from their respective legislatures, but all were on the document by November—all but Thomas McKean of the Delaware delegation, who didn't get around to signing until 1781, five years late.

Reproductive strategy of the truffle is to be eaten. It is delicious because it has evolved to be delicious. Since the truffle, a fungus, lives completely underground its spores cannot propagate in any of the usual ways. Continuation of the species depends on the spores, which are not digestible, passing through any insect or animal that eats the parent organism.

Though principally known today as a product of France's Périgord region—where they are sniffed out by specially adept pigs—truffles are found in abundance in the Kalihari desert.

Historically, the marketing of gem-cut rock crystal has depended on its being called by any fanciful name to disguise its humble nature. Usually "diamond" is worked into the description, preceded by a veritable gazetteer of place-names. The more honest have a certain plainness: Alaska diamond, Arkansas diamond, Bohemian, Brighton, Bristol, Buxton, Cornish, German, Hawaiian, Hot Springs, Irish, Isle of Wight, Lake George, Mexican, Pecos, Quebec, Rhine, Tasmanian, Trenton, and Washita diamond.

A little more deceptive, or at least with a romantic ring, are: Arabian, Baffa, Briancon, Dauphiné, Herkimer, Horatio, Mari, Marmarosch, Marmora, Mutzchen, Paphros, Schaumberg, Stolberg, Vallum, and Zabeltitzen diamond.

But it's still just crystal.

By 1818 the territory of Missouri had gained sufficient population to warrant its admission into the Union as a state. When the petition of the residents was put before the Sixteenth Congress in 1820, the difficult issue of slavery arose. Most of the settlers in the territory were from the South, and it was expected that Missouri would be admitted as a slave state. The debate on the matter was brutal and bitter, but in the end a compromise was reached, the so-called Missouri Compromise.

Just as the Congressmen were about to vote on this historic issue, Felix Walker, the Representative from Buncombe County, North Carolina, asked permission to speak. The speech he delivered had nothing whatsoever to do with Missouri, or slavery, or the compromise. In fact, the subject of the lengthy speech wasn't clear to anyone but Walker. When Walker finally ended this fatuous peroration, a weary Congressman asked him why he had delayed matters. Walker replied, "I was not speaking to the House, but to Buncombe." Thus, the word *buncombe* came into our language as a word for nonsense or foolish, insincere talk. The spelling eventually changed to *bunkum*, and the word usually appears in its shortened from, *bunk*.

Saccharin is 675 times sweeter than sugar.

Cure for the common cold, ca. 1850:

¼ pound raisins
2 ounces licorice

simmer the above in 2 quarts of water until one quart remains, then add:

¼ pound pulverized sugar candy
1 tablespoon old rum
1 tablespoon white vinegar or lemon juice

and drink a pint warm.

President Lincoln on March 2, 1861, signed a proposed Constitutional amendment to be styled "Article Thirteen" and providing: "No amendment shall be made to the Constitution which will authorize or give to Congress the power to abolish or interfere, within any State, with the domestic institutions thereof, including that of persons held to labor or service by the laws of said State."

In light of Lincoln's views on slavery and the fact that a presidential signature on any constitutional amendment is completely unnecessary (this is the only proposed amendment to which a presidential signature is affixed), his signature evidences his resolve to avoid, at any cost, the threatened splitting of the Union.

But General Beauregard opened fire on Ft. Sumter, April 12, 1861, anyway.

Albert Einstein died in a hospital in Princeton, New Jersey, early in the morning of April 18, 1955. He was not alone when he died. There was a nurse near him, and she heard his last words, but no one knows what he was saying. He was speaking German, and the nurse did not understand German.

Among the passengers aboard the *Titanic* during its ill-fated maiden voyage was the wealthy bibliophile Harry Elkins Widener. According to tradition, Widener went down clutching a 1598 edition of Bacon's essays. His library went by will to Harvard University, where it is installed with other collections as the Harry Elkins Widener Memorial Library.

The United States has landed troops in the Soviet Union twice, both in 1918. Five thousand went ashore at Archangel and 9000 in Siberia (at Vladivostok). The ill-fated expeditions were part of a confused international plan to overthow the new revolutionary (Bolshevik) government of Russia.

In the hope of speeding the mail, citizens in colonial America wrote, "Haste, post, haste," on the covers of their letters.

Flo and Pop:
Geography

The smallest of colonial possessions, until it reverted to the Dahomey Republic (now Benin) in 1961, was the Portuguese fort at Ouidah, garrisoned by one officer. This force was doubled in 1960.

Only one of New York City's five boroughs is connected to the US mainland: the Bronx. (The other boroughs—Manhattan, Brooklyn, Queens, and Staten Island—are all separated from the mainland by water.)

COLDEST PLACES

Rank/Place/Country	Lowest Recorded Temperature F
1 Eismitte, Greenland	−85
2 Yakutsk, USSR	−84
3 Fairbanks, USA	−66
4 Aklavik, Canada	−62
5 Ulaanbaatar, Mongolia	−48
6 Harbin, China	−43
7 Kuusamo, Finland	−40
8 Haparanda, Sweden	−34
9 Krakow, Poland	−28
10 Cluj, Rumania	−26

With only 108 acres of area, the Vatican City is the world's smallest independent country. It also has the world's smallest population. It is unlikely that the Vatican City's population will grow, for it is the only nation on earth that boasts a zero birth rate.

The oldest continuously inhabited city in the world is Damascus, Syria.

WARMEST PLACES

Rank/Place/Country	Highest Recorded Temperature in F
1 Arouane, Mali	130
2 Cloncurry, Australia	127
3 Abadan, Iran	127
4 Wadi Halfa, Sudan	127
5 Fort Flatters, Algeria	124

6	Aswan, Egypt	124
7	Mosul, Iraq	124
8	Cufra, Libya	122
9	Multan, Pakistan	122
10	Gabes, Tunisia	122

The islands now known as the Canary Islands were visited by Romans around 40 BC. Astounded by the number of wild dogs they found on the islands, the Romans named the islands *insulae canariae* ("islands of the dogs"). The Romans don't seem to have noticed an inordinate number of birds flying around the islands, but the little yellow finches known as canaries take their name from the islands.

Before settling down in Washington in 1800 the Congress was on the road a great deal. Cities in which this governing body convened include Philadelphia, 1774–76, 1778–83, 1790–1800; Baltimore, 1776–77; Lancaster, Pa., 1777; York, Pa., 1777–78; Princeton, N.J., 1783; Annapolis, Md., 1783–84; Trenton, N.J., 1784; and New York, 1785–90.

Indianapolis is the largest American city not located near a body of water.

Routes on air navigation charts, designated V(ictor) and J(et), share with surface highways a numbering rule: east-west routes bear even numbers, north-south odd.

Geometric figures laid out on a spherical surface (such as Earth) have larger angles than equivalent figures existing in a truly flat plane, e.g., triangle apexes sum more than their allotted Euclidean 180 degrees, rectangles more than 360 degrees, etc. The German mathematician Karl Gauss (1777–1855) demonstrated this to his own satisfaction by triangulating three widely separated church steeples.

A more striking demonstration is the regular, gridlike highway system of North Dakota, where east-west routes periodically zigzag to join road segments that could only have met each other on a flat planet. An overall plan could have avoided this, of course, but roads tend to grow from one locality into the next without making a transition from plane to spherical geometry.

The German mercenaries hired by the British during the Revolutionary War were called Hessians because more than half of them came from the German state of Hesse-Cassel.

The section of Paris known as the Latin Quarter got its name during the Middle Ages when it was home to crowds of students who spent most of their time debating various subjects in Latin.

The first gold strike in the United States was at Meadow Creek, North Carolina, in 1799.

Both the words *book* and *Bible* come from Byblos, an ancient Phoenician city that was located northeast of modern Beirut, Lebanon. The city was the principal port of Phoenicia during the second millennium BC and was the center of the worship of Adonis. Because of its papyruses, it was the source of the Greek word *biblos,* meaning the inner bark of the papyrus. From *biblos* comes Bible, which at first meant any book, and finally *book.* The name of the contemporary town on the site is Jebail, which comes from Gebal, the name given the city in the Old Testament.

Mexico City had an American governor, John Quitman, in the years 1847–48 immediately after the Mexican War.

During his travels in the East, Marco Polo was introduced to the East Indian redwood, or sappanwood tree. The wood of the tree yields a red dye, which became a favorite with European clothiers during the Renaissance. Until the sixteenth century, great quantities of the tree were imported to Europe. In 1500 Portuguese explorers under Pedro Alvares Cabral claimed a hunk of territory in the New World. Wandering through the jungles of their new South American realm, the Portuguese were delighted to find vast quantities of a tree very similar to the East Indian tree. They referred to the tree as *brasil,* from *brasa* ("live coals," a reference to the tree's color). There were so many of the trees in the new land that the Portuguese mariners began referring to it as *terra de brasil* ("land of brasil"). This later became Brazil.

Largest Cities by Population

Rank City	Population
1 New York City	16,120,023
2 Mexico City	13,993,866
3 Sao Paulo	12,578,045
4 Los Angeles	11,496,206
5 Shanghai	11,320,000

6	Paris	9,878,524
7	Buenos Aires	9,749,000
8	Rio de Janeiro	9,018,981
9	Beijing	8,706,000
10	Tokyo	8,646,520
11	Moscow	8,022,000

One of history's shortest-lived republics was that created in the German city of Schwartzenberg in May 1945. World War II had just ended, and the city was supposed to be occupied by American troops, but the Americans misread the demarcation line on their maps and stopped outside the city; on the other side were the Russians. For seven weeks, the town enjoyed its neutral position. Former Nazis were chased out, postage stamps were issued, and train schedules established. When Soviet military authorities learned the town had uranium resources, the Russian army moved in and crushed the tiny republic.

The Antarctic Treaty of 1961 recognized no claims of territorial sovereignty in the Antarctic. Countries supporting claims through exploratory ventures include Great Britain, Norway, Australia, New Zealand, and France. Chile and Argentina have announced claims that conflict with each other and with that of Great Britain.

Hell's Kitchen, once a tough district on Manhattan's west side, takes its name from Dutch Heinrich's Hell's Kitchen Gang, hijackers active in the area during the late 1860s.

The highest tides in the world are found in the Bay of Fundy in eastern Canada. The sea level there changes by as much as forty feet during the day.

The "Kingdom of St. Mary's," as it was known, is an island ten miles off the northeast corner of Madagascar where Atlantic and Indian ocean pirates went to retire. Many maintained palisaded homes there, taking up residence when business was slow or raising cattle and vegetables after leaving the trade.

In the early eighteenth century the island served as a clearinghouse for stolen goods. Several New York fortunes (e.g., Philpse, DeLancey) were made in transporting merchandise to markets and whiskey, supplies, and gunpowder to the stronghold.

In 1499, while exploring the northern coast of South America, Amerigo Vespucci came upon an island (probably Aruba) where he saw Indian villages built above the water on stilts. The villages reminded him of the Italian city Venice, so he named the place Venezuela, "little Venice." The name held and was soon applied to the mainland.

One of the most astute real estate transactions was managed by the British in 1890 when they traded to Germany Heligoland, 150 acres of red sandstone in the North Sea, for Zanzibar and Pemba, 1020 square miles, a chief spice producer off the east African coast.

The Commissioners of Northern Lights are not charged with maintenance of auroral displays, rather they were created in 1786 to oversee operation of lighthouses in Scotland and the Isle of Man.

The "Land of the Winds" is Seistan in eastern Iran, where northerly winds, up to 70–120 miles per hour, blow from late May to late September.

The Atlantic Ocean is widening at a rate of about one centimeter per year.

ROSTER OF THE UNITED NATIONS

Member	Year		
Afghanistan	1946	Bolivia	1945
Albania	1955	Botswana	1966
Algeria	1962	Brazil	1945
Angola	1976	Bulgaria	1955
Antigua and Barbuda	1981	Burma	1948
Argentina	1945	Burundi	1962
Austria	1955	Byelorussia	1945
Bahamas	1973	Cambodia (Kampuchea)	1955
Bahrain	1971	Cameroon	1960
Bangladesh	1974	Canada	1945
Barbados	1966	Cape Verde	1975
Belgium	1945	Central Afr. Rep.	1960
Belize	1981	Chad	1960
Benin	1980	Chile	1945
Bhutan	1971	China	1945

Colombia	1945	Kenya	1963
Comoros	1975	Kuwait	1963
Congo	1960	Laos	1955
Costa Rica	1945	Lebanon	1945
Cuba	1945	Lesotho	1966
Cyprus	1960	Liberia	1945
Czechoslovakia	1945	Libya	1955
Denmark	1945	Luxembourg	1945
Djibouti	1977	Madagascar (Malagasy)	1960
Dominica	1978	Malawi	1964
Dominican Rep.	1945	Malaysia	1957
Ecuador	1945	Maldives	1965
Egypt	1945	Mali	1960
El Salvador	1945	Malta	1964
Equatorial Guinea	1968	Mauritania	1961
Ethiopia	1945	Mauritius	1968
Fiji	1970	Mexico	1945
Finland	1955	Mongolia	1961
France	1945	Morocco	1956
Gabon	1960	Mozambique	1975
Gambia	1965	Nepal	1955
Germany, East	1973	Netherlands	1945
Germany, West	1973	New Zealand	1945
Ghana	1957	Nicaragua	1945
Greece	1945	Niger	1960
Grenada	1974	Nigeria	1960
Guatemala	1945	Norway	1945
Guinea	1958	Oman	1971
Guinea-Bissau	1974	Pakistan	1947
Guyana	1966	Panama	1945
Haiti	1945	Papua New Guinea	1975
Honduras	1945	Paraguay	1945
Hungary	1955	Peru	1945
Iceland	1946	Philippines	1945
India	1945	Poland	1945
Indonesia	1950	Portugal	1955
Iran	1945	Qatar	1971
Iraq	1945	Romania	1955
Iceland	1955	Rwanda	1962
Israel	1949	Saint Lucia	1979
Italy	1955	Saint Vincent and the	
Ivory Coast	1960	Grenadines	1980
Jamaica	1962	Samoa (Western)	1976
Japan	1956	Sao Tome e Principe	1975
Jordan	1955	Saudi Arabia	1945

153

Senegal	1980	Turkey	1945
Seychelles	1976	Uganda	1962
Sierra Leone	1961	Ukraine	1945
Singapore	1965	USSR	1945
Solomon Islands	1978	United Arab Emirates	1971
Somalia	1960	United Kingdom	1945
South Africa	1945	United States	1945
Spain	1955	Upper Volta	1960
Sri Lanka	1955	Uruguay	1945
Sudan	1956	Vanuatu	1981
Suriname	1975	Venezuela	1945
Swaziland	1968	Vietnam	1977
Sweden	1946	Yemen	1947
Syria	1945	Yemen, South	1967
Tanzania	1961	Yugoslavia	1945
Thailand	1946	Zaire	1960
Togo	1960	Zambia	1964
Trinidad & Tobago	1962	Zimbabwe	1980
Tunisia	1956		

Nations that are longstanding *non*-members of the United Nations are Andorra, North Korea, South Korea, Liechtenstein, Monaco, San Marino, Switzerland, Tonga, Vatican City, and Taiwan.

Two "nations" in the United Nations, Byelorussia and Ukraine, are considered republics within the Soviet Union.

The memory of the Roman occupation of Britain survives in many place-names. The Romans built fortified camps throughout Britain; they called them *castra* ("camp"). As these Roman camps grew and became larger settlements, the Roman *castra* was frequently attached to older Celtic names. In several variations, *castra* now forms a familiar element in such places-names as Chester, Winchester, Manchester, Lancaster, Gloucester, Worcester, and Rochester.

It was Martin Waldseemüller, a German humanist and mapmaker, who selected the name America for the western landmass "discovered" by European explorers. He chose the name based on letters printed in Europe that described the region and suggested that Amerigo Vespucci had discovered it. Waldseemüller sketched the New

World in two maps, the first to show North and South America separate from Asia. He labeled the southern portion America, from the Latin form *(Americus)* of Vespucci's first name. He published the maps in 1507 together with an explanatory treatise and Vespucci's account of his voyages to the New World. Vespucci's claims were widely disputed, however, and Waldseemüller soon changed his mind and omitted America from his later maps. Even so, the name stuck and was soon applied to both the northern and southern continents.

In 1513, while sailing around in the waters of the New World, Ponce de Leon noticed that the water around his ship was not remarkably deep. He therefore named the area *baja mar* (Spanish for "shallow water")—the Bahamas.

Rhodesia is named for Cecil John Rhodes, the British imperialist and businessman who developed the country.

Dallas, Texas, is named for George Mifflin Dallas, vice-president under James K. Polk.

The city of New York is named after York, England. The name *York* is the result of a long evolution, an evolution that provides insight into the history of the English language. The original Celtic name for the place that is now called York was *Eburacon,* which means "the place of the yew trees." When the Romans occupied the area, they changed this to the Latin *Eburacus.* Following the Roman withdrawal from Britain, Anglo-Saxons took over the place. They changed *Eburacus* to *Eofor-wic,* meaning "boar town." The Anglo-Saxons were followed by Viking invaders to whom *Eofor-wic* sounded like *Iorvik.* This was eventually shortened to *Iork,* which became *York.*

The islets of Langerhans are in the pancreas; they manufacture insulin. The crypts of Lieberkühn are in the small intestine; they supply fluid for digestion. Other exotic body geography includes the isthmus of His and the islands of Calleja, both in the brain.

The Carthaginians gave Spain its name. They named it *Span* or *Spania,* meaning "land of rabbits."

Kiev is the oldest city in Russia.

From 1832 to 1835 a northern area of New Hampshire styled itself a sovereign nation, the Indian Stream Republic. The US government chose to ignore its ambassadors and paid no attention to this new neighbor other than to send a few marshals into the short-lived republic.

Peru is the world's leading fishing nation, taking in more than 9 million metric tons each year; Japan is second with 6 million.

According to Washington, D.C., legend, the original Uncle Tom's cabin sits on Old Georgetown Road in Montgomery County, Maryland.

Sandusky, Ohio, is named for Jacob Sadowski, a Polish immigrant and one of the first Europeans to descend the Mississippi River.

"Beyond the pale" is, literally, anywhere in unconquered Ireland. The phrase refers to the limits of English rule in Ireland after the initial invasion of 1172. Some authorities believe that a real pale, or wall, may have from time to time marked the boundaries, around Dublin, of secure English holdings.

The bayonet is named for Bayonne, France, the city in which the weapon is said to have been first developed.

Nihon, or Nippon, the name of the country we call Japan, is derived from the Chinese ideograph for "the place where the sun comes from," or "the land of the rising sun." Marco Polo's attempt to repeat the Chinese pronunciation of Nihon gave us "Japan."

Council Bluffs, Iowa, was named for a meeting that took place there in 1804 between members of the Lewis and Clark expedition and some Otoe Indians.

Lincoln's Emancipation Proclamation, read to the cabinet July 22, 1862, but not formally issued until January 1, 1863, was not quite so broad as it might have been. Not wishing to alienate slaveholders in border regions, Lincoln exempted certain territories in Tennessee, Virginia, and Louisiana.

There is a hill in Massachusetts known as Cheese Rock. It happened that on February 7, 1652, Governor John Winthrop went on a little trip with his servant. When lunchtime came, Winthrop discovered that his servant had forgotten to bring along anything to eat. All he had was some cheese.

There is a hill in Oregon known as Deathball Rock. The name recalls an amateur cook's evidently unsuccessful attempts to bake biscuits.

Canada has more lakes than the rest of the world combined.

Nome, Alaska, got its name through a misunderstanding. While preparing a chart of the coast of Alaska, British naval officers aboard HMS *Herald* noted that one particular cape had no name. They therefore marked the spot on their chart "? name." The draftsman who inked in the names on the chart wrote this as C (for "cape") Name, and he made the *a* in Name indistinct. Back at the admiralty offices in Britain this became Cape Nome.

The Russo-Japanese War (1904–05) ended with the Treaty of Portsmouth, which was signed in Portsmouth, New Hampshire. (President Theodore Roosevelt acted as mediator at the peace conference and was awarded the 1906 Nobel Peace Prize for his efforts.)

The United Nations is an independent postal authority with its own post office at its New York headquarters.

On January 1, 1501, Amerigo Vespucci was sailing along the coast of what was to become known as Brazil. Sighting what he believed to be a river, he named the area Rio de Janeiro ("river of January"). What he was looking at was not a river, but a bay.

The African republic of Cameroon was named by Portuguese explorers. While traveling up a river in the area, the Portuguese found shrimp, so they named the area *Camaroes* ("shrimp").

During his second voyage to the New World, in 1493, Christopher Columbus discovered and named several islands. On one particular Sunday, he sighted and named the island of Dominica ("Sunday").

Florence Nightingale was named after Florence, Italy, the city in which she was born. Since her sister had been born in Naples, she was named Parthenope (Parthenope being the Greek name for Naples). The two girls were usually called Flo and Pop by their parents.

Men and Melons:
Good Advice

When Bob Hope met Anthony Dominick Benedetto, he told him to change his name to Tony Bennett. Anthony did.

Stephen Foster wrote a very nice song about the Yazoo River, but his brother complained that "Yazoo" wasn't a very musical name. So Foster changed the name and published the song as "Swanee River."

The motto under the photograph of Walter Mondale in his 1946 high school yearbook states, "A little nonsense now and then is relished by the best of men."

Potential art buyers at a Sotheby Parke-Bernet auction scrutinize the catalog for the small nuances of listing. If the attribution of a painting is to a full name, e.g., "Rembrandt van Rijn," then connoisseurs are agreed on its authenticity. As the name shortens—"R. v. Rijn" or "Rembrandt"—so do the odds of connecting the work to an illustrious artist.

Over the centuries artists agree nothing is superior for oil painting to a brush made of hair from the tail of the kolinsky, or Russian red sable. Less costly, but always less satisfactory, are brushes of ferret and skunk, goat and ox hair, and hog bristle.

Following the Great Fire of London, in 1666, the architect Christopher Wren opined that the devastation of the city was the result of the haphazard arrangement of its streets. According to Wren, the fire would have done less damage had the city had perpendicular streets. William Penn learned of Wren's pronouncements: the streets of Philadelphia were set at 90-degree angles to one another.

"Commonsense is the deposit of prejudice laid down in the mind before the age of 18."

—Albert Einstein (1879–1955)

When the Luftwaffe began bombing cities in Britain in reprisal for raids on Cologne and Lubeck, the navigators of the bombers used Baedeker guidebooks to make certain they would hit the buildings of greatest historic interest.

Admiral Nelson at Trafalgar wished to signal "Nelson confides that every man will do his duty." His signal officer pointed out that "expects" could be sent faster than "confides," because the latter would have to be spelled out letter by letter. Another officer suggested "England" for "Nelson," which pleased the admiral.

As it was finally sent, Nelson's signal required twelve hoists and a total of 31 flags; only "duty" had to be spelled, which has led to some puzzling reconstructions inasmuch as V precedes U in the signal system (Popham's Vocabulary) then in use—no one knows why.

Watch out for plutonium in liquid solutions, as it goes critical more easily than when in dry, solid form.

When, in 1848, Daniel Webster was offered the opportunity of running for vice-president, he declined, stating, "No, thank you. I do not propose to be buried until I am really dead and in my coffin."

To use Occam's Razor is to reason with as few concepts, causes, hypotheses, etc., as are barely necessary to attain or explain results. It is the method of William of Occam (1290–1350).

Physicists lost in dimensional quagmires, limping tensors, spaces shy a coordinate often rely on the Buckingham Pi. This curiously named theorem merely predicts for any dimensional problem how many terms of a certain kind are necessary for any potential solution to "look" right.

"The Captain" of The Captain and Tennille is Daryl Dragon (Tennille is his wife, Toni Tennille). Dragon was given his nickname by Mike Love of the Beach Boys when he played for that group.

The language spoken by Jesus Christ was Aramaic.

Isabella Beeton, author of the monumental *Beeton's Book of Household Management* (1861), explains in one paragraph the art of dressing for women.

Brunettes should prefer darker colors, blondes lighter, cool colors are not to be combined with one another, and: "The colors which go best together are green with violet; gold-color with dark crimson or lilac; pale blue with scarlet, pink with black or white; and gray with scarlet or pink."

Until they disappeared in the Babylonian sack of Jerusalem (607 BC) Urim and Thummim decided the will of God for the Hebrews. These were two stones, possibly precious, cast or drawn as lots to signify a simple yes or no.

For making pacts with the devil, the proper kind of ink is made from 10 ounces gallnuts, 3 ounces iron sulphate, 3 ounces alum or gum arabic. The ingredients are added to river water in an unused earthenware pot and set to boil over a fire kindled with virgin paper.

The signature, of course, is in blood.

Five US quarters weigh one ounce.

"It is either the end of the world or it is a mistake."

—Tucuna Indian saying

Paul Revere cleaned his silver with a homemade baking-soda paste.

Popular dream analysis in turn-of-the-century America interpreted symbols with a certain directness. Dreams of giraffes meant seeing a friend arrived from a distance, an accordion brings amusement, derricks are obstructions to success, dice foretell contagious sickness, amethyst warns of greed, scrubbing kettles a sign of having to apologize, and dreams of committing adultery portend a letter containing bad news. Ice cream, of course, signifies success in love.

A book was responsible for the great upsurge in Scandinavian immigration to the United States during the 1840s. Ole Rynning, a leader of Norwegian colonists, came to Illinois in 1837, where he wrote a book about America and its opportunities for immigrants. The book was published in Norway in 1838 and was later translated as *A True Account of America for the Information and Help of Peasant and Commoner*. Known among Norwegian peasants as the "America Book," Rynning's work was instrumental in encouraging the great Scandinavian migration.

A traditional French tongue twister:
Un chasseur sachant chasser sans son chien est un chasseur bien chaussé. ("A hunter knowing how to hunt without his dog is a well-shod hunter.")

"A collection of terms is infinite when it contains as parts other collections which have just as many terms in it as it has."

—Bertrand Russell (1872–1970)

162

Research has taken much of the guesswork out of begging. Thanks to a 1974 study the best strategies for panhandlers have been scientifically determined. A female, for example, who persists in a dominant approach to non-eating couples (15 percent success probability) may be forced to look for other work. The simple expedient of concentrating on couples who are in the act of eating may quadruple (60 percent success) her income; this is obviously a distinction worth making. And she must remember to approach single, eating males submissively but pairs of eating males dominantly. It is hardly worth the effort to even wish a good morning to people who are not eating: a success is scored only one-third to one-half as often.

In general, male beggars will fare much worse than females, except when the targets are exclusively female.

When in the field, Confederate general Stonewall Jackson always carried three books: the Bible, Webster's dictionary, and Napoleon's *Maxims of War*.

In his several municipal offices, including New York park commissioner and head of the Triborough Bridge and New York City Tunnel Authority, Robert Moses (b. 1888) was responsible for planning many of the highways, parks, beaches, bridges, and tunnels of New York City. He himself never learned to drive a car.

It was not Alfonso the Battler (d. 1134) or Alfonso the Catholic (693?–757) or Alfonso the Chaste (759–842) or Alfonso the Emperor (1104–57) or Alfonso the Fat (1185–1223) or Alfonso the Great (838?–911?) or Alfonso the Magnanimous (1396–1458) or either of the two Alfonsos called Noble (994?–1027 and 1155–1214), but, of course, Alfonso the Wise (1221–84), who said, "Had I been present at the creation, I would have given some useful hints for the better ordering of the universe."

"He that takes up conclusions on the trust of authors . . . loses his labor, and does not know anything, but only believeth."
—Thomas Hobbes (1588–1679), *Leviathan*

Alligators move with remarkable speed over the swampy ground they call home. Experts offer this advice: if chased by an alligator, zigzag.

Eluding a pursuing bear is another matter. If chased by a bear, you should endeavor to run downhill. Bears tend to trip themselves on inclines.

Benjamin Franklin's *Poor Richard's Almanack* included some memorable bits of wisdom, such as:

Men and melons are hard to know.
Fish and visitors stink in three days.
He that lives upon hope dies farting.
If you want to know the value of money, try to borrow some.
Hunger never saw bad bread.

Serves Nine Muses:
Good Manners

"Ah, Mr. President, I see you are teaching your dog to chew the rug."

——Henry Kissinger (to Richard Nixon, 1969)

Sir John Finett, appointed Master of Ceremonies to Charles I of England (he was the second person ever to hold the post) ruled once and for all that the head of any table was wherever the best man sat, location of the fireplace notwithstanding.

In an effort to keep the philanderings of Venus secret, Eros (also known as Cupid) once gave Harpocrates, the god of silence, a rose. From this mythical bribe, we get the expression "under the rose" (with its Latin form *sub rosa*), meaning "in secrecy." During the fifth century BC, roses were hung from the ceilings of council chambers to indicate that all present were sworn to secrecy. In Tudor England, the ceilings of banquet halls were decorated with roses or rosettes to let guests know that intimate conversations—and the words spoken by tongues loosened by wine—were to remain confidential.

Lyndon Johnson was fond of giving his friends electric toothbrushes.

The death of Tycho Brahe, the most prominent astronomer of the late sixteenth century, was the result of good table manners. On October 13, 1601, the Danish astronomer was invited to a banquet given by the Baron of Rosenberg. Brahe forgot to relieve himself before taking his seat at the table, and although he desperately needed to visit a bathroom, he remained in his place—it would have been impolite to get up and leave. Poor Brahe's bladder burst, an infection set in, and he died.

Benny Goodman was the first white bandleader to employ black musicians in his band. Black bandleader Charlie Mingus employed white musicians in his band: he called them "colorless."

The Renaissance banking family Chigi maintained in Rome a palace (later the Italian Foreign Ministry) of such concentrated magnificence that a visiting Spanish ambassador spat in the face of a servant, explaining he could find no other vacant place.

The Indian who killed Custer at the Little Big Horn was a Sioux named White Bull. He didn't brag about it, however: he was somewhat shy, and he feared reprisals.

Mark Twain met Winston Churchill when the latter was in New York. Twain presented Churchill to lecture audiences as "half American."

"The children of America must not see their president smoking," said William McKinley. Walter Mondale evidentally agrees with this maxim. He smokes cigars—but never in public.

Alexander the Great succeeded to the throne of Macedon in 336 BC. One year later, the city of Thebes rose up in revolt because of a false rumor that Alexander was dead. Very much alive, Alexander immediately attacked Thebes and ordered the city sacked. However, he directed that none of the city's temples be damaged, and, a lover of poetry, he gave instructions that the house where Pindar had lived (more than 100 years earlier) be spared.

Romans loved dinner parties and were very particular about the number of guests they invited. The formula they followed was "not less than the Graces nor more than the Muses"—between three and nine people.

Congress's first "leak" to the press occurred as early as 1795. The subject was a secret treaty with Great Britain, a treaty widely thought too "soft" after its exposure by the *Aurora,* a Philadelphia newspaper. As if to establish the form for posterity, it had become public when a senator (from Virginia) thoughtfully provided a copy of the treaty to politically interested parties.

The word *ciao,* used throughout the world both in greeting friends and in bidding them farewell, comes from the dialect of the Veneto, the region of northeast Italy once ruled by the republic of Venice. It was the habit of the citizens of the Venetian republic to greet and say good-bye to their acquaintances with the respectful phrase *"Schiavo vostro"* ("I am your slave"). In the dialect of the region, the first word was pronounced *s-ciao;* as use of the greeting spread across northern Italy, it became simply *ciao.*

"Who likes to insult people through his writing is like a sorceress; who likes to flatter people through his writings is like a fortune teller."

—Chinese proverb

Invited to seat themselves at the famous round table, Arthur's knights did not take their places haphazardly. More than mere manners determined their seating arrangement: one of the chairs was the Siege Perilous, a seat fatal to any occupant save the knight destined to find the Holy Grail.

Marie Antoinette's last words were a polite apology. As she made her way up the scaffold toward the guillotine, she accidentally stepped on the foot of the executioner, Henri Sanson. "I beg your pardon," she said, "I did not do it on purpose." Monsieur Sanson accepted her apology and then performed his duty.

From a Greek mathematics quiz, ca. AD 500:
"The Graces were carrying baskets of apples and in each was the same number. The nine Muses met them and asked for apples, and they gave the same number to each Muse, and the nine and three had each of them the same number. Tell me how many they gave and how they all had the same number."

Dumplings:
Gourmandise

Michael Jackson is a vegetarian.

The Austrian soprano Dame Nellie Melba had hordes of admirers, both in Europe and the United States. She sang regularly at Covent Garden in London from 1888 to 1926, and while in London she sometimes stayed at the Savoy Hotel. This habit delighted the hotel's famous chef, Auguste Escoffier (twice presented orders of the *Legion d'Honeur* by presidents of France), who was one of Melba's devoted fans. One evening, while dining alone at the Savoy, Melba was presented with a special dessert concocted by Escoffier and named in her honor: peach Melba. Dame Nellie Melba's name also appears in melba toast.

Americans of the newborn republic still labored under impressions of the French passed on by unfriendly British propagandists. Thus, on the occasion of entertaining officers of the much-appreciated French fleet, Nathaniel Tracy of Boston—wholly believing that Frenchmen absolutely required frogs—added frogs liberally and entire to the evening's soup. The words of the first officer to spoon one out are recorded as *"Mon Dieu, une grenouille!"* ("My God! a frog").

The first people to sample pepper pot soup, the soup for which Philadelphia is now famous, were some of George Washington's soldiers. The soup is said to have been created in 1778 by a cook at Valley Forge who put together what was at hand and added a few handfuls of pepper to feed the hungry Continentals.

Service à la russe, inscribed at the guarded portals of some great restaurants, means that meals will be orchestrated by the waiters and kitchen so that one hot dish, or course, after another is served to the guest. This is in contrast to the older *service à la francaise,* in which all the dishes arrive at the table in three huge courses—about half the evening's menu in the first course, half in the second, and a phalanx of desserts in the third.

This revolution in French tastes was brought about by the Russian ambassador to Paris during the time of Napoleon, Prince Alexander Borosovich Kurakin.

A great deal of thought and regulation has gone into the federally approved sizing of olives. As the scale now stands, olives possess twelve designations beginning with counts of 200 or more to the pound and ending at 32 or fewer. The list in ascending order of size is

Sub-Petite, Midget, Select, Medium, Large, Extra Large, Mammoth, Giant, Jumbo, Colossal, Super Colossal, and Special Super Colossal (28 or fewer to the pound), which is not often seen.

The dodo *(Didus ineptus)* became extinct around 1680–85, but was extinguished a second time in 1775, when the last stuffed dodo was burned. It had been the moldering property of Oxford's Ashmolean Museum.

A relative of the pigeon but larger than a turkey, the dodo bird existed in only one place, the island of Mauritius. Facing no predators, the obese, flightless birds knew nothing of self-defense and were thus easy prey for the Portuguese explorers who first landed on the island. Today, only a head, foot, and some random bones exist.

As to those who had the opportunity of dining on this fifty-pound species, none of them left Mauritius raving. "Tolerable eating," "flesh is very hard," "greasy stomachs," and merely "ample" are among recorded comments.

To add pungency, turpentine oil is occasionally present in manufactured candy, baked goods, and chewing gum, but always in microscopic amounts (rarely more than ten parts per million).

Other unlikely food ingredients, also added in nearly undetectable proportions, are:

musk oil—ice cream, candy, baked goods; has a musky flavor

ambergris—ice cream, candy, baked goods; from the stomachs of sperm whales, it has a sweet flavor

beeswax—in many dessert goods; has a sweet flavor

civet oil—ice cream, candy, baked goods, chewing gum; from civet cats, a sweet to slightly putrid flavor.

The members of the heavy-metal band Van Halen are very finicky about their backstage food. They require the promoters of their concerts to provide them with two pounds of M&Ms. What's more, they demand that all the brown-colored M&Ms be removed.

When France's Louis XIV died, in 1715, his heart was removed and his body buried in the Abbey of Saint-Denis. Seventy-five years later, the tomb was ransacked by a mob of Revolutionary fanatics; the king's heart was somehow lost in the confusion. Eighty-odd years later, the heart turned up in England, in the possession of Francis Buckland, a naturalist and dedicated gourmet.

Buckland was very fond of animals. While in school, he had kept monkeys and a bear in his room. He liked all kinds of animals, and he liked to eat them. He fed his friends such delicacies as sea slug and stewed mole, boiled trunk of elephant and rhinoceros pie. It is thus theoretically understandable that when Buckland got hold of Louis XIV's plundered heart, he did not proudly put it on display. He ate it.

Sailors' demands in the 1797 mutiny of the English fleet at Spithead and the Nore included, among other things, that they be fed no more salmon.

Haggis, the Scottish national dish, consists of a boiled sheep's stomach turned inside out and stuffed with boiled and minced sheep's heart, liver, and lungs. Serve in a well-starched napkin.

The first US diplomat to visit Japan after that country had been opened by Commodore Matthew C. Perry was Townsend Harris. Harris arrived in Shimoda in 1856. His desire to eat American-style cuisine led to two firsts in Japan. Shortly after his arrival, a calf was butchered, the first calf to be slaughtered in Japan. Harris also had a cow milked, the first time cow's milk had ever been obtained for human consumption in Japan.

Soldiers, slaves, and plebians in ancient Rome had a beverage all their own. It was called posca and was nothing more than vinegar mixed with enough water to make it palatable. The sponge that was offered to Christ on the cross was most likely steeped in posca.

William Pitt's last words were "I think I could eat one of Bellamy's pork pies."

Snails must be kept in captivity for awhile before they are eaten since the snail's diet often includes plants toxic to humans. Isolation affords the snail a chance for proper digestion.

Similarly, anchovies are "thronged" for three days before smoking and packing, that is, they are kept tightly bound in nets underwater, unable to eat until they are drawn in.

In early experiments to discover effects of radiation on animal tissue, researchers filled the target chambers of their synchrotrons (atom-smashers) with substances such as bacon. This is undoubtedly the most expensive way ever devised to prepare breakfast, but it also yielded valuable data in translating raw radiation measures (curies, roentgens, rads) into biological dosages (rem =   equivalent man).

The ability to regenerate amputated limbs is not limited to lizards and newts. With a surgical procedure to double its nerve supply to the limb, frogs can grow new legs.

Henry Ford refused to eat chicken. He had been raised on a farm, and his chores had included taking care of the chickens.

The so-called Caesar salad was invented in Tijuana, Mexico, during the 1920s. Its inventor was Caesar Gardini, local restaurateur.

Luisa Tetrazzini (1871–1940), Italian coloratura soprano and author of *My Life of Song* and *How to Sing,* is immortalized in the well-known dish chicken tetrazzini.

The roots of the pink-flowered perennial known as the marsh mallow (*Althea officinalis*) were once used to make the spongy confection called marshmallow. Today the place of the roots is taken by syrup, gelatin, and other ingredients.

Technically, the tomato is a fruit. It is considered a vegetable, however, because of the ways in which it is usually used. The US Supreme Court has ruled on this matter, declaring that, legally at least, the tomato is a vegetable.

Napoleon's favorite wine was Chambertin.

Somewhere on the northern coast of Africa lived the lotus-eaters, or Lotophagi, who subsisted on the lotus, the fruits of which brought forgetfulness and happy indolence. Odysseus, when he made landfall there, nearly lost some of his crewmen when they sampled the lotus, an incident made famous by Tennyson in his poem "The Lotus-Eaters." The fruit eaten by the lotus-eaters has been identified as the jujube, member of the buckthorn family.

Hippocrates (ca. 470–360 BC), author of that oath still taken by physicians, perhaps only shared a taste peculiar to his times when he claimed that the meat of puppies was the equal of fowl.

"I *am* the Emperor and I will *have* dumplings."

—Ferdinand I (1793–1875), Emperor of Austria

Tea for 84,000:
Group Activities

The "Locofocos" (radical faction of the New York Democratic party) in 1835 outwitted the "Hunkers" (conservative wing, same party) when they brought candles to a crucial caucus at which the Hunkers had turned off the gas. Loco-foco was a brand of matches then in use.

Though a decade later the radicals would be referred to as "Barn-burners," it is not because they continued to play with matches, rather they would "burn the party down" before tolerating members of pro-slavery opinion.

Only once in World War II did adversaries manage to get every-thing into place for what might be regarded a "strategic" tank battle. This was the Battle of Kursk, in which the Russians and Germans engaged between them 6300 tanks and 30,000 pieces of artillery. At its most intense, on July 12, 1943, the conflict cost Germany 350 tanks in one day.

The first recorded labor strike appears to have taken place in 1245 at Douai (in modern Belgium). In this case clothmakers walked out on the guild masters, their employers.

The first New Orleans Mardi Gras celebration took place in 1827.

At the siege of Mafeking (October 1899–May 1900) during the Boer War youths were dispatched around the city carrying the orders of the commander, Lord Baden-Powell. From the young messengers Baden-Powell drew his inspiration in founding the Boy Scouts in 1908.

Baden-Powell's example in quasi-military organization of youth was not lost on the daughter of Lord Gore-Booth, Constance Mar-kiewicz, who formed the Sons of Erin in 1909 to participate in the Irish revolutionary movement.

Oktoberfest, now celebrated all over Germany, was begun in Bavaria on the occasion, October 27, 1810, of King Ludwig I's wed-ding.

The Civil War draft imposed upon Americans (1863) was the cause of riots, particularly serious in New York City. General Meade was slowed in exploiting his victory at Gettysburg by the need to detach troops to put down the disturbances.

No draft had been in force since the end of the War of 1812, the first occasion on which Congress enacted a national levy.

The Althing of Iceland, established in 930, is the oldest parliament in the world.

The first battles of the American Revolution were fought at Lexington and Concord during the long and fateful day of April 19, 1775. The British went to Concord in the hope of capturing colonial military supplies. News of their plan was sent through the countryside by Paul Revere, William Dawes, and Samuel Prescott. Thus, when the British reached Lexington they found themselves facing a group of minutemen. After a brief exchange of gunfire, the British marched to Concord, where they did indeed destroy some supplies. They then turned around and marched back toward Boston. During their withdrawal to Boston they were fired on by American colonists. Although the minutemen and the colonists who fired on the passing column of British soldiers have become justly famous for their heroism, their aim was not very good. All together, they fired an estimated 75,000 rounds. Only 273 of those projectiles struck any part of the bright-red coats of the British soldiers. (The British sustained 273 casualties at Lexington and Concord; Americans 95.)

New Amsterdam had America's first police force. When it was established, in 1658, it numbered just eight men.

In an effort to stiffen the morale of a broken army, the World War I Russian War Ministry organized in 1915 a women's battalion. The unit participated in action at Tarnopol, taking 200 prisoners and heavy casualties. No improvement of morale was noticed, however, as male units on either side of the "Death Battalion" retreated.

Nineteenth-century Manhattan was the scene of well-organized mayhem. Most of the city's muggers, murderers, pickpockets, and thieves were members of gangs. Among the many such gangs terrorizing local citizens were the Dead Rabbits (Irishmen whose emblem was a dead rabbit impaled on a spike), the Plug Uglies, the Roach Guards, the Bowery Boys, the Daybreak Boys (they did most of their dirty work at dawn, and they really were "boys"—most were ten or younger), the Molasses Gang (whose trademark was a bucket of molasses, which they happily rammed over the heads of their victims), and the Swamp Angels (who used the sewer system for their forays).

177

By the end of the century, the most feared gang was the Whyos. It wasn't easy becoming a member of the Whyos; you had to prove you had committed at least one murder. Members of the gang passed their free time at a Bowery bar called the Morgue, the proprietor of which boasted that his liquor was as good for embalming corpses as it was to drink.

Among the army of doughboys sent to France in 1917 was the 15th New York Infantry, a black outfit. The 15th New York served alongside the French 162nd Division in the Meuse-Argonne. The black infantrymen were such courageous soldiers that their French comrades nicknamed them "the hell fighters" and awarded the entire regiment the croix de guerre.

When the SS *William Browne* hit an iceberg in 1841, only one lifeboat could be launched. The crew threw sixteen of the paying passengers overboard to keep the crowded boat afloat.

The common eels of Europe and America migrate to the Sargasso Sea to spawn and die. Such a journey, several thousand miles from the coasts of northern Europe, is arduous and mysterious, especially since the eels have never been observed en route.

It is theorized that this spawning ground remains from a time when the eel species was young, say 200 million years ago, and the Atlantic was little more than a large lake between two separating landmasses (Europe and North America). Spreading along the Mid-Atlantic Ridge added vast areas to the ocean floor, but the eels seem forever attached to their ancient haunt, no matter how displaced or changed in the geological process.

Researchers find that, on the average, an American's concept of intimate space extends to a radius of 1.5 feet, personal space to 4 feet, and social space to 12 feet.

The American Revolution ended with the Treaty of Paris in 1783. With the end of the war, the last soldiers of the Continental Army were disbanded. In 1784 the entire American army was composed of eighty guards—its senior officer was a Captain John Doughty. This situation came to an end when Indian troubles along the frontier required the formation of the First American Regiment, a unit composed of seven hundred men.

The cavalry unit that has become famous as the "Rough Riders" was also known in its day as "Teddy's Terrors," "Teddy's Terriers," and the "Cowboy Cavalry."

Anatomy lessons in the Renaissance were social occasions. The first step in throwing such a party was to obtain a papal indulgence permitting dissection of the cadaver. Invitations were sent out to prominent persons and officials. And a specimen, still living, had to be chosen from among condemned criminals.

The actual event was launched by an oration and the singing of an anthem by the physicians present. Dissection itself was generally carried out by a servant while a pointer-wielding doctor read from the approved text, usually Galen.

Afterward, everyone attended a small celebration.

The period before Lent has always been a period of frolics and feasts. The feasts are of particular importance because Lent is a period of fasting. The Italians called this pre-Lent merrymaking *carnelevare* ("the putting away of meat") and finally *carnevale,* giving us *carnival.*

Following the British retreat to Boston, not all of the minutemen went home. A few of them camped just outside Boston and waited to see what would happen. They were the first American army.

At Valley Forge, the desertion rate for black soldiers was lower than that for white. Following that disastrous winter, George Washington was more accepting of blacks in the Continental Army.

The first Jew to settle in New Amsterdam was Jacob Barsimson. Barsimson arrived in New Amsterdam from Brazil in August 1654. One month after Barsimson's arrival, twenty-three more Jews arrived in New Amsterdam from Brazil, and they established America's first Jewish community.

In the 1905 Battle of Tsushima (in the straits between Japan and Korea), a Japanese fleet consisting of four battleships and eight cruisers sank twelve of the twenty-one Russian ships involved, including six out of the eight Russian battleships. There were no Japanese losses.

There were nearly a dozen blacks among the minutemen who fought at Lexington and Concord on April 19, 1775, and at least two of them—Peter Salem and Lemuel Haynes—went on to fight in later battles. Haynes took part in the capture of Fort Ticonderoga; Salem fought at Bunker Hill and was credited with killing British major John Pitcairn.

The size of a classic Japanese tea room is about ten feet square. This is a size, mentioned in the *Vikramadytia Sutra,* that accommodated all at once 84,000 disciples of the Buddha.

The Devil's Egg:
Justice

To protect his tea monopoly Frederick II of Prussia created *Kaf-fee-Schnüffler,* coffee sniffers, to wander the streets with a nose out for the illicit aroma of coffee.

Saint Cassian of Imola was a Christian schoolteacher who refused to sacrifice to the Roman gods. As punishment, he was handed over to his pupils, who harbored more than the usual schoolboy hatred for their mentor. They stabbed him to death with their iron pens.

Jay Gould was educated in a seminary in Delaware County, New York. He wrote his senior essay on the praiseworthy theme "Honesty Is the Best Policy." Gould's first business venture was a leather goods firm that he set up with two partners. When the time was right, he swindled his partners and went on to bigger things—he printed and sold counterfeit shares in the Erie Railroad.

Among the ancient Persians a physician was allowed to challenge a colleague's competence by means of a test in which each administered to the other a poison of choice. Physicians not quickly and correctly diagnosing their own symptoms, and so preparing the proper antidote, faced a dire censure.

The infamous Massacre of St. Bartholomew (August 24, 1572) inspired Charles IX to issue general commands for the extermination of all Huguenots. But the governor of Bayonne, Vicomte Dorte, wrote the king he could not find among the troops and the people a single murderer and concluded he would be unable to carry out his orders.

The following menu, reproduced by a former inmate, was an average bill of fare at the Bastille in the eighteenth century:

Green pea soup, garnished with lettuce and a joint of fowl
Sliced roast beef, garnished with parsley
Meat pie, garnished with sweetbreads, coxcombs, aspara-
gus, mushrooms, and truffles
Sheep's tongue *en ragoût*
Biscuit, Fruit, Burgundy wine

Lionel Barrymore died while reading *Macbeth* aloud.

The epitaph over the grave of Ben Jonson, English dramatist and poet, was supposed to read *Orare Ben Jonson* ("Pray for Ben Jonson"). Unfortunately, either the stonecutter didn't know his Latin or was moved by a more personal inspiration: the epitaph reads "O rare Ben Jonson."

The first black elected to the US Senate was Hiram Revels of Mississippi—he took the seat left vacant by Jefferson Davis.

The Roman emperor Commodus, son and successor of Marcus Aurelius, was exceedingly vain. He was particularly fond of showing off his muscles in gladiatorial combats. To get the respect he deserved, he decreed that he should be worshipped as Hercules Romanus. He changed his name to Marcus Commodus Antoninus and wanted to rename Rome Commodiana after himself. Quite understandably, everyone wanted to kill him, but all the assassination attempts failed until one of his advisers hit on the bright idea of taking advantage of the emperor's fondness for sports—he had a wrestler strangle him to death.

The flag of Cuba was designed in New York City. In June 1849 a group of Cuban revolutionaries led by Narciso Lopez was living in New York. They got together and designed the flag; in 1902 it became the official flag of Cuba.

When he was in his last year at Duke University Law School, Richard Nixon worried constantly about his grades. To ascertain his class standing, he broke into the dean's office. He was pleased to find that he was at the top of his class, and he wasn't punished for his little break-in.

Turkish Sultan Murad IV instituted the punishment of pouring molten lead down the throats of tipplers (alcohol is not permitted to Muslims).

Bethlehem Hospital for the insane in London, which gave the word *bedlam* to the language, moved to new quarters in 1930. The old bedlam building was given over to the Imperial War Museum.

The "ship of fools" was a very real vessel along the rivers of medieval Europe. Often, it was made a condition of landing at river ports that mariners take away with them a number of the addled and insane who had by whatever means wandered into the city.

The net result, of course, was not satisfactory. Merchant shippers did not welcome the extra cargo, and towns achieved nothing more than an exchange of visiting idiots.

The Earl of Cardigan, the man who led the disastrous "Charge of the Light Brigade" at Balaklava, died fourteen years after that day of dubious glory of injuries suffered when he fell off his horse.

Etienne de Silhouette (1709–67) gave his name to the familiar picture. As a result of numerous unpopular economies imposed while he served Louis XV as finance minister, caricaturists named any representation stripped to its mere outlines a silhouette.

It does not follow, therefore, that the minor French painter Anton Mauve affixed his name to a rosy purple hue; the color term derives from mallow flowers.

In 1471 a chicken in Basel, Switzerland, made the mistake of laying a brightly colored egg. Horrified by this transgression of "natural law," the townspeople accused the chicken of being "a devil in disguise" and put it on trial. Found guilty, the bird was burned at the stake.

The Scarlet F:
Law and Crime

To "read the riot act" was in fact to read the Riot Act of 1715, an English law that required of itself an actual reading in the presence of any illegally gathered crowd before police action and serious charges were initiated.

Mid-eighteenth-century forgers of banknotes simulated official watermarks—once thought an infallible mark of authenticity by the banks that used them—by drawing them on counterfeit-grade paper with a pointed stick dipped in a mixture of whale oil and linseed oil.

The earliest Romans were permitted to expose deformed infants, but parents were legally bound to show them first to five neighbors.

Adolf Hitler was adamantly opposed to abortion. He sentenced Aryan women who had abortions to hard labor after the first offense. If the woman had another abortion, she was sentenced to death.

Pennsylvania was the first state to abolish slavery. A 1780 law provided that no child could be born a slave, thus gradually eliminating slavery in the state.

The identification division of the American FBI contains the largest collection of fingerprint records in the world: over 169 million.

In Sweden, it is against the law for parents to spank their children.

By an English statute of 1341 royal courts might try dead usurers, ecclesiastical courts live ones. Live usurers did not appear in the king's courts until the reign of James I (r. 1603–25).

Convicted killer Gary Gilmore, first to be executed in ten years in the United States, died by firing squad—the law of Utah—in 1977. His last words were, "Let's do it."
In 1960, when James W. Rodgers faced the Utah firing squad, he was asked if he had a last request. His last words were, "Why, yes—a bulletproof vest."

Body-snatchers in Scotland were careful to take the body only, never clothing or possessions buried with their owners. There being, under Scottish law, no property rights in a corpse, these so-called resurrectionists were protecting themselves against charges of robbery.

Salic law, that venerable symbol of male domination, has taken a bad rap. As a body Salic law is that of the Salian Franks (as opposed to Ripuarian Franks, the other great branch of the "barbarian" group that settled in France during the Roman Empire's decline). But more particularly it was resurrected to justify the naming exclusively of male heirs in the early fourteenth century by Philips V and VI of France, who faced female competition in the succession.

In fact, the Salic laws do favor inheritance by direct male descent, but in the absence of sons or daughters bestow property on female relatives in preference to surviving males.

Salic law was also quite modern, and nearly unique in the post-Roman world, in requiring that persons making accusations bring evidence, and when evidence was produced, in causing the accused to do more than multiply oaths and swear innocence.

This idea of multiplying oaths—as many as 72 friends and relatives might be produced—led naturally to the expedient of trial by combat when everyone was equally sworn out. The early Church, though it countenanced and officiated at trials by combat, was far too sophisticated to allow such hocum in its own ecclesiastical courts. It insisted, like the Salians, upon evidence and proof.

In 1981 major reported crimes (per 100,000 population) were lowest in the state of West Virginia, highest in the District of Columbia (2619 versus 10,934).

The USSR was the first country to legalize abortion, in 1920.

Pirates signing on with Bartholomew Roberts (1679–1722), often thought the most successful of buccaneers, made a written compact with his captain and shipmates.

These pirate articles provided, among other things, equal division of captured provisions, a graduated scale of monetary compensation for loss of limb or crippling injury "on the job," and strict prohibitions against gambling, quarreling, desertion, and smuggling women aboard ship.

Marooning was a popular punishment for breach of the contract.

In ancient Rome, laws determined the height of buildings. No privately owned building was permitted to be higher than twice the width of the street on which it stood. This law insured that sunlight always reached the street.

Marm Mandelbaum fenced perhaps $10,000,000 worth of stolen goods in the years 1870–84. Apprehended by Pinkerton men in New York, she jumped bail (on her lawyer's advice) and fled to Canada, establishing other businesses there.

The Chou (1122–256 BC) rulers of China considered certain crimes so repugnant as to admit of no defense; punishment was a swift and certain death. To bewilder and perplex the multitude was the greatest crime, whether by wearing strange clothes, playing unusual music, inventing new tools and machines, or spreading false information about the days and seasons.

Tampering with names and lawyerly tinkering with words of the laws headed the list of capital offenses.

A *mortgage* ("dead pledge") was distinguished in the Middle Ages from a *vif gage* ("live pledge"), in which revenues from pledged property counted toward reducing the principal of a debt. Mortgages were more favorable to lenders since revenues were paid over to the mortgage holders without shrinking the mortgagee's debt.

Anyone living in or near the forests in the time of Henry I of England (1068–1135) might keep a dog but was required by law to declaw it. This would prevent its use in poaching on the king's forest preserves.

English kings were no less hard on human poachers: by the time of Richard I, the Lion Heart (1157–99), the punishment consisted of blinding and castration.

Hawthorne made notorious the punishment of adultery by branding with the "scarlet letter" A. But pity the poor forger, who was still punished as late as 1835 in Rhode Island by cropping the ears, branding with the letter C, pillory, imprisonment of up to six years, and a fine. Adulterers paid then up to $200 and six months confinement.

Delaware had also adopted the pillory for forgers, as well as solitary imprisonment and a fine, but also required the prominent wearing of a scarlet F on outside garments for a period of from two to five years after release. Adulterers paid $100.

The Arm of God:
Lost and Found

Walled up somewhere in the Spanish royal palace are the crown jewels of Spain. They were hidden there to prevent their being carried off by Napoleon during the French occupation. But the rooms were completely redecorated by the French, and no useful clues remain to identify the treasure room.

England's Queen Elizabeth I (1533–1603) did not wear dentures. When she lost her front teeth, she took to stuffing pieces of cloth under her lips to fill out her face.

U. S. Grant's second vice-president was Henry Wilson. Wilson was a self-made man, and he was self-named, too. Born Jeremiah Jones Colbath, he had been indentured to a farmer at the age of 10. For eleven years, he worked for the farmer. He passed his spare time reading books, and one of the books he read was the biography of a certain Henry Wilson. When he reached the age of 21, he escaped his indenture. One of his first acts was to have his name legally changed to Henry Wilson. The identity of the original Henry Wilson has been lost; no one knows who he was, but he certainly inspired the young Jeremiah Jones Colbath.

Between 1800 (John Adams) and 1913 (Woodrow Wilson) no president appeared before Congress. It was Wilson who reestablished the custom of delivering the Annual Message. Truman renamed it the State of the Union Message.

The first Japanese visitor to the United States was Manjiro Nakahama, who was one of five shipwrecked Japanese sailors rescued at sea by an American whaling ship in 1843. Nakahama's four companions were put ashore at Honolulu, but he stayed on the whaling ship and was eventually put ashore at New Bedford, Massachusetts. The first Japanese to become a naturalized US citizen, in 1850, was Hikozo Hamada, another shipwrecked sailor rescued at sea.

A safe kept in the Capitol was to have been opened in 1976 on the occasion of America's second centennial. Presented to the government after the 1876 Exposition, the so-called Centennial Safe is opened with a key entrusted to the Smithsonian Institute, and they can't find it.

To obtain green cloth a medieval artisan dyed first with weld (a vegetal yellow) and then with woad (vegetal blue). And the vexing problem of producing purple—the secret of true Tyrian purple was lost with the fall of Byzantium in 1453—could be solved by squeezing the right species of molluscs, as the Byzantines had done, or by dyeing first in blue and then in red.

John Deere made his first steel plow in 1837: he fashioned it from a discarded sawmill blade.

A 1688 census of England that compiled such useful figures as the number of papists fit to bear arms (4940) and the proportions of conformists to nonconformists, appeared under the title "The Telling of Noses." But the figures lied, inasmuch as this was really a census of 1676 that had been bureaucratically lost in the shufflings of the 1688 Glorious Revolution.

It took historians about two centuries to notice that a census appeared in a year in which no census was taken and to track down the error.

Thurgood Marshall, who became the first black American appointed to the Supreme Court, was born Thoroughgood Marshall. He himself shortened his name. "By the time I reached the second grade, I got tired of spelling all that out and had it shortened to Thurgood."

Only one American flag was displayed during the first battles of the American Revolution on April 19, 1775, and that flag was already more than one hundred years old. The so-called Bedford flag was made in England in the middle of the seventeenth century. It was used by the Three County Troop, a cavalry unit organized in 1659 in eastern Massachusetts to defend the colonists from Indians. The flag shows the "arm of God"—an armored arm holding a sword reaching out of a cloud—with the Latin motto *vince aut morire* ("conquer or die").

Nathaniel Page, standard bearer of the Bedford minutemen, grabbed this flag from a closet in his home as he rushed out to fight the British at Concord on the morning of April 19, 1775. Page lost sight of the flag during the fighting, and when he had finished tending the wounded he went to look for it. He found a group of children happily playing with the aged banner. Page took the flag and put it back in his closet. It stayed there for another hundred years, when it

191

was again taken out to celebrate the centennial of the Battle of Concord. The flag was donated to the town of Bedford in 1885 and is probably the oldest flag in the United States.

The Chair's Spell:
Magic

"No one has ever seen a bald headed Indian."

—from an advertisement for Kickapoo Indian Remedies

In the early 1960s French astronomers twice reported the presence of sulphur in the sun—a thing seriously at variance with prevailing theories of solar operation. What the French had not taken into account with their improved spectrometer was that it detected and analyzed the striking of a match anywhere in the same room with it. "No Smoking" signs were posted. No more sulphur was found in the sun.

In 1970 the Rhine Institute of Parapsychology in Durham, North Carolina, produced lab results to demonstrate that fertilized chicken eggs possessed psychokinetic abilities and hard-boiled eggs did not. But it later transpired that the data had been tampered with.

Heisenberg's Uncertainty Principle, which allows that an experimenter may determine a sub-atomic particle's position or velocity with great accuracy, but not both, applies fully to larger, everyday reality. Its effects, however, are not likely to be noticed. In dropping a baseball from a third-story window the uncertainty as to its whereabouts when it lands is less than one tenth the radius of a baseball atom's nucleus.

The greenhouse effect—the often cited mechanism by which heat is captured by Earth's atmosphere—works something like this: solar radiation, largely at the frequencies of visible light, is admitted through the atmosphere; the earth reradiates much of this energy but at lower (infrared) frequencies, to which the atmosphere is highly absorptive, not transparent. Heating results.

This, as it turns out, is *not* what happens in a greenhouse. Recent scientific putterers report that heating in glassed enclosures is predominantly the result of more mundane convective and insulating processes.

In 1970s medical studies of wart cures, people with large numbers of warts distributed over the whole body were given instructions under hypnosis to "will" them away, but only on one side of the body. Results were spectacularly successful, even with a subject who couldn't distinguish left from right and unconsciously banished the warts from the wrong side of his body.

Dr. Wilhelm Fliess (1858–1928) held that the root of most disease and aberration was in the membranes of the nose. He operated on his friend Sigmund Freud twice for nasal infections.

Later in life Fliess became obsessed with the idea of twenty-three- and twenty-eight-day cycles in human affairs. From his observations and writings is derived the modern notion of biorhythms.

Although historians are often agreed in ascribing the course of witch hunts to the mixed action of superstition, hysteria, factionalism, and downright fraud, that isn't always enough to get the process started. L. R. Caporael suggested a physiological cause for the famous outbreak at Salem, Massachusetts, in late 1692.

Ergotism, the toxic effects of eating grains, very often rye, infected with the ergot fungus, produces symptoms remarkably similar to those described and witnessed during the Salem episode. In addition to causing crawling sensations of the skin, tingling in the fingers, vertigo, headaches, and sudden muscular contraction, ergot may produce hallucinations and a range of altered mental states.

A high proportion of the affected persons and accusers at Salem lived in the damper, marshy areas nearer the river than did accused witches and their defenders. The fungus thrives in warm wet weather (the spring and summer of 1691 were especially rainy and hot) and develops equally well in grains stored in damp places.

To their credit, the clergy warned against testimony consisting merely of apparitions and seizures, but the magistrates were inclined to accept it.

During the eighteenth century, many sailors had crucifixes tattooed on their backs. They didn't do so out of religious zeal, however. It was the custom at that time to punish wrongdoing sailors with the lash, and the sailors believed that officers would be reluctant to whip the image of Christ. (The more superstitious sailors also believed that the image would turn away the whip.)

Rice Krispies in Dutch-speaking countries do not go "snap, crackle, pop" but "pif, paf, pof."

King Alfonso of Spain was believed to possess the dreaded "evil eye." His reign was certainly marked by mishaps. On his wedding day in 1906, an attempt was made to kill Alfonso and his bride, the first of several assassination attempts. His wife introduced hemophilia into his family. His first and fourth sons died of minor accidents.

When, in 1923, Alfonso decided to pay an official visit to Italy, Italian dictator Mussolini was not pleased. Mussolini was terrified of the evil eye and refused to meet with Alfonso—all their business had to be carried out by intermediaries. Mussolini's fears seemed justified. A fleet of Italian ships was sent to greet the Spanish monarch: several sailors were washed overboard and drowned; a cannon fired in the king's honor exploded, killing its crew; an officer who bravely shook Alfonso's hand died shortly after the experience.

Techniques employed by Marcel Duchamp to produce *The bride stripped bare by her bachelors, even* (more conveniently referred to as the *Large Glass*) included firing paint-tipped matchsticks at the glass from toy cannon, photographic studies of wind-blown curtains, and allowing the piece to accumulate dust for a year on the floor of his New York apartment.

Jack be nimble
Jack be quick
Jack jump over
The candlestick

In medieval England, people did indeed jump over lighted candles—it was believed to be a way of telling fortunes. It was a good omen if the candle stayed lit; if it went out, dark days lay ahead.

Jean (Hans) Arp, seizing upon the laws of chance as esthetic grist, claimed to produce his striking collages of 1918–20 by randomly dropping squarish pieces of paper to the floor. But the odds against their being truly random compositions exceed the credibility of all save a few art lecturers. (Arp modified his telling of the feat to later biographers.)

If all the zeros, exceeding sixty by a minimal estimate, in the odds against Arp were to be dropped from a height of nine meters, the result might well resemble the work of Larry Poons.

During the famous 1972 championship chess match between Boris Spaasky and Bobby Fischer the Russians made formal complaints concerning the chair Fischer had brought with him. It was their position that secret properties of the chair, perhaps chemical or electronic, were weakening Spaasky's performance. Examination of the chair at the seventeenth game turned up two dead flies.

Two Pipée and Then Turn Left: Measurement

A jackpot was originally an English measure of about two jiggers of whiskey.

The following system of cowrie exhange was in use in the 1790s for the Dahomey slave trade:

40 cowries = tockey
5 tockey = gallino
1 gallino = ackey
4 ackey = cabess
4 cabess = ounce
the last-named measure being worth abut £2.

Food cans come in about nine standard sizes. In order of ascending size they are called: 8 ounce, Picnic (10 ounce), 12 ounce, No. 300 (14 ounce), No. 303 (16 ounce), No. 2 (18 ounce), No. 2¼ (26 ounce), No. 3 Cylinder (46 ounce), and No. 10 (about three quarts).

John Wayne had a size 18 neck.

When particles are accelerated in an atom-smasher toward targets of interest physicists express the probability of hitting anything (the "cross section") in barns—as in to hit the broad side of. A smaller unit of measure is the shed.

US and British measures for beverage alcohol content look similar but are not the same. British measure of, say, 100 proof is equal to 114 proof American, i.e., British measure is 14 percent stronger than American.

The most divergent system of all, however, is the Spanish Cartier measure, in which all degrees of alcohol content are compressed non-linearly into a scale running from 10 to 44. Numbers around the bottom end of this scale signify increases in alcohol content about five times as large as numbers at the top end.

The nomenclature of mental deficiency is quite precise and should be kept in mind when formulating epithets: an "idiot" is a feeble-minded person who performs at the potential age of 3 years; an "imbecile" displays a mental age of 3 to 7 years; and a "moron" has a potential mental age of between 8 and 12 years.

COMMON WEIGHTS AND MEASURES
LENGTH

American and British units *Metric system*

1 inch (in.) = 1/12 foot
1 foot (ft.) = 1/3 yard
1 yard (yd; basic unit of length)
1 rod (rd) = 5½ yards
1 furlong (fur.) = 220 yards = 1/8 mile
1 mile (mi) = 1,760 yards = 5,280 feet
1 fathom (fath) = 6 feet
1 nautical mile = 6,076.1 feet

1 millimeter (mm) = 1/1000 meter
1 centimeter (cm) = 1/100 meter
1 decimeter (dm) = 1/10 meter
1 meter (m; basic unit of length)
1 dekameter (dkm) = 10 meters
1 kilometer (km) = 1,000 meters

Conversion factors

1 centimeter = 0.39 inch
1 inch = 2.54 centimeters
1 meter = 39.37 inches = 3.28 feet = 1.094 yards
1 foot = 0.305 meter

1 yard = 0.914 meter
1 kilometer = 0.62 mile
1 mile = 1.609 kilometers
1 nautical mile = 1.852 kilometers

AREA

American and British units *Metric system*

1 square inch (sq in.) = 1/2296 square yard = 1/144 square foot
1 square foot (sq ft) = 1/9 square yard = 144 square inches
1 square yard (sq yd; basic unit of area) = 9 square feet
1 square rod (sq rd) = 30¼ square yards
1 acre = 4,840 square yards = 160 square rods
1 square mile (sq mi) = 3,097,600 square yards = 640 acres

1 square centimeter (sq cm) = 1/10000 square meter
1 square decimeter (sq dm) = 1/100 square meter
1 square meter (sq m; basic unit of area)
1 are (a) = 100 square meters
1 hectare (ha) = 10,000 square meters = 100 area
1 square kilometer (sq km) = 1,000,000 square meters

Conversion factors

1 square centimeter = 0.155 square inch
1 square inch = 6.45 square centimeters
1 acre = 0.405 hectare

1 hectare = 2.47 acres
1 square kilometer = 0.386 square mile
1 square mile = 2.59 square kilometers

VOLUME AND CAPICITY *(liquid and dry)*

American and British units

1 cubic inch (cu in) = $\frac{1}{46656}$ cubic yard = $\frac{1}{1728}$ cubic foot

1 cubic foot (cu ft) = $\frac{1}{27}$ cubic yard = 1,728 cubic inches

1 cubic yard (cu yd; basic unit of volume) = 27 cubic feet

1 U.S. fluid ounce (fl oz) = $\frac{1}{128}$ U.S. gallon = $\frac{1}{16}$ U.S. pint

1 gill (gi) = $\frac{1}{32}$ gallon = $\frac{1}{4}$ pint = 4 fluid ounces

1 pint (pt) = $\frac{1}{8}$ gallon = $\frac{1}{2}$ quart = 16 fluid ounces

1 quart (qt) = $\frac{1}{4}$ gallon = 32 fluid ounces

1 U.S. gallon (gal; basic unit of liquid capacity in the U.S.) = 231 cu in.

1 dry pint (dry pt) = $\frac{1}{64}$ bushel = $\frac{1}{2}$ dry quart

1 peck (pk) = $\frac{1}{4}$ bushel

1 U.S. bushel (bu; basic unit of dry capacity in the U.S.) = 2,150.4 cubic inches

1 cup = $\frac{1}{4}$ quart = $\frac{1}{2}$ pint = 8 fluid ounces

1 tablespoon = $\frac{1}{2}$ fluid ounce = 3 teaspoons

1 teaspoon = $\frac{1}{3}$ tablespoon

1 British imperial fluid ounce (fl oz) = $\frac{1}{160}$ imperial gallon

1 imperial gallon (gal; basic unit of liquid capacity in some Commonwealth nations) = 277.4 cubic inches

1 imperial bushel (bu; basic unit of dry capacity in some Commonwealth nations) = 2,219.4 cubic inches

Metric system

1 cubic centimeter (cc) = $\frac{1}{1000000}$ cubic meter

1 cubic decimeter (cu dm) = $\frac{1}{1000}$ cubic meter = 1,000 cubic centimeters

1 cubic meter (cu m) = 1 stere (s; basic unit of volume)

1 milliliter (ml) = $\frac{1}{1000}$ liter = 1 cubic centimeter

1 centiliter (cl) = $\frac{1}{100}$ liter = 10 milliliters

1 deciliter (dl) = $\frac{1}{10}$ liter

1 liter = 1 cubic decimeter (basic unit of capacity)

1 dekaliter (dkl) = 10 liters

1 hectoliter (hl) = 100 liters = $\frac{1}{10}$ cubic meter

1 kiloliter (kl) = 1,000 liters

1 cubic centimeter = 0.06 cubic inch
1 cubic inch = 16.4 cubic centimeters
1 cubic yard = 0.765 cubic meter
1 cubic meter = 1.3 cubic yards
1 milliliter = 0.034 fluid ounce
1 fluid ounce = 29.6 milliliters
1 U.S. quart = 0.946 liter
1 liter = 1.06 U.S. quarts
1 U.S. gallon = 3.8 liters

1 imperial gallon = 1.2 U.S.
 gallons = 4.5 liters
1 imperial bushel = 1.03 U.S.
 bushels = 36.37 liters
1 liter = 0.9 dry quart
1 dry quart = 1.1 liters
1 dekaliter = 0.28 U.S. bushel
1 U.S. bushel = 0.97 imperial
 bushel = 35.24 liters

WEIGHT OR MASS

American and British units:
avoirdupois

Metric system

1 grain = $\frac{1}{7000}$ pound = $\frac{1}{4375}$ ounce
1 dram (dr) = $\frac{1}{256}$ pound = $\frac{1}{16}$ ounce
1 ounce (oz) = $\frac{1}{16}$ pound
1 pound (lb; basic unit of weight or
 mass)
1 short hundredweight = 100 pounds
1 long hundredweight = 112 pounds
1 short ton = 2,000 pounds
1 long ton = 2,240 pounds

American and British units; troy and
apothecaries'

1 grain = $\frac{1}{7000}$ avoirdupois pound
 $\frac{1}{480}$ troy ounce
1 pennyweight (dwt) = 24
 grains = $\frac{1}{20}$ troy ounce
1 apothecaries' dram (dr ap) = 60
 grains = $\frac{1}{8}$ apothecaries' ounce
1 troy or apothecaries' ounce (oz t or
 oz ap)= 480 grains = $\frac{1}{12}$ troy or
 apothecaries' pound
1 troy or apothecaries' pound (lb t or
 lb ap) = 5,760 grains = 12 troy or
 apothecaries' ounces

1 milligram (mg) = $\frac{1}{1000000}$
 kilogram = $\frac{1}{1000}$ gram
1 centigram (cg) = $\frac{1}{100000}$
 kilogram = $\frac{1}{100}$ gram
1 decigram (dg) = $\frac{1}{10000}$ kilogram =
 $\frac{1}{10}$ gram
1 gram (g) = $\frac{1}{1000}$ kilogram
1 dekagram (dkg) = $\frac{1}{100}$ kilogram =
 10 grams
1 hectogram (hg) = $\frac{1}{10}$ kilogram =
 100 grams
1 kilogram (kg; basic unit of weight or
 mass)
1 metric ton (t) = 1,000 kilograms

1 milligram = 0.015 grain
1 grain = 64.8 milligrams
1 gram = 0.035 avoirdupois ounce
1 avoirdupois ounce = 28.35 grams
1 troy or apothecaries' pound = 0.82
   avoirdupois pound = 0.37 kilogram
1 avoirdupois pound = 1.2 troy or
   apothecaries' pounds =
   0.45 kilogram
1 kilogram = 2.205 avoirdupois
   pounds
1 short ton = 0.9 metric ton
1 metric ton = 1.1 short tons

The problem of expressing degrees of physical pain is approximately solved in a system that assigns the unit "jnd" to a "just noticeable difference." Two jnds equal one "dole."

To express the resistance to passage of an electrical current the ohm (after George Ohm) is used. If, instead, the ease of current passage is a more convenient measure ("conductance"), physicists merely invert the formula and the measure—ohm becomes mho. But mhos must not be confused with mohs (measures relative hardness of substances on a scale of ten) named after Friedrich Mohs.

A faggot is not a single piece of kindling but a bundle of sticks three feet long and two feet in circumference (as measured by a two-foot length of string, specified by centuries-old English law to insure uniformity).

While an American A is 440 cycles per second (officially adopted in 1936), an international A is 435 cycles. Both are in use.

Oceangoing ships are described sometimes by gross tonnage, sometimes by deadweight tonnage. The gross ton is not at all a measure of weight but of capacity; each gross ton is equal to 100 cubic feet of permanently enclosed space. Deadweight, however, is expressed in real tons. It is the weight of all that a ship may carry when laden to its Plimsoll line.

Displacement tonnage is something else again, usually only of interest as applied to warships. This measure is equal to the weight of water displaced by the ship, in other words, its actual weight.

Though it has fallen into disuse the measure, two quarts, that lies between the gallon and the quart is the pottle.

One sixteenth-century English barrel (30 gallons) of eels is equal to ½ a salmon pipe or ¹⁄₁₂ a salmon last, which is a little less than four firkins, or two kilderkins, of haddock (well, because haddock shippers adopted the 32-gallon ale barrel standard; others were using beer barrels). Pilchard and mackerel obeyed laws unlike any other, growing finally into 50-gallon barrels, about a hogshead.

Left over, and still used, from the early days of experimental atomic physics are the names for fission products: alpha particle for a helium nucleus, beta particle for an electron, and gamma ray for extremely short wavelength electromagnetic energy. Missing from the list is the delta ray, once a designation for electrons above 100 electron volts but now fallen into disuse.

Between 1900 and 1940 the stature of the average 20-year-old Japanese male increased from 160 centimeters (63 inches) to 164.5 centimeters (64¾ inches). For females the growth rate was from 147.9 centimeters (58 inches) to 152.7 centimeters (60 inches). This is also the period in which Western dress was adopted in Japan.

For a brief period during the technological infancy of the laser, researchers expressed the relative power of their beams in gillettes, that is, the number of razor blades pressed together that the beam would penetrate.

The National Bureau of Standards unofficially proposed in 1970 certain uniform measures for trivia. The smallest is the femto-bismol, one quadrillionth of a bismol—a suitable fraction for the significance level of most trivia.

An easier, more natural unit, also proposed, is the pede, with its obvious overtones of pedantry. And it provides workable units in the millipede to centipede range.

"Wind chill factor," developed from 1941 experiments of Siple and Passel, is really all about freezing a half-pint of water in the Antarctic. This is the uniform sample size that was exposed to a range of temperature and wind conditions in the Antarctic weather to derive the now-familiar table used in winter forecasts.

The scale does not take into account effects of high humidity or perspiration on chilled humans.

One metric measure that has been in British and American use since 1914 is the carat, unit of weight for gemstones. Previously the carat varied from place to place by as much as 10 percent—expensive misunderstandings did arise.

The metric carat is equal to 200 milligrams, a measure small enough that even diamonds are not generally weighed to more than two decimal points.

Standard architectural height for the seat of a chair is seventeen inches. It must be drawn up to a table or desk twenty-nine inches high.

In grading milk, government inspectors award demerits for degrees of taste in nine categories: butter, chalky, feed, flat, oxidized, scorched, stale, storage, and utensil.

For the uninitiated, oxidized is a flavor resembling cardboard, scorched is a definite burnt aftertaste, and flat lacks sweetness or fullness of flavor.

The four primary taste sensations are sweet, sour, salty, and bitter. In establishing relative strengths of taste sensations substances used in each category—given an arbitrary index value of one—are sucrose (sweet), salt (salty), quinine (bitter), and dilute hydrochloric acid (sour).

Telling the temperature by the song of crickets is done by counting the number of chirps in a fourteeen-second interval and adding forty. The total is the temperature in Fahrenheit degrees—useful only in the 20-30-degree temperature range in which crickets feel like chirping.

Paper sizes larger than average book size, e.g., octavo, quarto, folio, are not often heard of anymore. Once in use but now obsolescent, some of those sizes were (in ascending order) crown, demy, royal, elephant, and imperial, the last being usually 22 inches by 30 inches.

A brilliant-cut diamond has 58 facets, 33 above (crown) and 25 below (pavillion) the girdle. The magna cut, a complex variation, has 102 facets, 61 above and 41 below. The topmost facet is always the "table," and the bottommost, the "culet."

Though most striking for diamond's natural crystal form, the brilliant cut is most wasteful: from 50-60 percent of the stone is cut away in the faceting process.

The difficult formal hieroglyphics of the Maya possess a unique set of number symbols. To each number corresponds a face. A bulging eye and snaggle tooth, for example, is the face of four. Nine is pock-marked; zero cups his hand to his chin, thoughtful.

Numbers between ten and twenty add together facial features from one to nine and the skeletal lower jaw of ten—though their number system was based on a counting unit of twenty.

These are visages of the gods, patrons of the various numbers. More convenient for the Maya was a bar-and-dot notational system also used to record sums.

To mind one's ps and qs was actually, in an old English pub, to keep an accounting of a customer's consumption by pints and quarts.

Until 1891 the US Census Bureau took great care to distinguish among people of mixed black and white ancestry: *mulatto* referred to the first-generation offspring of black and white parents; *quadroon* was a person of one-quarter black ancestry; *octoroon* was a person of one-eighth black ancestry. There was even a category called *griffe*, composed of persons "lighter" than octoroons.

The rating of eggs—AA, A, B, C, I, II—under the Egg Products Inspection Act of 1970 is a dynamic system. An egg that is US Grade AA, for example, at its point of origin may have matured biologically into a Grade A or less by the time it reaches its destination. Generally, in each grade, 85 percent of the eggs must start out in their labeled classification and no more than 5 percent move into a lower grade during shipment.

Grades I and II are not lower quality eggs than US Grade C, the lowest, they are the allowed mixes of the various grades in large shipments.

Before 1958 there was no agreement on what actually constituted an inch. In the United States it was 2.540005 centimeters; in Britain it was 2.5399956; in Australia and Canada it was 2.54 centimeters. In 1958 all countries agreed to standardize to 2.54.

The French have within recent history used the *pipée* as a rough unit of length. It is the distance a man can walk while smoking one pipeful of tobacco.

Through Clenched Teeth: Medicine

Acupuncture, the ancient Chinese remedy, has caught on in the West. But acupuncture is a yin cure, and where there is a yin there is always a yang. In this case it is ignipuncture, or lighting a fire on the patient.

The fire is a small one kindled with a cone of powdered dry leaves; it is allowed to burn while the fuel lasts. As with its historical complement, acupuncture, the choice of precise points on the body to apply the cure is of chief importance.

Though still seen in China this treatment did not find favor in the West.

Verruga, also known as Oroya fever and Carrion's disease, is often fatal, contracted only at night, and only in the Andes at altitudes between 3000 and 8000 feet. Its rather mysterious occurrence was explained in 1913, when researchers connected the habitat and nocturnal activity of the disease vector, a South American sandflea, to its outbreak.

Deep canyons on the Andean west slope are still to be avoided after dark, as screening against the minute sandflea is often ineffective.

An ancient Roman cure for hiccups is to put a ring on the middle finger. Authorities are split upon the question of which hand should receive the ring. Roman physicians say the left, some philosophers the right.

People with Münchhausen's syndrome invent realistic tales of affliction to gain admission to hospitals. With enough practice and discernment in choosing diseases they are often detected only by uncovering a pattern of admissions to a large number of hospitals.

But people exhibiting *factitious* Münchhausen's syndrome are even more sophisticated: showing up in emergency rooms with painted lesions or surgical scars and sham symptoms, such a patient pretends, with calculated imprecision, to suffer from Münchhausen's syndrome. A doctor discovers, thus, the patient is pretending at the pretense of being ill, and that all this has been exactly contrived just to be discovered. Is the patient ill?

The names of these dizzying afflictions are taken from an immensely popular collection of children's tales, *Baron Münchhausen's Narrative of his Marvellous Travels and Campaigns in Russia,* published in 1785 by Rudolf Erich Raspe. Raspe had collected and embellished the reminiscences of none other than Baron H. K. F. von Münchhausen (1720–97), a Prussian officer who told of his fabulous exploits so often that he eventually came to believe in them

---

The magical "powder of sympathy," thought in the seventeenth century to heal wounds, was ferrous sulphate heptahydrate, sometimes mixed with a gum base. Also called green vitriol, its magical quality lay in its application, which was strictly to some article soaked in blood of the wound, never to the wound itself.

The Renaissance was a time of great art and expensive medicines. For those who could afford them, the most popular medicines were concoctions made of crushed jewels. Indeed, the more expensive or rare a remedy, the more effectual it was believed to be. The lives of several famous people were cut short by the ingestion of these costly and ineffectual—if not absolutely detrimental—potions.

Pope Clement VII, patron of Raphael, Michelangelo, and Benvenuto Cellini, became ill in 1534. He might have recovered had his physicians not prescribed crushed gems. Over a period of fourteen days, Clement swallowed roughly $3 million worth of precious stones, including one large diamond. He died.

In 1626 a very sick but usually more sensible Francis Bacon was prevailed upon to take, as medicine, a mixture composed of ground-up pearls and lemon juice. Although the pearly paste probably did him little harm, Bacon soon perished.

Abraham Lincoln's mother died when he was 9 years old. Lincoln never knew the cause of his mother's death. He knew that she died of "the trembles" and that the malady was somehow connected to milk. In fact, the cause of the disease was not identified until 1927. Mrs. Lincoln died from drinking poisonous milk. The Lincoln family was poor and lived in an area where there were no pastures. Since there was no grass, their cows had to forage in the woods, and they ate what they could find, including poisonous white snakeroot. Mrs. Lincoln's death was thus a result of her family's poverty. The young Lincoln must have drunk the milk, too, and it is only an accident of fate that he did not die.

Modern man is not really taller than his ancestors. The average modern man is five feet eight inches tall; the average Paleolithic man stood five feet nine inches.

Tuberculosis, at least in one of its forms, scrofula, was thought curable by the touch of the English king's hands, a belief arising in the time of the very pious Edward the Confessor (d. 1066). Other and earlier kings, notably in France, had a go at it, but the laying on of the royal hands persisted in England through the reign of Queen Anne (1665–1714). In England the disease came to be referred to as King's Evil, that is, an evil reserved to the king's mercy.

Among the last to take the cure, and receive a protective medal, from the hands of Queen Anne was Samuel Johnson in 1712, aged nearly 3. Johnson's chief recollection of the trip was of having become sick in the coach.

Dragon's brains, when mixed with the earth, produced a white substance once sold in Chinese apothecaries for tongue ailments. The material is asbestos.

Queen Elizabeth I was billed by her druggist for "a confection made like mannas Christi, with bezoar stone and unicorn's horn." These unpalatable ingredients were, respectively, an animal's gallstone and ivory.

Also popular, even into the nineteenth century, were remedies containing usnea—moss scraped from a criminal's skull (lingering deaths made for greater potency)—eunuch's fat, and pieces of mummy.

Among the famous people who have suffered the agony of kidney stones are Michelangelo and Montaigne.

In the late nineteenth century a course of treatment for consumption (tuberculosis) might include the surgical removal of one or two of the lowest ribs. Though a desperate expedient, the resulting partial collapse of the lungs seemed to slow progress of the disease.

The famous American actress Anna Held (1837–1918) did not have the disease but, like some other women of fashion, underwent the operation to give herself that unnaturally slender "hourglass" waist thought most attractive at the time. She died not long afterward from slow suffocation.

Charles Darwin thought himself afflicted with Chaga's Disease, contracted from the bite of a benchuga bug (of the assassin bug family) while he worked in South America. The disease was at that time impossible to diagnose, and his acquaintances leaned to the view that he suffered from hypochondria. Inasmuch as the chief symptom of both is often a general, lifelong malaise, neither sickness can be excluded.

Henry VIII's physicians reported regularly from his deathbed that the king was not seriously ill. They were neither deluded nor incompetent, and especially not stupid, since it was high treason to predict the king's death.

There were, as well as midwives, midmen in seventeenth century Europe. They were quite the fashion at Louis XIV's court (and delivered Louis's heir), where they were called *accoucheurs*.

Daniel Hale Williams, a black physician working at Chicago's Provident Hospital, performed the world's first successful heart operation on July 9, 1893.

During the Prohibition era, the government failed in a suit against the manufacturers of Blackdraught, a patent medicine that the government claimed was no better than pure hooch with a medicinal label. Blackdraught showed in court, however, that the government had bought their product by the freight-car load to treat wounded and ill soldiers during the Civil War. The court found this product endorsement persuasive.

A surgical technique reported in India, South America and other tropical locales utilizes Leaf-cutting ants instead of sutures. While a wound is held closed, worker ants are applied; when the jaws have taken a proper grip, the bodies are twisted off or cut away, leaving a row of ant mandibles that fall away, later, as the wound heals. Even very large gashes are successfully treated in this way.

Physicians of the eighteenth century often carried a cane with a hollow bulb in the handle. When visiting the sick its top might be unscrewed, releasing the fumes of vinegar (contained in the bulb), which were thought to protect against infectious diseases.

That delivery of an infant by abdominal surgical incision is called caesarean section does not mean Julius or any other Caesar was born in this way. The operation was not then performed on living mothers, but it was an ancient Roman law that in any advanced pregnancy the child, alive or dead, must be recovered from the womb. Passing from older republican into imperial, or Caesarean, law it bore merely a legalistic denotation.

Queen Victoria was the first royal personage to be anesthetized, delivering Prince Leopold in 1853 under chloroform.

A cure for stammering, promulgated in the mid-nineteenth century by the Boston Society of Natural History, consisted of nothing more than tapping with the finger once for each syllable. Less professional but widely held opinion was that stammerers might improve by reading aloud two hours a day through clenched teeth—for about three or four months.

She Never Sang Again:
Mid-Life Crisis

Vaslov Nijinsky (1888–1950), the legendary dancer, was forced into retirement as early as 1917 from advancing insanity. While away from the stage he looked for new outlets, inventing, among other things, a windshield wiper and an automatic pencil.

In August 1768 something happened to William Brodie. The son of a wealthy cabinetmaker in Edinburgh, a member of the city council and deacon of the mason's guild, Brodie was a well-respected man—until that fateful summer, when he began to lead two very different lives. By day, he was Deacon Brodie, leading citizen; by night, he was the leader of a gang of vicious thieves. No one knew about Brodie's secret nightlife—not even his two mistresses. He maintained his schizophrenic existence for eighteen years. The end came when he and his gang were caught trying to break into the Scottish customs and excise office. Brodie was hanged. In 1884 Robert Louis Stevenson and William E. Henley wrote a play based on Brodie's career called *Deacon Brodie, or The Double Life*. In 1886 Stevenson used Brodie as the basis for *The Strange Case of Dr. Jekyll and Mr. Hyde*.

Charles Alkan (French composer, 1813–88) did die as a result of pulling down on himself a bookcase laden with Talmudic texts. There is no truth to the assertion that he had, after a life of tasteful dissipation, just then decided to become a rabbi.

According to Christian doctrine, the world will end on Judgment Day, also known as Doomsday. On this day, the dead will be raised up in a general resurrection, and Christ will come in glory to judge the living and the dead; the sinners will be cast into hell, and the righteous will live forever in heaven. When the dead are brought back to life, they won't be the age they were at their death: medieval theologians reckoned that everyone resurrected will be 32, the age of Christ when he died.

In one of the most famous scenes of the antiwar classic *All Quiet on the Western Front* (1930), the German soldier Paul (Lew Ayres) stabs a French soldier and then spends a terrible night listening to the man die. The role of the French soldier—who groans but never says a word—was given to Raymond Griffith. It was Griffith's last film role, and he was ideally suited for the part: he had made a name for himself as an actor in silent films but had had to stop acting with the arrival of sound—he suffered from a voice affliction.

On September 6, 1901, Leon F. Czolgosz shot and fatally wounded President William McKinley. Czolgosz did not originally intend to kill the president. He wanted to kill a priest, but when he had told a friend of his plan, the friend had remarked, "Why kill a priest? There are so many priests." So Czolgosz had chosen a more particular target.

The last song Jimi Hendrix wrote, the song he was working on the night he died, was called "The Story of Life."

The only pirate actually known to have made prisoners walk the plank was Stede Bonnet. Until 1715 Bonnet was a well-to-do and well respected farmer, and his sudden change of character startled his neighbors. They blamed his nagging wife for having driven him mad.

Mark Twain served in the Confederate Army for about one week. He deserted.

Willa Cather decided to become a novelist after an accidental meeting with Stephen Crane when she was 21. Before that, she had planned to become a doctor.

Prince Carlo Gesualdo in 1590 murdered his first wife and her lover. He spent the rest of his life confined to the family estate, composing madrigals rich in odd harmonies not to be heard again in Europe for a century or more.

Cat Stevens stopped singing when he became religious. He even changed his name: Yusef Islam.

Victor Hugo (1802–85), that towering figure of 19th-century French literature, once told a friend, "I missed my calling. I should have been an interior decorator."

William Herschel (1738–1822) thought up the idea of using lead weights to sustain long organ notes in the bass while his fingers were busy elsewhere. And for the instruction of singers he invented a stick that props the mouth open, the better to make round, clear sounds. His sister was the first to study voice in this painful manner. After some success in England she returned to her native Germany. Though she never spoke ill of her brother, she never sang again.

William, naturally, became court astronomer to George III of England.

Fish Breath and Bird Spittle: Offworld

Some pious intellects of the Enlightenment were inclined to search among the stars for Hell. In a curious letter of 1787 to William Herschel, a correspondent refers to the "outer darkness" into which the Bible says the disobedient shall be cast and wonders if there may not be indigo stars "without one ray of cheerful light."

Which we now know, of course, as indigo holes.

Bird migration was not well understood even by the seventeenth century. Some theories held that instead of flying south for the winter months birds hibernated or perhaps buried themselves in the clay of river bottoms (which is not unlike the habits of crabs).

The most fanciful idea, however, was that of Bishop Francis Godwin, who maintained that birds wintered on the moon. Though Godwin's theory was part of an elaborate adventure tale, *The Man in the Moone,* it nonetheless won a few adherents.

Twenty-six astronauts have reported sighting UFOs while in orbit around the earth.

The temperature of interstellar space is 3.18 degrees Kelvin; that is -269.82 Centigrade, or -453.67 degrees Fahrenheit, and 6.33 degrees Rankin.

If molten iron is allowed to cool extremely slowly, as for instance during eons of travel through empty space, it exhibits an uncommon sign of its crystalline form. These are the hexagonal widmanstaetten lines in iron-bearing meteorites. Such a phenomenon is achieved on Earth only on a small scale and only with the most stringent of temperature controls.

Utopia is the ancient Greek word for "nowhere."

The Lunar Roving Vehicles (better-known as Moon Buggies) used by American astronauts on the moon in 1971 and 1972 were electric powered.

The constellations Ursa Major ("great bear") and Ursa Minor ("little bear") have been known to earthlings since ancient times and have had various names. In the United States, part of Ursa Major is called the Big Dipper (or the Drinking Gourd), and part of Ursa Minor is called the Little Dipper. The Big Dipper is known as the

Casserole in France, the Plough in Britain, and the Celestial Bureaucrat in China. In medieval Europe, these same stars were seen as Charles's Wain, or Wagon. The ancient Greeks and native Americans saw them as the tail of a bear. The ancient Egyptians saw in them a bull followed by a horizontal man.

THE NEAREST STARS

Name	Distance (light-years)	Proper motion ("/yr)	Visual magnitude	Abs magnitude	Spectral Type
Proxima Centauri	4.28	3.85	11.05	15.45	M5
α-Centauri A	4.37	3.68	−0.01	4.35	G2
α-Centauri B	4.37	3.68	1.33	5.69	K5
Barnard's Star	5.90	10.31	9.54	13.25	M5
Wolf 359	7.60	4.71	13.53	16.68	M8
Lalande 21185	8.13	4.78	7.50	10.49	M2
Sirius A	8.80	1.33	−1.45	1.41	A1
Sirius B §	8.80	1.33	8.68	11.56	A
Luyten 726—8 A	8.88	3.36	12.45	15.27	M5
UV Ceti	8.88	3.36	12.95	15.80	M6
Ross 154	9.44	0.72	10.60	13.30	M4
Ross 248	10.28	1.59	12.30	14.80	M6
ε-Eridani	10.76	0.98	3.73	6.13	K2
Luyten 789-6	10.76	3.26	12.18	14.60	M7
Ross 128	10.83	1.37	11.10	13.50	M5
61 Cygni A	11.09	5.21	5.22	7.58	K5
61 Cygni B	11.09	5.21	6.03	8.39	K7

§ White dwarf

THE BRIGHTEST STARS

Name	Designation	Visual magnitude	Abs magnitude	Spectral Type	Distance (light-years)
Sun	—	−26.74	4.83	G2	—
Sirius	α-Canis Majoris	−1.45	1.41	A1	8.8
Canopus	α-Carinae	−0.73	−4.70	F0	196
Rigil Kent	α-Centauri	−0.10	4.35	G2	4.37
Arcturus	α-Bootis	−0.06	−0.20	K1	37
Vega	α-Lyrae	0.04	0.50	A0	26
Capella	α-Aurigae	0.08	−0.60	G8	46

Rigel	β-Orionis	0.11	−7.00	B8	815
Procyon	α-Canis Minoris	0.35	2.65	F5	11.4
Achernar	α-Eridani	0.48	−2.20	B5	127
Hadar	β-Centauri	0.60	−5.00	B1	391
Altair	α-Aquilae	0.77	2.30	A7	16
Betelgeuse	α-Orionis	0.80	−6.00	M2	652
Aldebaran	α-Tauri	0.85	−0.70	K5	68
Acrux	α-Crucis	0.90	−3.50	B1	260
Spica	α-Virginis	0.96	−3.40	B1	261
Antares	α-Scorpii	1.00	−4.70	M1	424

The globe on the flag of Brazil shows actual constellations: the Southern Cross, Scorpio, the Southern Triangle, and parts of other constellations can be identified. The stars are shown as they appear over Rio de Janeiro, but in mirror image. Unlike the stars on the flag of the United States, which do not correspond to specific states, the stars on the flag of Brazil correspond to specific political entities. Furthermore, the stars on the flag of Brazil are not all the same size: there are five different sizes.

The first words spoken when US astronauts landed on the moon were "Tranquility Base. The Eagle has landed."

Ironically, the man most responsible for the existence, in theory at least, of black holes was also the first to think of a way of getting rid of them. (They must occasionally vanish in some natural way or clearly they would have swallowed most of the universe by now.)

Stephen Hawking speculated thus: pairs of particles, e.g., an electron and positron, are often spawned from nothing, exist for a brief time, and annihilate each other, restoring their original nothingness. This much of the story has been experimentally observed.

Surely some of these twins can become separated, one perhaps falling into a black hole before its "borrowed" existence is extinguished. Instead, if it is, say, a positron it will annihilate the first electron it encounters within the black hole.

On the scale of cosmological time such events are frequent enough to cause evaporation of black holes. Hawking believes any black holes left over from the birth of the universe smaller than a hundred million tons are now completely evaporated.

The middle star in the handle of the Big Dipper is called Mizar. Next to Mizar is a fainter star named Alcor. These two stars were observed from ancient times. The eyesight of Roman soldiers was tested by having them point out Alcor.

The Great Wall of China is the only manmade structure big enough to be visible from space by astronauts.

"Amazonia, women's land, is a country part in Asia and part in Europe, and is nigh to Albania, and hath that name of Amazonia . . ."

—Bartholomew (ca. 1250), *De Proprietatibus*

FAMOUS COMETS

Name	First seen	Orbital period (years)
Halley's Comet	240BC	76
Encke's Comet	1786	3.3
Biela's Comet	1806	6.7
Great Comet of 1811	1811	3,000
Pons-Winnecke Comet	1819	6.0
Great Comet of 1843	1843	512.4
Donati's Comet	1858	2,040
Schwassmann-Wachmann Comet	1925	16.2
Arend-Roland Comet	1957	10,000
Ikeya-Seki Comet	1965	880
Kouhoutek's Comet*	1975	

* observed from Skylab and Soyuz spacecraft

The stars on the flag of Australia represent the constellation of the Southern Cross.

Alexander Courage wrote the theme song for "Star Trek."

Million Dollar Legs, W. C. Fields' 1932 comedy, and his second sound feature, was set in the mythical nation of Klopstokia, where all the women are named Angela, and all the men George.

One lesser-known puzzle about the moon is a faint red glow occasionally seen on the lunar surface. As a result of seismographic data gathered by Apollo 12 (1969), scientists theorize that during moonquakes gases are released through fissures torn in the lunar crust.

This explanation also accounts for why, through the centuries, the orange-red glow has been observed when the moon is closest to Earth: moonquakes are far likelier at such times, triggered by the waxing tidal forces acting upon the moon's surface as the earth nears.

Gleipnir was made by dwarves of fish breath and bird spittle, the roots of a mountain, beard of a woman, and the sound of cat's footsteps. Gleipnir is the chain that holds Fenris, the Norse wolf who will swallow Odin at the end of the world, and Gleipnir is the reason why so many of these things are scarce.

Looking into Shadows:
Order and Chaos

Melville Louis Kossuth Dewey was born December 10, 1851, in Adams Center, New York. His father was a bootmaker and owner of a small general store; his mother was sternly religious. Young Dewey flashed the first sparks of his fervent, lifetime devotion to saving time and setting things in order when he dropped the "Louis" from his name. Still dissatisfied by the unwieldy moniker, he dropped "Kossuth." Then he trimmed the "le" off Melville. His name remained Melvil Dewey for the rest of his life, although he tried spelling Dewey "Dui" at one point.

Having made his name less wasteful of time, he went after another time thief, tobacco. He made his father stop selling tobacco in his general store. The store promptly failed, but young Dewey gleamed, proud of being, as he spelled it, "morally ryt." The simplification of English ("We hav the most unsyentifik, unskolarli, illojocal and wasteful spelling ani languaj ever ataind," he wrote) and the extinction of tobacco were only two of his crusades. Alcohol, another notorious promoter of idleness, was also among his targets. And he was ardently in favor of the metric system.

When he attended Amherst, he was shocked by the disorder in the college's library. Chaos reigned: the books were organized according to size, title, author, accession date—even color. Dewey had thought of becoming a missionary, but he now saw his lifework. When he graduated, in 1874, he went to work on Amherst's library. He evolved a system of classification, using numbers from 000 to 999 to cover the general fields of knowledge and designating more specific subjects by the use of decimal points. The Dewey decimal system was born. It was easy for librarians to use, and it was easy for library users to understand.

Dewey went on to serve as librarian of Columbia College, where he established the first library training school. As librarian at the New York State Library at Albany, he founded another important library school. He never gave up on his plan to simplify English. According to Dewey, too much precious time was being wasted on unnecessarily long educations.

Together with his wife, he opened the Lake Placid Club, which soon became one of the nation's most famous resorts (although the menu, written by Dewey, was sometimes hard to decipher). Dewey applied his categorizing skills to the membership of his exclusive club. He excluded anyone against whom there was "physical, moral, social or race objection." As Dewey said, he found it "impractical" to admit Jews.

EXPLORERS OF THE NEW WORLD

Year	Explorer	Discovery or exploration
1492	Christopher Columbus	San Salvador, Cuba
1497	John Cabot	Newfoundland or Nova Scotia
1498	John and Sebastian Cabot	Labrador to Hatteras
1499	Alonso de Ojeda	South American coast Venezuela
1500, Feb.	Vicente y Pinzon	South American coast Amazon River
1500, Apr.	Pedro Alvarez Cabral	Brazil (for Portugal)
1500–02	Gaspar Corte-Real	Labrador
1501	Rodrigo de Bastidas	Central America
1513	Vasco Nunez de Balboa	Pacific Ocean
1513	Juan Ponce de Leon	Florida
1515	Juan de Solis	Rio de la Plata
1519	Alonso de Pineda	Mouth of Mississippi River
1519	Hernando Cortes	Mexico
1520	Ferdinand Magellan	Straits of Magellan, Tierra del Fuego
1524	Giovanni da Verrazano	Atlantic coast-New York harbor
1532	Francisco Pizarro	Peru
1534	Jacques Cartier	Canada, Gulf of St. Lawrence
1536	Pedro de Mendoza	Buenos Aires
1536	A.N. Cabeza de Vaca	Texas coast and interior
1539	Francisco de Ulloa	California coast
1539–41	Hernando de Soto	Mississippi River near Memphis
1539	Marcos de Niza	Southwest (now U.S.)
1540	Francisco V. de Coronado	Southwest (now U.S.)
1540	Hernando Alarcon	Colorado River
1540	Garcia de L. Cardenas	Grand Canyon of the Colorado
1541	Francisco de Orellana	Amazon River
1542	Juan Rodriguez Cabrillo	San Diego harbor
1565	Pedro Menendez de Aviles	St. Augustine
1576	Martin Frobisher	Frobisher's Bay, Canada
1577–80	Francis Drake	California coast
1582	Antonio de Espejo	Southwest (named New Mexico)
1584	Amadas & Barlow (for Raleigh)	Virginia
1585–87	Sir Walter Raleigh's men	Roanoke N.C.
1595	Sir Walter Raleigh	Orinoco River
1603–09	Samuel de Champlain	Canadian interior, Lake Champlain
1607	Capt. John Smith	Atlantic coast
1609–10	Henry Hudson	Hudson River, Hudson Bay
1634	Jean Nicolet	Lake Michigan, Wisconsin
1673	Jacques Marquette, Louis Jolliet	Mississippi S to Arkansas
1682	Sieur de La Salle	Mississippi S to Gulf of Mexico
1789	Alexander Mackenzie	Canadian Northwest

The acronym *snafu*, US Army slang for "*situation normal, all fouled (f——ed) up*," has become part of the English language. Snafu is only one of several such acronyms that were used throughout World War II; among the less well remembered are:

Fubar: "*fouled up beyond all recognition*"
Jaafu: "*joint Anglo-American foul-up*"
Jacfu: "*joint American-Chinese foul-up*"
Janfu: "*joint Army-Navy foul-up*"
Susfu: "*situation unchanged, still fouled up*"
Tarfu: "*things are really fouled up*"

In 1923 Garrett A. Morgan, the first black to own a car in Cleveland, Ohio, invented the automatic traffic light. It was not his first invention, for he had already invented the Morgan inhalator, a gas mask that was adapted for military use in World War I.

Cervantes and Shakespeare died on the same day, April 23, 1616.

Alexandre Dumas père wrote his poetry on yellow paper, his novels on blue paper, and his nonfiction on rose-colored paper.

Timothy Dexter, American eccentric and merchant, made his fortune during the American Revolution by buying up depreciated continental currency that later regained its full value. His shrewd mercantile transactions included selling warming pans to the already warm islands of the West Indies (they were used as cook pots). Admiring friends styled him "Lord" Timothy Dexter; he happily accepted the title.

Dexter wrote a book in which he explained why America needed an emperor and why he was the perfect choice for the role. He entitled the book *A Pickle for the Knowing Ones; or Plain Truths in a Homespun Dress*. Published in 1802, the book is remarkable for its individual spelling, randomly located capital letters, and complete absence of punctuation. In the second edition of this masterly work, Dexter added a page full of nothing but periods so that readers might "pepper and salt it as they please."

"What we cannot speak of we must pass over in silence."

—First and last lines of Ludwig Wittgenstein's
(1889–1951) *Tractatus Logico-Philosophicus*

There are sixty-five alphabets in use throughout the world. The alphabet with the most letters is Cambodian, which has seventy-two; Rotokas, spoken on Bougainville, has the least: eleven.

The American presidential election process miscarried badly in the 1876 contest between Samuel Tilden (Democrat) and Rutherford B. Hayes (Republican). Tilden had a clear plurality of the popular vote and an almost certain claim to several contested electoral votes. The final tally was 184–185 after a Republican-dominated special committee distributed all of twenty questioned ballots to Hayes.

More than 1000 languages are spoken in Africa.

"The great Senate shall decree a triumph to one who afterwards shall be driven out vanquished: his followers shall have their property advertised at the sound of the trumpet, and be driven out as enemies."
—Nostradamus, ca. 1655 *(X, 76)*

The *Encyclopedia Britannica* has nothing to do with Britain. The first editions were put together and published by Scotsmen, and from 1928 to 1943 it was owned by Sears, Roebuck. Since then, it has been the property of the University of Chicago.

The letter tiles used in the Scrabble board game are made of Bavarian maple from Germany's Black Forest. The tight grain of the wood makes it difficult to mark—whether purposely or accidentally— the backs of the tiles.

In Italy and Spain the traditional four suits in a playing-card deck are swords, batons, cups, and coins. German suits are hearts, bells, leaves, and acorns. It is the French choice of suits that makes up an American deck: hearts, clubs, spades, and diamonds.

Ytterby, a Swedish village not far from Stockholm, inspired the names of four elements: erbium (no. 68), terbium (no. 65), ytterbium (no. 70), and yttrium (no. 39). All were first identified in samples drawn from a local quarry.

But the names are confusingly similar. Erbium and terbium had swapped identities by 1877; ytterbium and nearby (no. 71) lutetium were bandied about for years as aldebaranium and cassiopeium by German scientists wishing to start the naming over again with a clean slate.

Plotted on official charts are 3500 wrecks in the English Channel.

Flowering in bamboo—which signifies death of the plant—is almost perfectly synchronized in each species. Plants widely separated by distance and climate nonetheless blossom and decline by the same genetic clock, dying within a week or so of each other.

A cycle of 120 years has been established, with a millennium's worth of Japanese records, for the brief blossoming of black bamboo.

A small Indian tribe of the American northwest coast, the Nootka, possess a language without nouns or pronouns. All is assumed to be in a state of motion or change. Expressed approximately in a more conventional language, Nootka thoughts still sound strange: "(it) skies bluely," "(it) forests thickly."

Presumably, modern Nootka find ways of lamenting "(it) televisions awfully" or maybe "(it) sofas greenful dreadly."

Until recently the standard rendering of Chinese into English employed a system (Wade-Giles) adopted by the British Post Office in China. Making the subtle distinctions among Chinese consonants proved difficult, thus *p, t, k, ch,* and *ts* are pronounced, respectively, *b, d, g, j,* and *dz* unless they happen to be followed by an apostrophe, in which case they are sounded in the usual English manner.

And buzz a little bit extra wherever you see a *z*.

In India, 845 languages and dialects are spoken.

The difference between flotsam and jetsam is one of intent: jetsam has been deliberately thrown overboard—it belongs to whomever may find it—flotsam is lost accidentally or through sinking. Rights to flotsam were once reserved to governments but no longer.

If something is thrown overboard and perhaps attached to a buoy so that it can later be retrieved it is neither flotsam nor jetsam but lagan.

All the Chinese dialects and Japanese share the same written language; texts are mutually comprehensible. Between Urdu and Hindi the opposite relation holds: though Pakistanis and Hindi-speaking Indians may converse intelligibly, they cannot read each other's books.

During the Civil War, 373 Lithuanians fought for the Union, and forty-four fought for the Confederacy.

Chaos chaos is the proper name of the voracious giant amoeba. Discovered in 1775, the organism is biologically curious in having a triple-nucleus within its single cell. Though not often encountered, it is large enough to be seen by the naked eye.

The reading of tea leaves requires that an adept first discern pictures—flowers, clouds, animals, objects, etc.—in the leaves. Prognostications are then based on a preferred symbolism for the various parts of the picture. People who just can't see the "picture" may improve with practice.

"Gobbledygook" is what one conservative Representative from Texas (Maury Maverick) had to say about the New Deal. The word, at least, has lived on.

Ancient Indian culture took a rather surprising view of the question of absolute pitches, i.e., are some sounds philosophically more correct than others, and if so which one is A, which B, etc., and how many of them should there be? In the West a few Greeks and medieval scholars worried over the same problem, though centuries later we have settled on an A around 440 cycles, and certainly not for any metaphysical or spiritual reasons.

The Sanskrit scholar Sarngadeva devised this system of pitches: first note tuned to the call of a peacock, second to the sound of the fever bird (heard in the rainy season), third to the bleat of a goat, fourth to the cry of the crane, fifth to the sound of the Indian woodpecker, sixth the call of a frog in love, and seventh an elephant's response when he is beaten on the head.

Western musicians have never been tutored to hear the difference between a loving frog and a flirtatious frog, nor do they strike elephants for the right reason. Perhaps this accounts in part for our divergent musical traditions.

Mathematical game theory provides unquestionable proof that a best possible chess strategy exists. Unfortunately, the number of calculations is so huge, the strategy cannot be discovered. Whether white or black is the inevitable winner, or whether stalemate must result, remains beyond the capability of the largest computers to answer.

The only person in history known to have invented an alphabet for a living language was Sequoyah (also known as George Guess), a half-breed Cherokee who created an alphabet for his people's language. It took him twelve years to devise the eighty-five-character alphabet, and he used it to print parts of the Bible and a newspaper, *The Cherokee Phoenix*. The alphabet was so simple that it could be learned within a few days.

The official languages of Cameroon are French and English, but 283 other languages are spoken.

Among history's more fanciful sciences of divination were:

lithomancy—casting stones
kleromancy—by lots
logarithmancy—yes, by logarithms
sternomancy—by marks on the torso
omphalomancy—navel reading
kapnomancy—visions in smoke
katoptromancy—done with mirrors
chartomancy—paper, especially valentines
sciomancy—looking into shadows
koskinomancy—from the residues on sieves

Ear Chawing, Cheap:
Parts of the Body

Fra Filippo Lippi (1406–69) acquired fame as a painter of the Renaissance but with the curious reputation of painting hands poorly. Complaints, claims Vasari, led Fra Lippi to conceal hands in folds of drapery, behind objects, etc., in later works.

When Sir Walter Raleigh was executed—by decapitation—his body was buried near the altar of a church in Westminster, but his head—in a red velvet bag—was given to his widow. She had it embalmed and put on display. His son, Carew, wanted the head to be buried with him, but somehow it got lost.

Chopin's body is buried in Paris, but his heart, as he had requested, is buried in the wall of the Church of the Holy Cross in Warsaw.

Although it lasted only two years, King Philip's War (1675–76) was the most devastating Indian war in colonial New England. The war ended with the death of King Philip, whose Indian name was Metacom. His body was drawn and quartered, and his head was stuck on a pole and displayed outside the gates of Plymouth. It remained there for twenty-five years.

A halo that encircles an entire (holy) person is a mandorla.

Responding to a new scent the human nose loses 50 percent of the new sensation within a second or two and ceases to register the smell after about a minute. This seems to indicate that the nose in humans has evolved little beyond a kind of alarm device.

What the nose detects is still hard to classify. Unlike the four basic tastes, and three primary colors, candidates for primary smells range in number from about seven to fifty or more.

Percy Bysshe Shelley drowned when his schooner, the *Don Juan,* capsized in the Gulf of Spezia. His body washed ashore ten days later and was cremated on the beach. The poet's heart was not burned—it was given to his widow, who carried it around in a silken shroud wherever she went for the rest of her life.

The first medical book printed in color, albeit by a laborious wood-block method, was Gasparo Aselli's *De Lactibus* (1627), concerning the physiology of the breasts.

The hands have a greater capacity to cool themselves than any other body surface. They lose up to 63.5 Btu/hr to maintain themselves at their preferred temperature of 83.5 degrees Fahrenheit. The head can radiate only about 15.9 Btu/hr, while maintaining a desired surface temperature of 94.4 degrees Fahrenheit.

Jacques Antoine Arlaud (1688–1743), chiefly renowned for his painting of a Leda, suffered a religious turn and decided to destroy his lascivious work. But he took it apart anatomically, selling arms, legs, head, and so forth to eager buyers.

Saint Agatha is the patron saint of bell-founders, but she had little to do with bells during her lifetime. According to legend, Agatha was the daughter of a noble Sicilian family. When she refused the marriage proposals of a well-to-do consul named Quintian, he got furious and denounced her for being Christian. Agatha was cruelly tortured. At one stage, her breasts were sliced off. In memory of her suffering, she is often presented in paintings carrying her breasts on a platter. It is because of the resemblance of the breasts to bells that she became the bell-founders' special saint.

At birth, a human baby has 305 bones; some of these later fuse together until there are about 206 in an adult.

Samuel Johnson's dictionary defined *pastern* as a horse's knee. It is not; the term refers, rather, to the part between fetlock and hoof. A puzzled admirer asked the distinguished scholar for an explanation. Johnson replied, "Ignorance, Madam, pure ignorance."

The four Hs in 4-H Clubs come from the pledge given by members: "My Head to clearer thinking, my Heart to greater loyalty, my Hands to larger services, and my Health to better living."

Although theft was their chief source of revenue, the nineteenth-century New York street gang known as the Whyos also performed certain "services" for paying clients. Members of the gang passed out handbills on the street, advertising the gang's special prices:

Punching: $2
Both eyes blacked: $4
Nose and jaw broke: $10
Jacked out (blackjacked): $15

Ear chawed off: $15
Leg or arm broke: $19
Shot in leg: $25
Stab: $25
Doing the big job (murder): $100 and up

Pluck Your Koras: Pomp

Flags that have been flown over the Capitol Dome in Washington, D.C., are such popular souvenirs that a special department, called the Flag Office, was created in 1955. The number of requests for flags that year was 2766; in 1983 there were 83,984 requests. To meet the demand, a work crew climbs to the base of the Capitol Dome for an hour or two every day and flies flags. Each flag is run up an eighteen-foot flagpole, is held there for a few seconds, and is then hauled down and tucked away (officials monitor the crew on closed-circuit television to make certain the flags really fly). As many as 300 flags fly over the capitol on any given day.

The Greek national anthem has 158 verses. Most Greeks know only the first four. The words are from a poem, "Ode to Liberty," by Dionysios Solomos.

The army of Andorra consists only of officers. All able-bodied men who own firearms are required to serve, which is to say, to carry out ceremonial duties on state occasions.

This army has not fought in seven hundred years.

The first woman to appear on a US postage stamp, in 1893, was Queen Isabella of Spain. The first American woman to appear on a US postage stamp, in 1902, was Martha Washington.

Ronald Reagan was the president of the student body in both high school and college; so was Richard Nixon.

New York State has an official animal (beaver), official state beverage (milk), state bird (blue jay), state fish (trout), state flower (rose), state fruit (apple), state gem (garnet), state tree (sugar maple), and—like a few other states—official state fossil: *Eurypterus remipes.*

On the tomb of a bishop are seven crosses; priests rate five; ordinary Christians one.

At the dawn of the African slave trade, in the early sixteenth century, King Manuel of Portugal and a great African ruler, the Mani-Congo Nzinga Mbemba, exchanged letters as royal equals.

Manuel decided that Nzinga needed an accelerated course in European kingship and furnished instructions for wholesale creation of princes, dukes, marquises, counts, viscounts, and barons—with correct distinctions thoughtfully provided.

Nor did the Portuguese monarch neglect the necessary doings between kings and popes. He suggested that Nzinga choose one son to be sent off to Rome and be made a bishop. This was actually accomplished in 1518, when Pope Leo X bestowed the mitre upon Prince Henry of Congo.

Masquerading as a member of an imperial suite, Virginia Woolf participated in the notorious and successful 1910 hoax in which young English pranksters boarded and inspected the battleship *Dreadnought* in the guise of a visiting Emperor of Abyssinia and his retinue.

President Theodore Roosevelt's inspection trip to the Panama Canal in 1906 was the first time an incumbent president had left the country. Public apprehension was soothed only by the news that the president would never be out of telegraphic touch with Washington. (This trip marked the first, and probably the last, occasion on which a president took charge of operation of a steam shovel, a niney-five-ton behemoth at the canal excavation.)

But Roosevelt never really left American territory: he traveled on the battleship *Louisiana* and toured only the American-leased Canal Zone. The first incumbent to visit a foreign country was Woodrow Wilson, who went to Paris in 1919 to participate in drafting the Versailles Treaty.

"God Save the King," national anthem of Great Britain, was borrowed in the early nineteenth century not only by the United States ("My Country Tis of Thee"), but by Germany and Poland.

Pope John XXIII left behind him, in the way of worldly possessions, a pectoral cross and one fountain pen.

Isabella, daughter of Philip II of Spain, swore not to change her underwear until Ostend (in the rebellious Spanish Netherlands) was recaptured. The siege lasted three years.

Perhaps the spirit of the Spanish army was not properly ignited by this declaration, but the public imagination was. A light yellowish brown may still be called isabella—*isabeau* in French.

At 6 feet 2½ inches Thomas Jefferson was America's tallest president. The shortest were Martin Van Buren and Benjamin Harrison, both 5 feet 6 inches.

The heaviest president was undoubtedly William Taft, whose

weight climbed as high as 332 pounds. He is the only president to have become stuck in the White House bathtub.

The sign in heraldry of illegitimate descent is a narrow baton slanting downward from the viewer's right to left. It does not touch the borders of the design.

Each day during the French bombardment of Vienna in May 1809, the ailing Franz Joseph Haydn was carried to his piano to play the Austrian imperial anthem.

George M. Cohan was not born on July 4; he was born on July 3, 1878. His father changed the record to the fourth out of patriotic fervor.

The French national anthem, the "Marseillaise," was written in 1792 in the city of Stasbourg. The song was composed by a certain Claude Joseph Rouget de Lisle, a captain of engineers. He wrote the song overnight in response to a request from the city's mayor, P. F. Dietrich, for a marching song that might be sung by the revolutionary troops. He called his composition "War Song for the Army of the Rhine." It was taken up by militiamen from Marseilles as they marched on the Tuileries, on August 10, 1792. The men from Marseilles sang the song with such fiery gusto that the Parisians attributed it to them and dubbed it "La Marseillaise." In 1795 the song was decreed France's national anthem; it was then outlawed by Napoleon because of its revolutionary tone. The song reemerged during the July Revolution of 1830 only to be banned again by Napoleon III. In 1879 it was again made the French national anthem. (The man who originally commissioned the song, Monsieur Dietrich, mayor of Strasbourg, did not survive the revolution. He was an aristocrat and, his revolutionary fervor notwithstanding, he was guillotined. Rouget de Lisle, also considered a royalist, very nearly met the same fate.)

The melody to the "Marseillaise" remains something of a mystery. Scholars concede the lyrics to Rouget de Lisle but are generally of the opinion that the tune is too fine to have been made up so quickly. Little-known composers proposed, and rejected, for the honor include Méhul, Grétry, and Dalayrac.

It was said of England's Queen Elizabeth I that she did "bathe herself once a month whether she required it or not."

During his term as president, Richard Nixon designed special uniforms for the White House guards. Derisively described as "Hessian-style," the uniforms, which were worn only at state dinners, consisted of white tunics, black gunbelts, visored caps, and lots of gold braid. When Nixon left the White House, the uniforms were put in storage and were eventually sold as surplus government property to a high school in Iowa, where they are worn by the school's marching band.

Under rules in force since 1634 proof of four miracles is necessary for canonization (sainthood); two is enough for beatification.

Dr. Clarence E. ("Ed") Hemingway announced the birth of his son Ernest (the future novelist) by stepping out on the porch of his home and giving a cornet salute.

"There is no settling the point of precedency between a louse and a flea."

— Samuel Johnson (1709–84)

The custom of flying the American flag over schoolhouses began during the Civil War.

Among those present in the Cathedral of Notre Dame when Napoleon crowned himself emperor was Simon Bolivar, soon to become famous as "the Liberator" of South America.

While president, Franklin Roosevelt had a special railroad car, named the *Ferdinand Magellan,* and a personal plane, called the *Sacred Cow.*

The job of members of the Académie Francaise, the "Forty Immortals," is to wear magnificent green uniforms, bask in honor, and to work on the *Dictionaire,* court of last appeal in the French language.
But it is not expected that work of such cultural eminence will proceed speedily, or even smoothly. Accounts of the Académie in the 1950s relate that in pondering the word "white"—defined in previous editions as "that which is the color of snow, of milk"—physicist Louis De Broglie informs all that white is not really a color; the poet Paul Claudel wishes to observe that in Paris milk is blue; but biographer André Maurois has seen on farms that milk is yellow. *Eh bien,* on to the next word.

Abigail Adams dried her family's laundry in the East Room of the White House.

Louis XIV bathed only once a year.

George Washington's family motto was *Exitus acta probat* ("the end justifies the means").

The oldest uniforms in the world are those worn by the Vatican's Swiss Guards: they were designed by Michelangelo.

The tune to "The Star-Spangled Banner " is derived from an Irish drinking song, "Anachreon in Heaven."

President Grover Cleveland personally answered the White House telephone during working hours.

At the court of a Chou–dynasty (1122–256 BC) Chinese emperor were found such luminaries as the Officers of Dried Food, Director of the Silk, Physician of Ulcers, Officer of the Feathers, Chief Turtle Catcher, and the Superintendent of Violence.

The noble figure of Britannica that appeared on English copper coins was modeled by the noble Frances, Duchess of Richmond (d. 1702).

In order of precedence the English aristocracy are ranked: duke, marquess, earl (an earl's wife is a countess), viscount, baron, and knight. "Peers," entitled to sit in the House of Lords, are only those who bear the title of viscount or better.

Among those national anthems most seldom heard are:
"In the Thunder Dragon Kingdom" (Bhutan)
"Chadians, Up and To Work!" (Chad)
"Let's Walk Through the Arbor Of Our Immense Happiness" (Equatorial Guinea)
"Pluck Your Koras, Strike the Balafons" (Senegal)
The Maldive Republic makes do with a piece titled "National Anthem," and several Islamic nations—Kuwait, Saudi Arabia, and the United Arab Emirates—use tunes without titles or lyrics.

Side by Side:
Relatives

John Stuart Mill knew Greek by the age of 4. At 8, he was teaching his brothers Latin.

The first statesman to be popularly known as "the father of his country" was Cicero.

Among the Old West's most notorious outlaws were the Younger brothers—Cole, John, James, and Robert. They grew up in pre-Civil War Missouri; Cole later served with the vicious raider Quantrill. After the war, the Youngers got together with the James brothers, Frank and Jesse, and went into business robbing banks and trains. Their career together ended following their raid on Northfield, Minnesota, during which the outraged townspeople shot the gang to pieces. The surviving Youngers were caught and imprisoned. The last of the Younger brothers, Cole and James, were given pardons in 1901 and released from prison.

James committed suicide; Cole worked for a while selling tombstones, wrote his autobiography, and ultimately returned to Missouri, where he got back together with Frank James. The two onetime outlaws assembled a Wild West show and went on tour with it. Frank eventually quit, got a job as the doorman of a theater, and sold souvenirs at his farm. Cole continued to work in carnivals. He died in 1916.

Wolfgang Amadeus Mozart never went to school. His father taught him music and mathematics.

When Marco Polo, along with his father and uncle, finally returned to Venice after being away for nearly a quarter of a century, they were not recognized by their family and friends, and their servants refused to let them enter their own home. To prove to their fellow Venetians that they were who they claimed, the Polos gave a large banquet. At the right moment, the three Polos suddenly threw off their shabby Tartar robes and tore open the seams and linings—a flood of emeralds, rubies, and pearls poured out and swept across the floor. Their dinner guests began to believe their story.

Using their combined assets of $68, Henry and Clement Studebaker founded the Studebaker Brothers Manufacturing Company in

1852. The two brothers specialized in chuck wagons. In 1868, joined by more Studebaker brothers—John, Peter, and Jacob—the brothers' company became the world's largest producer of wagons and carriages. Having made more than 750,000 horse-drawn conveyances, the Studebaker Brothers made their first horseless carriage—an electric car—in 1902.

Van Gogh sold only one of his paintings during his lifetime; his brother, Theo, acting as Vincent's agent, likewise sold one.

Coffee was first decaffeinated in 1900 by Ludwig Roselius. His father had been a coffee taster, and Ludwig believed his father's death to have been caused by caffeine.

Fidel Castro's sister Juanita lives in Miami, Florida. An anti-Communist, she left Cuba in 1964 and went into business running a drugstore in the Miami area.

National Football League football is truly a family affair, and sibling rivalry may explain some of the more aggressive tackles. The following twenty sets of brothers played—some together but most on opposing teams—during the NFL's 1984 season:

Chris Bahr (Los Angeles Raiders)
Matt Bahr (Cleveland Browns)

Brian Baldinger (Dallas Cowboys)
Rich Baldinger (Kansas City Chiefs)

Mark E. Bell (Indianapolis Colts)
Mike J. Bell (Kansas City Chiefs)

Lyle Blackwood (Miami Dolphins)
Glenn Blackwood (Miami Dolphins)

Jeff Bostic (Washington Redskins)
Joe Bostic (St. Louis Cardinals)

Pete Brock (New England Patriots)
Stan Brock (New Orleans Saints)

Joey Browner (Minnesota Vikings)
Keith Browner (Tampa Bay Buccaneers)
Ross Browner (Cincinnati Bengals)

Don Dufek (Seattle Seahawks)
Joe Dufek (Buffalo Bills)

Tony Eason (New England Patriots)
Bo Eason (Houston Oilers)

Jim Fahnhorst (San Francisco 49ers)
Keith Fahnhorst (San Francisco 49ers)

Charley Hannah (Los Angeles Raiders)
John Hannah (New England Patriots)

Victor Heflin (St. Louis Cardinals)
Vince Heflin (Miami Dolphins)

Jay Hilgenberg (Chicago Bears)
Joel Hilgenberg (New Orleans Saints)

Doug Martin (Minnesota Vikings)
George Martin (New York Giants)

Bruce Matthews (Houston Oilers)
Clay Matthews (Cleveland Browns)

Cle Montgomery (Los Angeles Raiders)
Wilbert Montgomery (Philadelphia Eagles)

Scott Pelluer (New Orleans Saints)
Steve Pelluer (Dallas Cowboys)

John Tice (New Orleans Saints)
Mike Tice (Seattle Seahawks)

Jimmy Williams (Detroit Lions)
Toby Williams (New England Patriots)

George Wonsley (Indianapolis Colts)
Otis Wonsley (Washington Redskins)

The Marx brothers' given names are Julian (Groucho), Arthur (Harpo), Leonard (Chico), Milton (Gummo), and Herbert (Zeppo).

Herb Alpert named his son after the first two notes of the musical scale: Dore.

When Stephen Marciszewski emigrated to the United States from Poland in 1903, he changed his name to Muskie; Edmund Muskie is his son.

Marilyn Monroe never knew who her father was.

David Niven's father was killed in the battle of Gallipoli.

Lincoln Logs were invented in 1916 by John L. Wright, son of architect Frank Lloyd Wright.

The sole authority for the venerable tale of Newton and the gravitating apple is his niece, a Mrs. Conduitt, who related the event to Voltaire, among others.

To "bring home the bacon" became a popular expression in 1910, after it was quoted from Jack Johnson's mother describing her son's world heavyweight title victory over James J. Jeffries.

Adolf Hitler's father died when he was 13; his mother died when he was 17.

Stephen Crane's wife ran a brothel in Florida.

Walter F. Mondale is the grandson of Frederik Mundal, a Norwegian farmer who arrived in the United States in 1856.

When Douglas MacArthur left home for West Point, his mother went with him. She rented an apartment overlooking his dormitory room so that she could make certain he did his studying. He did: he graduated first in his class.

"Hail and farewell." The words, *ave atque vale* in Latin, are from the elegy of Catullus (87–ca. 54 BC) on the death of his brother in the Troad, rocky wastes of Turkey's northwest coast.

Cotton Mather entered Harvard at 12, the youngest student ever admitted. He went on to write more than 450 works, including histories, biographies, essays, sermons, fables, verses, theological treatises, and books of philosophy, science, medicine, and piety. His father, Increase Mather, wrote only 130 books.

The mother of Mary Shelley, neé Godwin, published as Wollstonecraft *(Frankenstein)*, was Mary Godwin, neé Wollstonecraft, also an author. Her third book, *A vindication of the rights of WOMAN, with strictures on political and moral subjects,* appeared in 1792.

Frances Trollope (1780–1863), mother of two prolific English novelists, Anthony and Thomas, sojourned with her husband for three years in Cincinnati. Their eccentric fancy goods store was a failure, and they returned to England. There, Frances wrote *Domestic Manners of the Americans;* though Mark Twain thought it accurate, the American nation was enraged by this highly unflattering portrait.

F. Scott Fitzgerald was named after one of his distant relatives, Francis Scott Key, author of "The Star-Spangled Banner."

Louisa Adams, wife of John Quincy Adams, was the only First Lady to be born abroad.

Although distant cousins, Theodore Roosevelt and Franklin D. Roosevelt did not pronounce their common family name the same way. Theodore pronounced his last name to rhyme with "goose": "Ruse-a-velt." Franklin pronounced the name to rhyme with "rose": "Rose-a-velt."

Lenin's brother Alexander was executed at the age of 21 for his participation in a plot to kill Czar Alexander III.

Jimmy Carter's brother Billy is allergic to peanuts.

Saint Austin holds a rather singular distinction in being the offspring of a canonized mother, Saint Monica.

El Exigente, the formidable coffee expert in Savarin Coffee commercials, is played by Carlos Montalban, brother of Ricardo Montalban.

There is a town on the Mohawk River in New York State named Fonda. It was founded during the 1700s by Douw Fonda, an ancestor of actor Henry Fonda.

There were three Andrews Sisters: Patricia, LaVerne, and Maxine. LaVerne was the oldest.

It was Dick Clark's wife who gave Chubby Checker his name—she devised it as a take-off on Fats Domino.

One of the characters on the soap opera "General Hospital" is played by Georganna La Pere, Cher's sister.

Frank Lloyd Wright's mother decided he should be an architect even before he was born. While she was still pregnant with him, she hung engravings of famous cathedrals on the walls of what was shortly to be his room.

No one knows what Martha Jefferson, wife of Thomas Jefferson, and Margaret Taylor, wife of Zachary Taylor, looked like, for no portraits of them exist.

Calvin Coolidge is the only president thus far who was sworn into office by his own father.

Lucy Hayes, wife of Rutherford B. Hayes, was the first First Lady to have a college diploma.

The War of Jenkins's Ear (1739–41) is named for one of the ears of Robert Jenkins. Jenkins, his ear carefully wrapped in a handkerchief, appeared before the English House of Commons in 1738 with a sad tale. He explained that in 1731, while sailing his ship, *Rebecca,* near Havana, he had been stopped and boarded by Spanish authorities. The Spaniards accused him of smuggling and searched his ship. When he complained, one of them, a captain named Frandino, sliced off Jenkins's ear and told him to return with it to his masters. As evidence, Jenkins unwrapped his dried and wrinkled ear and displayed it to the assembly.

Already eager for war with Spain, the English leaped on this unique piece of propaganda: Jenkins's severed body part thus provided both the impetus and name for the conflict.

One of those most eager to grapple with the Spanish was Admiral Edward Vernon. As soon as war was declared, Vernon sailed to the West Indies and, in 1739, won a great victory, capturing the city of Portobelo.

Vernon, an old sea dog, had the habit of pacing the deck in a tattered old grogram coat during stormy weather. Because of the coat, his men called him Old Grog. In 1740 Vernon ordered that the British navy's daily rum ration be diluted (as established in 1731, the daily rum ration for a British seaman was half a pint in two equal tots). It was Vernon's remarkable belief that the watered liquor would somehow prevent scurvy. It didn't, and it didn't please his sailors, who referred derisively to the weak liquid as Old Grog's drink (giving us, eventually, the words *grog, groggy, grogshop*, etc.).

Perhaps because of his sailors' lingering wrath (or because their increased sobriety made them more cautious), Old Grog's next ventures, sieges of Cartagena and Santiago de Cuba, were absolutely unsuccessful. These failures led to Vernon's recall.

Before taking leave of the Americas, Vernon took the time to distribute awards to those who had performed well during the campaign. One of those to receive a decoration was a captain from the Virginia colony named Lawrence Washington. The proud and thankful Washington returned home to his plantation on the Potomac River. Until then he had called the place Green Mountain; he now renamed it, in honor of his admiral, Mount Vernon. Shortly thereafter it was inherited by Lawrence's younger half-brother, George.

More than 9400 Americans are buried in the cemeteries at Normandy, France, site of the D-Day invasion of Europe. Among the Americans are thirty-three pairs of brothers and, buried side by side, one father and son.

Emperor Norton I:
Royalty

"It's hard for a king to find a job."

—King Michael of Rumania (1921–   ).

The last of the small number of history's female court jesters was Kathrin Lise (d. ca. 1722), fool to the Duchess von Sachsen-Weissenfels.

CHINESE DYNASTIES

Dynasty

Hsia, c. 1994–c.1523 B.C.
Shang or Yin, c.1523–c.1027 B.C.
Chou, c.1027–256 B.C.
Ch'in, 221–207 B.C.
Han, 202 B.C.—A.D. 220
Three Kingdoms, A.D. 220–265
Tsin or Chin, 265–420
Sui, 581–618
T'ang, 618–906
Five Dynasties and Ten Kingdoms, 907–960
Sung, 960–1279
Yüan, 1260–1368
Ming, 1368–1644
Ch'ing or Manchu, 1644–1912

King Christian X (1870–1947) of Denmark rode horseback unescorted every morning for thirty years through the streets of Copenhagen. (The name of his favorite horse was Rolf.)

On April 9, 1940, he shut himself into his palace, refusing to come forth until the Nazi occupation of his kingdom was brought to an end.

Lob-sang Gya-tso (d. 1680), fifth Dalai Lama of Tibet, rebuilder of the Potala, strong administrator, and first ruler of the whole of Tibet, is remembered simply as the Great Fifth.

RUSSIAN RULERS FROM 1462 TO 1917

House of Rurik

Ivan III, (the Great), 1462–1505
Vasily III, 1505–33
Ivan IV (the Terrible), 1533–84
Feodor I, 1584–98

House of Godunov

Boris Godunov, 1598–1605
Feodor II, 1605

Usurpers

Dmitri, 1605–6
Vasily IV, 1606–10

Interregnum, 1610–13

House of Romanov

Michael, 1613–45
Alexis, 1645–76
Feodor III, 1676–82
Ivan V and Peter I (the Great), 1682–96
Peter I (the Great), 1696–1725
Catherine I, 1725–27
Peter II, 1727–30
Anna, 1730–40
Ivan VI, 1740–41
Elizabeth, 1741–62
Peter III, 1762
Catherine II (the Great), 1762–96
Paul.I, 1796–1801
Alexander I, 1801–25
Nicholas I, 1825–55.
Alexander II, 1855–81
Alexander III, 1881–94
Nicholas II, 1894–1917

Napoleon designed the flag of Italy. He made it the banner of his Italian National Guard when he invaded Lombardy in 1796. The flag was later adopted by Victor Emmanuel, who added his coat of arms to the center.

RULERS OF THE ROMAN EMPIRE

Augustus, 27 B.C.–A.D. 14
Tiberius, A.D. 14–A.D. 37
Caligula, 37–41
Claudius, 41–54
Nero, 54–68
Galba, 68–69
Otho, 69
Vespasian, 69–79
Vitellius, 69
Titus, 79–81
Domitian, 81–96
Nerva, 96–98
Trajan, 98–117
Hadrian, 117–38
Antoninus Pius, 138–61
Marcus Aurelius, 161–80
Lucius Verus, ruled jointly with Marcus Aurelius, 161–69
Commodus, 180–92
Pertinax, 193
Didius Julianus, 193
Severus, 193–211
Caracalla, 211–17
Geta, son of Severus, 211–12
Macrinus, 217–18
Heliogabalus, 218–22
Alexander Severus, 222–35
Maximin, 235–38
Gordian I, 238
Gordian II, 238
Balbinus, 238
Pupienus Maximus, 238
Gordian III, 238–44
Philip (the Arabian), 244–49
Decius, proclaimed 249–51
Hostilianus, 251
Gallus, 251–53
Aemilianus, 253
Valerian, 253–60
Gallienus, son of Valerian, 253–68
Claudius II, 268–70
Aurelian, 270–75
Tacitus, 275–76
Florianus, 276
Probus, 276–82

Carus, 282–83
Carinus, 283–85
Numerianus, 283–84
Diocletian, 284–305
Maximian, 286–305
Constantius I, 305–6
Galerius, 305–10
Maximin, 308–13
Licinius, 307–24
Maxentius, 306–12
Constantine I (the Great), 306–37
Constantine II, 337–40
Constans, 337–50
Constantius II, 337–61
Magnentius, 350–53
Julian (the Apostate), 361–63
Jovian, 363–64
Valentinian I, ruled in the West, 364–75
Valens, ruled in the East, 364–78
Gratian, coruler in the West with Valentinian II, 375–83
Maximus, 383–88
Valentinian II, ruler of the West, 375–92
Eugenius, 392–94
Theodosius I (the Great), 375–95

Emperors in the East

Arcadius, 395–408
Theodosius II, 408–50
Marcian, 450–57
Leo I, 457–74
Leo II, 474

Emperors in the West

Honorius, 395–423
Maximus, 409–11
Constantius III, 421
Valentinian III, 425–55
Petronius Maximus, 455
Avitus, 455–56
Majorian, 457–61
Libius Severus, 461–65
Anthemius, 467–72
Olybrius, 472
Glycerius, 473–74
Julius Nepos, 474–75
Romulus Augustulus, 475–76

HOLY ROMAN EMPERORS

Saxon Dynasty

Otto I, 936–73
Otto II, 973–83
Otto III, 983–1002
Henry II, 1002–24

Salian or Franconian Dynasty

Conrad II, 1024–39
Henry III, 1039–56
Henry IV, 1056–1105
Henry V, 1105–25
Lothair II, duke of Saxony, 1125–37

Hohenstaufen Dynasty and Rivals

Conrad III, 1138–52
Frederick I, 1152–90
Henry VI, 1190–97
Philip of Swabia, 1198–1208
antiking: Otto IV (Guelph), 1198–1208
Otto IV (king, 1208–12; emperor, 1209–15), 1208–15
Frederick II (king, 1212–20; emperor, 1220–50), 1212–50
Conrad IV, 1237–54
antiking: Henry Raspe, 1246–47
antiking: William, count of Holland, 1247–56

Interregnum, 1254–73

Richard, earl of Cornwall, and Alfonso X of Castile, rivals

Hapsburg, Luxembourg, and Other Dynasties

Rudolf I (Hapsburg), 1273–91
Adolf of Nassau, 1292–98
Albert I (Hapsburg) 1298–1308
Henry VII (Luxembourg), 1308–13
Louis IV (Wittelsbach), 1314–46
Charles IV (Luxembourg), 1346–78
Wenceslaus (Luxembourg), 1378–1400
Rupert (Wittelsbach), 1400–1410
Sigismund (Luxembourg), 1410–37

Hapsburg Dynasty

Albert II, 1438–39
Frederick III, 1440–93

Maximilian I, 1493–1519
Charles V, 1519–58
Ferdinand I, 1558–64
Maximilian II, 1564–76
Rudolf II, 1576–1612
Matthias, 1612–19
Ferdinand II, 1619–37
Ferdinand III, 1637–57
Leopold I, 1658–1705
Joseph I, 1705–11
Charles VI, 1711–40

Interregnum, 1740–42

Wittelsbach-Hapsburg and Lorraine Dynasties

Charles VII (Wittelsbach-Hapsburg), 1742–45
Francis I (Lorraine), 1745–65

Hapsburg-Lorraine Dynasty

Joseph II, 1765–90
Leopold II, 1790–92
Francis II, 1792–1806

RULERS OF ENGLAND AND GREAT BRITAIN

Saxons and Danes

Egbert, 802–39
Æthelwulf, 839–58
Æthelbald, 858–60
Æthelbert, 2d, 860–65
Æthelred, 3d, 865–71
Alfred, 4th, 871–99
Edward (the Elder), 899–924
Athelstan, 924–39
Edmund, 3d, 939–46
Edred, 4th, 946–55
Edwy, 955–59
Edgar, 959–75
Edward (the Martyr), 975–78
Æthelred (the Unready), 978–1016
Edmund (Ironside), 1016
Canute, by conquest, 1016–35
Harold I (Harefoot), 1037–40
Harthacanute, 1040–42
Edward (the Confessor), 1042–66
Harold II, 1066

House of Normandy

William I (the Conqueror), by conquest, 1066–87
William II (Rufus), 3d, 1087–1100
Henry I, youngest, 1100–1135

House of Blois

Stephen, 1135–54

House of Plantagenet

Henry II, 1154–89
Richard I (Coeur de Lion), 1189–99
John, youngest, 1199–1216
Henry III, 1216–72
Edward I, 1272–1307
Edward II, 1307–27
Edward III, 1327–77
Richard II, 1377–99

House of Lancaster

Henry IV, 1399–1413
Henry V, 1413–22
Henry VI, 1422–61, 1470–71

House of York

Edward IV, 1461–70, 1471–83
Edward V, 1483
Richard III, 1483–85

House of Tudor

Henry VII, 1485–1509
Henry VIII, 1509–47
Edward VI, 1547–53
Mary I, 1553–58
Elizabeth I, 1558–1603

House of Stuart

James I (James VI of Scotland), 1603–25
Charles I, 1625–49

Commonwealth and Protectorate

Council of State, 1649–53
Oliver Cromwell, lord protector, 1653–58
Richard Cromwell, 1658–59

House of Stuart *(restored)*

Charles II, 1660–85

James II, 1685–88
William III, 1689–1702
Mary II, 1689–94
Anne, 1702–14

House of Hanover

George I, 1714–27
George II, 1727–60
George III, 1760–1820
George IV, 1820–30
William IV, 1830–37
Victoria, 1837–1901

House of Saxe-Coburg

Edward VII, 1901–10

House of Windsor

George V, 1910–36
Edward VIII, 1936
George VI, 2d, 1936–52
Elizabeth II, 1952–

RULERS OF FRANCE SINCE 987

The Capetians

Hugh Capet, 987–96
Robert II (the Pious), 996–1031
Henry I, 1031–60
Philip I, 1060–1108
Louis VI (the Fat), 1108–37
Louis VII (the Young), 1137–80
Philip II (Augustus), 1180–1223
Louis VIII, 1223–26
Louis IX (Saint Louis), 1226–70
Philip III (the Bold), 1270–85
Philip IV (the Fair), 1285–1314
Louis X (the Quarrelsome), 1314–16
John I (the Posthumous), 1316
Philip V (the Tall), 1317–22
Charles IV (the Fair), 1322–28

House of Valois

Philip VI, 1328–50
John II (the Good), 1350–64
Charles V (the Wise), 1364–80

Charles VI (the Mad or the Well Beloved), 1380–1422
Charles VII (the Victorious or the Well Served), 1422–61
Louis XI, 1461–83
Charles VIII, 1483–98
Louis XII, 1498–1515
Francis I, 1515–47
Henry II, 1547–59
Francis II, 1559–60
Charles IX, 1560–74
Henry III, 1574–89

House of Bourbon

Henry IV (of Navarre), 1589–1610
Louis XIII, 1610–43
Louis XIV, 1643–1715
Louis XV, 1715–74
Louis XVI, 1774–92

The First Republic

The National Convention, 1792–95
The Directory, 1795–99
The Consulate (Napoleon Bonaparte, First Counsul,
    1802–4), 1799–1804

The First Empire

Napoleon I (Napoleon Bonaparte), 1804–15

Bourbon Restoration

Louis XVIII, 1814–24
Charles X, 1824–30

House of Bourbon-Orléans

Louis Philippe, descendant of Louis XIII, 1830–48

The Second Republic

Louis Napoleon Bonaparte, nephew of Napoleon I,
    president, 1848–52

The Second Empire

Napoleon III (Louis Napoleon Bonaparte), 1852–70

The Third Republic *(presidents)*
Louis Jules Trochu (provisional), 1870–71
Adolphe Thiers, 1871–73
Marie Edmé Patrice de MacMahon, 1873–79
Jules Grévy, 1879–87
Sadi Carnot, 1887–94
Jean Paul Pierre Casimir-Périer, 1894–95
Félix Faure, 1895–99
Émile François Loubet, 1899–1906
Armand Fallières, 1906–13
Raymond Poincaré, 1913–20
Paul Eugène Louis Deschanel, 1920
Alexandre Millerand, 1920–24
Gaston Doumergue, 1924–31
Paul Doumer, 1931–32
Albert Lebrun, 1932–40

The Vichy Government
Henri Philippe Pétain, chief of state, 1940–44

The Provisional Government
Charles De Gaulle, president, 1944–46

The Fourth Republic *(presidents)*
Georges Bidault (provisional), 1946
Vincent Auriol, 1947–54
René Coty, 1954–58

The Fifth Republic *(presidents)*
Charles De Gaulle, 1958–69
Georges Pompidou, 1969–74
Valéry Giscard d'Estaing, 1974–1981
François Mitterrand, 1981–

Wives and Children of the Presidents
Listed in order of presidential administrations

Name	Sons	Daughters
Martha Dandridge Custis Washington	. . .	. . .
Abigail Smith Adams	3	2
Martha Wayles Skelton Jefferson	1	5

Dorothea "Dolley" Payne Todd Madison	. . .	. . .
Elizabeth Kortright Monroe	. . .	2
Louise Catherine Johnson Adams	3	1
Rachel Donelson Robards Jackson	. . .	. . .
Hannah Hoes Van Buren	4	. . .
Anna Symmes Harrison	6	4
Letitia Christian Tyler	3	4
Julia Gardnier Tyler	5	2
Sarah Childress Polk	. . .	. . .
Margaret Smith Taylor	1	5
Abigail Powers Fillmore	1	1
Caroline Carmichael McIntosh Fillmore	. . .	. . .
Jane Means Appleton Pierce	3	. . .
Mary Todd Lincoln	4	. . .
Eliza McCardle Johnson	3	2
Julia Dent Grant	3	1
Lucy Ware Webb Hayes	7	1
Lucretia Rudolph Garfield	4	1
Ellen Lewis Herndon Arthur	2	1
Frances Folsom Cleveland	2	3
Caroline Lavinia Scott Harrison	1	1
Mary Scott Lord Dimmick Harrison	. . .	1
Ida Saxton McKinley	. . .	2
Alice Hathaway Lee Roosevelt	. . .	1
Edith Kermit Carow Roosevelt	4	1
Helen Herron Taft	2	1
Ellen Louise Axson Wilson	. . .	3
Edith Bolling Galt Wilson	. . .	. . .
Florence King De Wolfe Harding	. . .	. . .
Grace Anna Goodhue Coolidge	2	. . .
Lou Henry Hoover	2	. . .
Anna Eleanor Roosevelt Roosevelt	4	1
Bess Wallace Truman	. . .	1
Mamie Geneva Doud Eisenhower	1	. . .
Jacqueline Lee Bouvier Kennedy	1	1
Claudia "Lady Bird" Alta Taylor Johnson	. . .	2
Thelma Catherine Patricia Ryan Nixon	. . .	1
Elizabeth Bloomer Warren Ford	3	1
Rosalynn Smith Carter	3	1
Anne Frances "Nancy" Robbins Denis Reagan	1	1

On January 16 and 17, 1893, Hawaiian queen Liliukoalani was overthrown in a bloodless revolution led by American annexationists.

The American planters were aided by US Marines, landed without US government approval at the request of the American envoy to Hawaii. The queen abdicated, and on July 4 of the next year the Republic of Hawaii was declared. Its first president was Judge Sanford Ballard Dole. (The Hawaiian Pineapple Company was founded in 1902 by Drummond Dole, son of a first cousin to Sanford Dole.)

The so-called penny black was the world's first postage stamp. It **was** issued in 1840 by Great Britain and had the picture of a woman on it: Queen Victoria.

In November of 1724, Peter the Great, founder of the Russian empire, went on a cruise in the Gulf of Finland. When he caught sight of a foundering ship, the great leader, without hesitation, leaped overboard and swam through the icy water to help rescue the shipwrecked sailors. He caught a bad cold. He was still suffering from the cold at the end of the year, and following a New Year's party at which he drank too much, he got sick and died.

Alexander the Great (356–323 BC) learned his lessons from a good tutor: Aristotle (384–322 BC).

In the days when Louis XIV spent most of his time there, Versailles had no indoor kitchens—or bathrooms.

The Hapsburg generation that ruled Austro-Hungary in its last half century was an unlucky one:

Archduke Charles Louis—died of dysentery in 1871 after drinking untreated water from the River Jordan (he was visiting the Holy Land).

Archduke Ferdinand Maximilian—executed by firing squad in 1867 in Mexico City after being unsuccessfully installed by the French as Emperor of Mexico. His empress, Carlotta, went mad but survived until 1927.

Archduke Rudolph—suicide in 1889 at Mayerling: his love affair with Maria Vetsera, who also died at Mayerling, had been forbidden by Emperor Franz Joseph.

Empress Elizabeth—assassinated in 1898 by an Italian anarchist at Geneva.

Archduke Franz Ferdinand—assassinated in 1914 at Sarajevo by a Slav nationalist.

Few monarchs are remembered so rosily as, say, John the Perfect of Portugal (1455–95) or William the Delightful of Austria (d. 1406), or even Philip the Amorous of France (1052–1108). Some of history's lesser known losers were:

Overweight kings—Alfonso the Fat (Alfonso II of Portugal), Charles the Fat (Charles III of France, son of Charles the Bald), and Louis the Fat and Wide Awake (Louis VI of France).

Speech-impaired kings—Louis the Stammerer (Louis II of France), and Michael the Stammerer (Michael II of Byzantium).

Unappreciated despots—Charles the Bad (Charles II of Navarre), Christian the Angry (Christian II of Denmark and Norway; he was angry with the Swedish nobility, whom he massacred), and Isabella the She-Wolf (Isabella of France, bad-news consort to Edward II of England, whom she had murdered).

Dissolute monarchs—Louis the Lazy (Louis V of France), Frederick the Indolent (Frederick III of Germany), Louis the Foolish (Louis VII of France), Robert the Bleary (Robert II of Scotland), and Ethelred the Unready (Ethelred II of England; what he was unready for was, of course, the Danes, but his sobriquet really refers to his lack of good counsel).

And what excuse can there be for Isabella the Great Sow (wife of Charles the Mad—Charles VI of France), a.k.a. Isabella of Bavaria, who signed away France to a king of England.

Mad King Ludwig II of Bavaria (1845–86), he of the cast-zinc peacock-feather throne, midnight sleigh rides, and fairyland castles, gave five royal orders to his guards concerning the commission appointed to look into his mental state: skin them, scalp them, blind them, chain them, fling them into a dungeon.

Finally in custody, he walked by Lake Starnberg one day in 1886 attended by Dr. Guden. Poor Guden was found strangled lying in the shallows; drowned and farther out was Ludwig.

Babe Ruth was, of course, the Sultan of Swat, but the real ruler was the Wali of Swat (a former state in Pakistan).

Although he was thoroughly detested by just about everyone, Ferdinand Maximilian, the Austrian archduke who became emperor of Mexico in 1864, showed courage when he was finally put before a firing squad. He looked at the six men who were about to kill him and then turned to the officer in charge and said, "Poor fellows. They have an unpleasant task." He drew six $20 gold pieces from his pocket and gave them to the officer. "Please give one to each man after I am shot," he requested.

But the soldiers' aim was not good. Maximilian expired in pain; his last utterance: "Hombre."

Joshua Abraham Norton was born in London in 1819. His family soon moved to South Africa. When his father died in 1848, Joshua Norton sold all his belongings and, with $40,000 in his pocket, booked passage for San Francisco on the steamer *Franzika*. The gold-rush-crazed city Norton arrived in was full of opportunities, and he invested his money well. By 1853, working as an agent, broker, and land speculator, he had accumulated $250,000.

Deciding to use all his money in one final effort to become rich, he bought up all the rice in the city and all the rice on ships coming to the city. The price of rice promptly shot up, but Norton, waiting for the right moment, refused to sell. His greed led to his downfall. An unexpected shipment of rice arrived from South America, and the price of rice plummeted. Norton (and those of his friends who had joined him in the scheme) was ruined. He emerged from the long lawsuits a bankrupt and mentally broken man. He disappeared.

He reappeared in September 1859. Dressed in a shabby colonel's uniform, he strode into the offices of the San Francisco *Bulletin* and, with great solemnity, handed the editor a piece of paper. He explained that it was a proclamation, and that it was to be published in the next issue. Amused by the small stocky man in the ancient uniform, the editor read the proclamation: "At the peremptory request and desire of a large majority of the citizens of these United States, I, Joshua Norton . . . declare and proclaim myself Emperor of these United States." Joshua Abraham Norton had become Norton I, Emperor of the United States and Protector of Mexico.

The editor ran Norton's proclamation, and Norton thus began his twenty-year reign. He became the most beloved eccentric in a city known for its eccentrics. The citizens of San Francisco embraced their emperor and never allowed anyone to even suggest that he was not what he claimed to be. When Norton passed through the streets, his saber rattling on the sidewalk behind him, his imperial person followed by stray dogs, he would accept the humble bows of his subjects with the requisite gravity.

Indeed, he took the job of emperor very seriously and showed obvious concern for the welfare of his subjects. He periodically inspected the city's drains, checked streetcar timetables, and continued to issue proclamations for the betterment of his empire. He printed his own money (usually in denominations of 50 cents) and levied minuscule taxes; his money was accepted throughout the city, and the taxes were paid. Norton ate free of charge in the best restaurants and drank gratis in the best saloons. Theaters reserved special seats for him, and when he entered a theater the patrons would all rise and wait for him to take his seat before sitting down again. The state legislature made a special chair for him, the railroads and streetcars let him ride free. The best tailors in the city made uniforms for him (they would then advertise themselves as "by appointment to His Majesty"). He visited a different church every Sunday. He never overstayed his welcome and never showed an instance of greed. (When he decided that protecting Mexico was becoming too difficult, he dropped "Protector of Mexico" from his title.)

When he died in January 1880, the city was heartbroken. "Le Roi Est Mort," ran the headline in the San Francisco *Chronicle*. Thirty thousand people attended his funeral. The reason for his popularity was partly explained by one editorial: "The Emperor Norton killed nobody, robbed nobody and deprived nobody of his country—which is more than can be said for most fellows in his trade."

Riches to Rags:
Ruin

An early eighteenth-century English handwriting contest between a Mr. More and a Mr. German ended in a dead heat. The judges were unable to award the prize, a gold pen, until one noticed in German's entry a single undotted *i*. And this is the whole recorded extent of calamities befalling those who are careless about dotting *i*s.

Gustave Courbet (1819–77) was ruined by an act of France's National Assembly. Courbet, the center of a group of artists called Realists, was an active socialist in the Paris Commune of 1870 and responsible for damage to a monument at the Place Vendôme. The government assessed him fr323,000 in costs. Courbet fled to Switzerland, destitute.

James Fenimore Cooper was dismissed from Yale during his third year for misbehavior.

The most rejected cabinet nominee was Caleb Cushing, Tyler's choice for secretary of treasury. He was denied confirmation by the Senate in three successive votes all on one day, March 3, 1843, and rejected—under Grant—for appointment as chief justice in 1874.

James Capen Adams gained fame for his close rapport with bears—he is best known as "Grizzly" Adams. In 1860 he brought his so-called California Menagerie to New York, where Phineas T. Barnum had arranged a special tour. The tour began with a parade through the city. The locals were thrilled to see Adams mounted on one of his bears while holding two others by chains—all of them riding on a platform without bars. Adams barely survived the ten-week tour: he was constantly being mauled by his coperformers.

Among gamblers and mathematicians a martingale is a betting system in which losses are covered by successively higher wagers. The system in which each loss is doubled in the amount of the next bet is a grand martingale.

Private suites on the *Titanic* cost $4350.

The thirteenth vice-president of the United States, William Rufus De Vane King, was a very unlucky man and has become perhaps the most unknown vice-president in US history. King was elected to the office of vice-president under Franklin Pierce, but he never made it to Washington, D.C., for his inauguration. He was a dying man and an alcoholic. In an attempt to restore his health, he had gone to Cuba, and it was there, in Havana, that he took the oath of office, the first and thus far only executive officer of the country to be sworn in in a foreign land. He died the next month.

In AD 9 Quintilius Varus, Roman governor of Germany, led three legions across the Rhine to suppress an uprising. As the Romans struggled through the pathless, dark woods of Teutoburg Forest, they were attacked by a horde of fierce German warriors. The Romans were slaughtered; Varus committed suicide. This defeat was a major catastrophe for the Romans, and it ended forever their hopes of further expansion to the north. The emperor Augustus, who had himself appointed Varus to the post of governor, was tormented by dreams of the battle. Years afterward he would awake with a start, crying out, "Varus, Varus, bring me back my legions!"

George Washington, Thomas Jefferson, and James Madison all came dangerously close to becoming bankrupt after their terms as president; James Monroe died bankrupt; Andrew Jackson died in debt; William Henry Harrison was penniless when he died.

"Alas, poor Mexico, so far from God, so near to the USA."
— Porfirio Diaz (1830–1915), President of Mexico

Alaska, "the last frontier," is the most heavily bureaucratized of the fifty states and the District of Columbia. In 1979 Alaska employed 775 state and local government workers for every 10,000 inhabitants. Not surprisingly, Alaska also ranked number one in per capita property taxes.

Napoleon died possessed of fewer francs than he supposed, the actual sum being near 3 million francs. To preserve the honor of France the government forty years later appropriated 10 million francs to fulfill, and indeed overpay, the bequests of Bonaparte.

US astronauts are supplied with special fireproof playing cards.

The famous western lawman Bat Masterson was born Bartholomew ("Bat") Masterson in Quebec, Canada, in 1853. Although he was known as Bat, he changed his name to William Barclay Masterson for reasons clear only to himself. He grew up in New York, Illinois, and Kansas. Out west, he worked as a buffalo hunter, army scout, and saloonkeeper before turning to the law. He is most famous as a marshal, but his favored role was that of gambler. When he tired of life out west, he returned to New York, where Theodore Roosevelt, always a fan of men of the frontier, appointed him deputy US marshal (he was later removed by Taft). He then became sports editor of the New York *Morning Telegraph* (he was considered an authority on boxing).

To the end of his life, Masterson drank too much, gambled, and was forever getting himself into trouble. He died of a heart attack in October 1921 while working at his desk. His last words were found on a sheet of paper he had been writing on: "There are many in this old world of ours who hold that things break about even for us. I have observed, for example, that we all get about the same amount of ice. The rich get it in the summertime, and the poor get it in the winter."

The Emperor Nero did not fiddle while Rome burned. Any evidence of Nero's musicianship notwithstanding, he was out of town when the fire raged.

"Building a battleship" is what Wobblies sometimes did when in jail. That is, members of the International Workers of the World, who often found themselves confined wholesale in the years 1908–20, might sing, lock arms, and jump up and down until the building literally rocked.

Seventy-two Wobblies confined in late 1916 at the Everett jail (in Seattle) caused structural damage, desisting only when their calls for food and blankets were met.

On July 9, 1864, 20,000 Confederate troops led by Jubal A. Early surrounded the city of Frederick, Maryland. The Rebels threatened to destroy the city unless the townspeople paid them a ransom of $200,000. The citizens managed to raise the—at that time—enormous sum, and the Confederates, true to their word, withdrew. Paying off the Confederates set the city back financially, and every year for the past twenty-four, a bill—Senate bill 2804—has been introduced in Congress to have the money—with interest—paid back.

Accurately, the Delphic Oracle predicted in AD 363 that it would make no further predictions.

Marie Antoinette did not say, "Let them eat cake." The phrase was used by Rousseau in his *Confessions* around the time Marie was 11. (In Rousseau's original the word was not *cake,* but *brioche.)*

Few examples survive today of the Renaissance lute. Not only was this instrument fragile, it suffered terribly from the enthusiasms of amateurs who converted lutes into hurdy-gurdies (i.e., instruments plucked and stopped by a crank-operated mechanism) or theorboes.

To last, theorboes must be solidly built from the ground up, engineered to support as many as 23-25 strings, some of them crossing in the void alongside the fingerboard to a precariously cantilevered extension of the tuning head. These innovations were, literally, explosive for the lightly built lutes of an earlier generation.

When he was in his late twenties, Dostoyevsky became involved with a group of radical utopians. When the group's illegal printing press was discovered, they were arrested and put in front of a firing squad. At the last moment, the prisoners were reprieved. Dostoyevsky was then sentenced to four years of hard labor in a Siberian penal colony.

"A head-on collision is not an act of God."

—John Riley (1984, litigating against AMTRAK)

The Museum of Modern Art in New York City hung Matisse's *Le Bateau* upside-down for forty-seven days before they were alerted to their error.

It is the fate of conquered peoples not to eat as well as conquerors, or so the English language seems to illustrate. Words for farm animals, cow, pig, calf, etc., are all of Anglo-Saxon origin, but they are eaten as beef, pork, bacon, and veal, words of the Norman conquerors.

John Fitch, considered the inventor of the first American steamboat, committed suicide in his despair at being unable to obtain either recognition or financial backing for his invention.

Most contemporary children are familiar with the playful rhyme:

Ring a ring of roses
A pocket full of posies
A-tishoo! a-tishoo!
We all fall down

The four lines began as a song sung in the plague-ravaged London of 1665. The first line refers to the red, rashlike sores that appeared on victims of the plague; the second line refers to the prevalent belief that the putrid breath of victims was the cause of the malady—to avoid it, people carried pocketfuls of sweet-smelling herbs, or posies; the "a-tishoo" of the third line is the sneezing of the victims; the last line is a straightforward indication of what happened to a large portion of the city's population—they fell down and died.

Harry Truman received the first presidential pension in 1956, three years after leaving the White House. Until then, Congress had made no provision for former presidents.

There was an Associated Press correspondent named Mark Kellogg with Custer at the Battle of the Little Big Horn.

"Racket," signifying an unpracticed din, is also the name of a more or less failed baroque musical instrument. It belonged to the famously difficult family of the double reeds, along with tenoroons and hautbuoys and such, and was perhaps the most intractable of them all.

Made from a rounded block of wood, rather proportioned like a fruitcake tin, the racket was honeycombed with tortuously folded air passages and pocked over its circumference with fingerholes. Connecting this contraption to the world outside was a short tube, capped with a double reed mouthpiece.

One contemporaneous description relates that such an instrument "blew up" when its drain was inadvertently omitted in the manufacture. And, as might be expected, its level of tonal stability compares favorably only with that of a Swiss cheese, which its engineering resembles, played through a gasoline syphon.

Londoners credited the Great Fire of 1666 with putting an end to the plague that had been ravaging the city. They were somewhat correct. Before the fire, most of the city's houses had had thatch roofs, popular dwelling places for rodents and their attendant fleas. Following the fire, the thatch roofs were replaced with tiles.

270

On the evening of July 22, 1934, John Dillinger, America's first "public enemy number one," walked out of Chicago's Biograph Theater into the sweltering summer heat. As he walked away from the theater, someone stepped out from behind a lamppost, lit a cigar, and whispered, "Hello, John." In that instant, a half-dozen guns opened fire, and Dillinger fell to the sidewalk, dead. A crowd gathered around his body; women dipped handkerchiefs and the hems of their skirts in his blood.

The film Dillinger had just seen was *Manhattan Melodrama,* a gangster film starring Clark Gable, William Powell, and Mickey Rooney. The G-man who lit the cigar as the signal to open fire later committed suicide. The Biograph Theater is still there: the chair Dillinger sat in on that fateful evening is painted silver, the only silver chair in the theater.

John Duns Scotus (known to his admirers as "Doctor Subtilis") was one of the greatest philosophers and theologians of the Middle Ages. He taught at Oxford, Paris, and Cologne, and gathered around him a large number of followers, called Scotists. His teachings, which involved subtle ways of distinguishing among different aspects of any one thing, dominated scholastic teaching until the fifteenth century. They then fell under attack, and the few adherents of his teachings began to be ridiculed for their absurd quibbling. These last followers of the brilliant John Duns Scotus were derisively known as *Dunsmen,* or *Dunses*—hence our word *dunce.*

There really was a Casey Jones or, at least, a John L. Jones of Cayce, Kentucky, who died braking his Illinois Central *Cannonball* (Memphis to Canton, Mississippi) in a 1900 crash. The passengers survived, as did his crewman, whom he ordered to jump from the cab.

A palimpsest is a piece of parchment whose original—often more valuable—contents have been scraped or washed off to allow reuse of the material. Some Latin works were lost forever when zealous monks erased the parchments and copied out pious works onto them.

German artist Christo sent an artwork, *The Parcel,* to London for a showing. But this parcel was opened for inspection by an English customs officer. Insurance agents agreed that no art inhered in what was left and paid up.

In the printing trade to "pi" the type is to mix it up accidentally in its ordered storage trays.

Horatio Alger (1832–99), though he sold over 20 million copies of his 130 rags-to-riches tales, gave away most of his money and died in poverty.

I Have Seized the
Light: Science

If that promised Hell reserved to unbelievers really is situated around a burning brimstone lake (Rev. 21:8), then the temperature thereabouts is in the vicinity of 445 degrees Centigrade (833 degrees Fahrenheit).

First to attempt daily weather forecasts was Cleveland Abbe (1838–1916). He compiled his reports from telegraph dispatches while with the US Signal Service.

In 1869, when paper technology had captivated the public imagination, not only household objects and clothing were being manufactured but paper coffins, carpets, machine belts, and railway wheels. That is, between the metal hub and metal rim laminated rye-straw paper was employed; one such set of wheels traveled 300,000 miles.

But the first toilet paper in a roll was not introduced until 1871.

In 1844 Samuel F. B. Morse demonstrated to Congress the practicability of his invention—the telegraph—by transmitting the famous message "What hath God wrought" over a wire from Washington to Baltimore. Morse did not choose the words; it was Annie Ellsworth, daughter of the commissioner of patents, who selected the phrase.

Cosmic radiation is about twelve times as intense at 6000 feet (say, Denver) as at sea level.

Thomas Edison produced small phonographs that could be fitted into the body of a French doll.

The temperature at the core of the earth—7200 degrees Fahrenheit—is just a little less than the temperature at the surface of the sun.

Plutonium is warm to the touch.

At the equator the centrifugal force acting to throw things off the planet is only 1/289 as strong as the attraction of gravity.

William Sydney Porter (later famous as O. Henry) was born in Greensboro, North Carolina, on September 9, 1862. His father, a doctor, was so obsessed with the theory of perpetual motion that when his mother died he became a virtual orphan.

SPACE FLIGHTS

Crew date	Mission name	Remarks
Yuri A. Gagarin (4/12/61)	Vostok 1	First manned orbital flight
Alan B. Shepard, Jr. (5/5/61)	Mercury-Redstone 3	First American in space.
Virgil I. Grissom (7/21/61)	Mercury-Redstone 4	Spacecraft sank. Grissom rescued.
Gherman S. Titov (8/6–7/61)	Vostok 2	First space flight of more than 24 hrs.
John H. Glenn, Jr. (2/20/62)	Mercury-Atlas 6	First American in orbit
M. Scott Carpenter (5/24/62)	Mercury-Atlas 7	Manual retrofire error caused 250 mi. landing overshoot
Andrian G. Nikolayev (8/11–16/62)	Vostok 3	Vostok 3 and 4 made first group flight
Pavel R. Popovich (8/12–15/62)	Vostok 4	On first orbit it came within 3 miles of Vostok 3
Walter M. Schirra Jr. (10/3/62)	Mercury-Atlas 8	Closest splashdown to target to date (4.5 mi.)
L. Gordon Cooper (5/15–16/63)	Mercury-Atlas 9	First U.S. evaluation of effects on man of one day in space
Valery F. Bykovsky (6/14–19/63)	Vostok 5	Vostok 5 and 6 made 2d group flight
Valentina V. Tereshkova (6/16–19/63	Vostok 6	First woman in space
Vladimir M. Komarov, Konstantin P. Feoktistov, Boris B. Yegorov (10/12/64)	Voskhod 1	First 3 man orbital flight: first without space suits
Pavel I. Belyayev, Aleksei A. Leonov (3/18/65)	Voskhod 2	Leonov made first "space walk" (10 min.)
Virgil I. Grissom, John W. Young (3/23/65)	Gemini-Titan 3	First manned spacecraft to change its orbital path
James A. McDivitt, Edward H. White 2d, (6/3–7/65)	Gemini-Titan 4	White was first American to "walk in space" (20 min.)
L. Gordon Cooper, Jr., Charles Conrad, Jr. (8/21–29/65	Gemini-Titan 5	First use of fuel cells for electric power; evaluated guidance and navigation system.
Frank Borman, James A. Lovell, Jr. (12/4–18/65)	Gemini-Titan 7	Longest duration Gemini flight

Walter M. Schirra, Jr.		
Thomas P. Stafford		Completed world's first space
(12/15–16/65)	Gemini-Titan 6-A	rendezvous with Gemini 7
Neil A. Armstrong		First docking of one space vehi
David R. Scott		cle with another; mission
(3/16–17/66)	Gemini-Titan 8	aborted, control malfunction
John W. Young,		First use of Agena target vehi-
Michael Collins		cle's propulsion systems, ren-
(7/18–21/66)	Gemini-Titan 10	dezvoused with Gemini 8
Charles Conrad, Jr.,		Docked, made 2 revolutions of
Richard F. Gordon, Jr.		earth tethered, set Gemini Alti-
(9/12–15/66)	Gemini-Titan 11	tude record (739.2 Mi.)
James A. Lovell, Jr., Edwin		Final Gemini mission; record 5
E. Aldrin, Jr. (11/11–15/66)	Gemini-Titan 12	hrs. of extravehicular activity
Vladimir M. Komarov		Crashed after re-entry killing
(4/23/67)	Soyuz 1	Komarov.
Walter M. Schirra, Jr.,		
Donn F. Eisele,		First manned flight of Apollo
R. Walter Cunningham		spacecraft command-service
(10/11–22/68)	Apollo-Saturn 7	module only
Georgi T. Beregovol		Made rendezvous with unman-
(10/26–30/68)	Soyuz 3	ned Soyuz 2.
Frank Borman, James A.		First flight to moon (command-
Lovell, Jr., William A.		service module only); views of
Anders (12/21–27/68)	Apollo-Saturn 8	lunar surface televised to earth
Thomas P. Stafford, Eugene		
A. Cernan, John W.		
Young (5/18–26/69)	Apollo-Saturn 10	First lunar module orbit of moo
Neil A. Armstrong,		First lunar landing made by Ar
Edwin E. Aldrin, Jr.,		strong and Aldrin collected 48.
Michael Collins		lbs of soil, rock samples; lunar
(7/16–24/69)	Apollo-Saturn 11	stay time 21 h. 36m. 21 s.
Charles Conrad, Jr.		Conrad and Bean made 2d
Richard F. Gordon,		moon landing, collected 74.7 lb
Alan L. Bean		of samples; lunar stay time 31 l
(11/14–24/69)	Apollo-Saturn 12	31 m.
Alan B. Shepard, Jr.,		Shepard and Mitchell made 3d
Stuart A. Roosa,		moon landing, collected 96 lbs.

Edgar D. Mitchell (1/31–2/9/71)	Apollo-Saturn 14	of lunar samples; lunar stay 33 h, 31 m.
Georgi T. Dobrovolsky, Vladislav N. Yolkov, Viktor·I. Patsayev (6/6–30/71)	Soyuz 11	Docked with Salyut space station; and orbited in Salyut for 23 days; crew died during re-entry from loss of pressurization.
David R., Scott, Alfred M. Worden, James B. Irwin (7/26–8/7/71)	Apollo-Saturn 15	Scott and Irwin made 4th moon landing; first lunar rover use; first deep space walk; 170 lbs. of samples; 66 h, 55 m. stay.
Charles M. Duke, Jr., Thomas K. Mattingly, John W. Young (4/16–27/72)	Apollo-Saturn 16	Young and Duke made 5th moon landing; collected 213 lbs. of lunar samples; lunar stay time 71 h, 2 m.
Eugene A. Cernan, Ronald E. Evans, Harison H. Schmitt (12/7–19/72)	Apollo-Saturn 17	Cernan and Schmitt made 6th manned lunar landing; collected 243 lbs. of samples; record lunar stay of 75 h.
Charles Conrad, Jr., Joseph P. Kerwin, Paul J. Weitz (5/25–6/22/73)	Skylab 2	First American manned orbiting space station; made long-flight tests, crew repaired damage caused during boost.
Alan L. Bean, Jack R. Lousma, Owen K. Garriott (7/28–9/25/73)	Skylab 3	Crew systems and operational tests, exceeded pre-mission plans for scientific activities; space walk total 13h, 44 m.
Gerald P. Carr, Edward G. Gibson, William Pogue (11/16/73–2/8/74)	Skylab 4	Final Skylab mission; record space walk of 7 h, 1 m., record space walks total for a mission 22 h, 21 m.
Alexi Leonov, Valeri Kubason (7/15–7/21/75)	Soyuz 19	
Vance Brand, Thomas P. Stafford, Donald K. Slayton (7/15–7/24/75)	Apollo 18	U.S.- USSR joint flight. Crews linked-up in space, conducted experiments; shared meals, and held a joint news conference.

The aqualung was invented by Jacques Yves Cousteau and Emil Gagnan. They developed the underwater breathing apparatus while fighting with the French Resistance during World War II.

Xerography was invented in 1937 by a prelaw student named Chester Floyd Carlson. The first message Carlson copied was "10–22–38 Astoria," the date and place where Carlson performed his experiments.

Because of the actions of currents, winds, tides, and even slight density differences, the Pacific Ocean is at an average sea level that is twenty inches higher than Atlantic sea level. But even the Atlantic has a sliding sea level, about fourteen inches higher at the Nova Scotia coast than on Florida beaches.

Benjamin Franklin was present in Paris during the first experiments with balloons. On August 27, 1783, he was part of a crowd of spectators at the first trial ascension of an unmanned balloon. One of the people standing near Franklin was unimpressed by the strange device and muttered "What good is it?" Franklin quickly responded with a question of his own. "What good is a new-born baby?" he asked.

That first balloon glided over the roofs of Paris and disappeared. The owner of the balloon had attached a note to it, asking that it be returned with an account of where it landed. What the owner had not foreseen was that the balloon did not impress the less-than-scientific peasants living on the periphery of Paris. The balloon was not warmly greeted when it finally hit the ground at Gonesse, twelve miles from the city. The locals threw stones at it and attacked it with knives and pitchforks. When it was finally "dead," they tied it to the tail of a horse and dragged it off. Someone who could read finally spotted and read the note, and the punctured balloon was returned to its owner.

That designers of dirigibles should risk using inflammable hydrogen to lift giant airships is readily understood when the price of inert helium—$2500 per cubic foot in 1915—is taken into account. (Present prices are about $35 per 1000 cubic feet.)

Helium is principally obtained by extraction from natural gas. Chemists in 1915 knew of only two American gas fields that produced helium; it was later discovered, though always in small proportions, in most gas wells.

"Aluminium," as some parts of the world call element number thirteen, was also spelled with the extra "i" in the US until 1925, when the word was changed by fiat of the American Chemical Society to "aluminum."

(In 1807, before the element had been discovered, the name "alumium" had been proposed by Sir Humphrey Davy.)

The average density of planet Earth is about 5.5 times that of water.

The zeroeth law of themodynamics was propounded after the more familiar first and second laws but considered more fundamental than either, hence its unique designation.

Einstein's famous $e=mc^2$ was not a surprise in 1905 when his special theory of relativity was published. Such an expression, though somewhat cryptic, is derivable from a well known equation published in 1902 by Lorentz and Fitzgerald. This equation, or transform, arose out of experimental necessity when theories of the universal "aether" proved untenable. It was rather Einstein's explanation of the result that changed the twentieth century.

Although it is thought that no particle can exceed the speed of light in empty space—such "tachyons" have been sought, unsuccessfully—it can happen that energetic particles exceed the somewhat reduced speed of light in other media (e.g., glass, water, quartz, etc.). Such an event is marked by a violet glow called Cerenkov radiation.

Tungsten is ideal for electric light filaments because it evaporates more slowly than any other element. (But Edison achieved good results also with bamboo.)

Because gravitational pull is equal in every direction at the earth's center, the gravitational force there is zero. Maximum pull is exerted at a depth of 2900 km below the earth's surface, a little less than halfway to the center.

A lightning bolt is from two to eight inches in diameter. Although the eye sees but one stroke, each flash may consist of up to forty quick exchanges along the same path from cloud to earth and back again.

If the mass of the earth were to be compressed to densities that would create a black hole, its diameter would be less than half an inch.

In dry air the atmosphere has a potential of 100–120 volts for every meter of altitude. Given the high resistance of dry air, however, current flow is scarcely measurable, amounting to no more than a few trillionths of an amp.

It is correct therefore to imagine, in an upright posture, that one's head might have an electrical potential of 200 volts or more in relation to one's feet.

Although it is often said that plutonium does not occur in nature, this is not strictly speaking true. Trace quantities of the element are formed in the earth's crust as a result of decay in uranium ores and through the action of cosmic ray bombardment.

Unlike charged particles, which damage living tissue most when most energetic, neutrons (electrically neutral) are most dangerous encountered at lower energies. The neutron's path is a straight line; the slower it moves (less energy) the longer it is in the neighborhood and the more likely to collide with something.

A low energy, or thermal, neutron moves on the average about eight inches in the human body before impacting.

When margarine was invented by Mège Mourièes in 1869 he had it patented simultaneously in France and England. The English patent (No. 2157) is for "The Preparation and Production of certain New Animal Fatty Bodies."

Like the oceans, the atmosphere experiences a lunar tide twice a day. These tidal effects are greatest at the equator, but amount to no more than six one-hundredths of a millimeter increase in atmospheric pressure.

Coriolis forces, effects of the earth's rotation, are responsible for counterclockwise circulation of large air masses in the northern hemisphere, clockwise in the southern half of the planet. And for those patient enough to undertake the experiment, the same forces can be seen at work in the swirling of draining bathtubs and toilets.

But there is a lesser known and somewhat controversial, Coriolis effect in rivers, Baer's Law. Rivers of the northern hemisphere are more eroded on the right-hand bank, those of the southern hemisphere on the left-hand bank. That is, in the northern hemisphere, when facing downstream the bank to the right is usually more eroded, no matter in which compass direction the river flows.

Coriolis-induced helical currents are proposed in theory to account for the phenomenon.

Blue-white, the most valuable of diamond colors, is now thought to be an effect of viewing the stone in sunlight, which has an ultraviolet component responsible for the color. But the blue-white showing is still an indicator of high value, since only the whitest, most perfect stones exhibit this slight fluorescence.

Black, gray, and green diamonds have been irradiated, either by natural or manmade processes, to produce their dark sheen. Energetic particles evict carbon atoms from their places in the diamond's crystal lattice, reducing transmission of light through the substance.

If you should try this in your own cyclotron, use alpha particles and remember that the diamonds are intensely radioactive for a few hours after the treatment. An electron accelerator might yield diamonds of bluish cast; exposure to neutrons, in an atomic pile, tends to produce green. Any sign of browning means the diamonds have reached too high a temperature.

When natural radiation acts on quartz the result is amethyst.

Peter Kapitsa, perhaps the leading Soviet physicist of the Stalinist era, seems to have refused Stalin's invitation to work on nuclear weapons (this job was given to Andre Sakharov, among others), and went to work instead on ball lightning.

No theory of ball lightning has proven satisfactory to physicists, but research is said to have important military applications.

Element 104, which has a half-life of 0.15 seconds, has also an unstable name: it is kurchatovium within Russian science and rutherfordium in American circles.

Though he is not so often remembered for it, Albert Einstein explained the sky's color:

The sky is blue because of the motions of molecules that make up the atmosphere. While these motions are random, and molecules never pile up in one place in preference to another, it does happen that some suitably microscopic region may be momentarily free of molecules or another may be over occupied. But viewed from any larger scale the atmosphere would "look" smooth, uniformly filled with gas molecules.

In fact, microscopic volumes small enough that unevenness begins to be theoretically noticeable are of precisely a size that interacts with the short wavelengths of blue light—blue light "sees" the atmosphere as grainy, bumpy, here more solid there less. Longer wavelengths are not affected nearly so much, as instantaneously empty or crowded regions large enough to be visible to these wavelengths are much less likely to form.

Blue light, then, has a rough ride through the atmosphere. It is scattered and deflected around the sky. The remaining components of sunlight, now relatively richer in red and yellow, arrive at the earth's surface without breaking up on the way.

Best estimates are that Earth's magnetic field has weakened about 15 percent since the mid-seventeenth century. It is thought the entire field has flipped no less than 170 times in the last 76 million years.

Researchers in 1979 put over five hundred ghosts into a machine, actually a computer used to statistically sort and group hundreds of spirit manifestations culled from the literature.

Traits shared most frequently by ghosts were movement of small objects (64 percent), rapping (48 percent), imitative noises (43 percent), and appearing as human phantasms (29 percent).

The rarest behaviors among the collated spooks were tampering with electric switches, ESP communication, animating objects, possession (all occurring in about 3 percent of cases); returning discarded objects, sitting on people in bed (both 2 percent occurrence); bending metal, damaging plants (only 1 percent each); and cutting hair (rarest, 0.4 percent).

Surprisingly, though spirits are usually associated with the hours of darkness, fully 42 percent of phenomena are recorded as having taken place in daylight hours.

In this research, investigators had chiefly wished to draw some quantitative distinction between poltergeists and other hauntings. The data were inconclusive.

When, in 1839, Louis J. M. Daguerre was finally successful in capturing a photographic image on a silver-coated copper plate, he is said to have exclaimed, "I have seized the light, I have arrested the flight!"

Lucky Rain Hat:
Seven

The Seven Mules of Notre Dame were the hardworking linemen on the 1924 Knute Rockne team more often remembered for its glamorous backfield, the Four Horsemen.

"Seventh Heaven," in the Ptolemaic system of astronomy, is the last of seven concentric spheres that make up the observable universe beyond Earth. The sun, moon, planets, and stars are mounted in the various independently revolving shells that surround Earth. In the last of these spheres lives God.

Jewish and Islamic theologians counted seven spheres; other astronomers and religious authorities believed in up to eleven.

The seven defense mechanisms are: conversion, regression, repression, projection, rationalization, identification, and sublimation.

Numbering seven, because it is a round, mystical number, were the original Pre-Raphaelite Brotherhood of 1848: Dante Gabriel Rossetti, John Everett Millais, William Holman Hunt, Thomas Woolner, James Collinson, William Michael Rossetti, and Frederick George Stevens.

Ship's bells announcing the time sound every half hour. At the beginning of each four-hour shipboard watch the bells begin again at one and run up to eight during the watch. The only exception is the split watch between 1600 and 2000 hours: bells sound four times at 1800 but start over again at one for 1830 and skip from three bells at 1930 to eight at 2000. Ship's watches are traditionally seven:

0000–0400—mid watch
0400–0800—morning watch
0800–1200—forenoon watch
1200–1600—afternoon watch
1600–1800—first dog watch
1800–2000—second dog watch
2000–2400—first watch

There are seven sacraments: baptism, confirmation, communion, penance, holy orders, matrimony, and extreme unction.

Unless a war is very long, e.g., Thirty Years War, Hundred Years War, or very short, e.g., Six Day War, it is apt to be remembered by its length, no one knows why, only if a seven is part of it. Examples: Seven Years War (Austria v. Prussia, 1756–63), Seven Months War (France v. Prussia, 1870), Seven Weeks War (Austria v. Prussia, 1866), and Seven Days' Battles (Union v. Confederacy, June 25–July 1, 1862).

The seven deadly sins are: gluttony, pride, covetousness, lust, anger, envy, and sloth. Others are merely venial.

"Seven Sisters," when this refers to the Pleiades of Greek myth, are the seven daughters of Atlas and Pleione: Alcyone, Asterope, Electra, Celaeno, Maia, Merope, and Taygeta. (But the constellation named for these sisters—or some authorities believe the sisters were named to fit the constellation—seems to consist either of eight or of six stars, if judged by like magnitudes.)

Speaking of oil companies, the seven sisters are: British Petroleum, Gulf, Mobil, Shell, Texaco, Exxon, and Standard Oil of California (Chevron).

And when speaking of American women's colleges, the seven are: Bryn Mawr, Smith, Vassar, Radcliffe, Wellesley, Mt. Holyoke, and Sarah Lawrence.

The seven electors of the Holy Roman Emperor (after 1356) were: the Count Palatine of the Rhine, Duke of Saxony, Margrave of Brandenburg, King of Bohemia, and Archbishops of Trier, Mainz, and Cologne. Much later additions were the Dukes of Bavaria and Hanover (who were also kings of England after 1713).

There are seven canonical hours:

> matins (now usually combined with lauds), at dawn or before
> prime, 6:00 AM
> tierce, 9:00 AM
> sext, 12:00 PM
> nones, 3:00 PM
> vespers, at supper or around 6:00 PM
> compline, before bed

More often than not a gaggle of wise men will number seven. We have, for example, the Seven Sages of the Bamboo Grove (Chinese sages renouncing the stress and strain of palace life), the Seven Sages of Rome, the Seven Viziers (from the tales of Sinbad), and the Seven Wise Men of Greece (Thales, Pittacus, Chilon, Myson of Chen, Solon, Cleobulus, and Bias).

The seven hills of the ancient city of Rome are: the Palatine, Capitoline, Quirinal, Viminal, Esquiline, Caelian, and Aventine. It was not by accident that the great city was founded on hills: the rest of the surrounding area was composed of malaria-infested swamps.

Seven fates for seven children are:

Monday's child is fair of face,
Tuesday's child is full of grace,
Wednesday's child is full of woe,
Thursday's child has far to go,
Friday's child is loving and giving,
Saturday's child works hard for his living,
And the child that is born on the Sabbath day
Is bonny and blithe, and good and gay.

The Seven Sleepers of Ephesus—Christians persecuted by the Roman emperor Decius (ca. AD 250)—took refuge in a cave, falling into a miraculous sleep until awakened two hundred years later by the Byzantine emperor Theodosius II. Clerics of the Middle Ages interpreted the story as a strong confirmation of the doctrine of resurrection.

The Japanese have seven gods of luck. Their names are Daikoku, Ebisu, Jurojin, Hotei, Bishamon, Fukurokuju, and Benten (who is actually a goddess). Associated with this blessed group are their lucky treasures: a hat of invisibility, keys to the heavenly treasure house, cloves, books, an inexhaustible purse, brocade, and a lucky rain hat.

Eagles Mating:
Sex and Love

"I've started other trends besides sex, you know."

—Mae West

Louis IX vowed to give up women, excepting his wife. Not for nothing was he known as Louis the Saint: he declared she was "not at all one of those in whom one could take great pleasure."

The honeymoon, the sweet first month of marriage, gets its name from an ancient northern European custom of drinking mead—honeyed wine—as an aphrodisiac during the first month of marriage.

The handwriting of Napoleon Bonaparte was notoriously illegible. Thus, the chief task of his secretary, Méneval, in behalf of them both was to learn how to decipher it.

Josephine was never able to read it and complained once that the emperor had sent her a campaign map, though a more careful scrutiny revealed it to be a love letter.

But Marie Louise read aloud and very quickly through Napoleon's letter proposing marriage to her, indicating that she at least had made a prolonged study of the imperial handwriting.

The Marquis de Sade (1740–1814) gave the language sadism; its opposite was contributed by Leopold von Sacher-Masoch (1835–95), a German novelist now remembered only for his name and a fetish about furs.

Venice in 1509 distributed a directory of its 11,654 prostitutes listed by name, address, and fee.

The modern wedding ring is a direct descendant of the *annulus pronubus,* which was a Roman betrothal ring. This first came into existence in the third century AD. At first it was made from iron, but gold became increasingly popular. By the ninth century, when Christianity adopted it, the ring was most commonly made from either gold or silver. It wasn't until the seventeenth century that it became customary to wear an unadorned ring. Until the sixteenth century, Christians placed the wedding ring on the third finger of a woman's right hand. This was directly against the pagan tradition of wearing the betrothal ring on the third finger of the left hand. The reason for the confusion was no more complex than a belief (created by Aulus Gellius in the second century AD) that there was a vein that flowed from the third finger on the right hand directly to the heart.

"Man is the only animal for whom mating for the first time is followed by repugnance."

—Pliny, *Historia Naturalis*

The search for a wife for the future Edward VII of England, then Prince of Wales, began in 1859. Relatives and confidantes of Queen Victoria scoured Europe for princesses and grand duchesses. Among those dismissed in private memoirs were:

Princess Elizabeth of Wied—"rather dowdy"
Princess Augusta of Meiningen—"undeveloped"
Princess Marie of Hohenzollern-Sigmaringen—"Catholic"
Princess Louise of Sweden—"too young"
Princess Marie of Saxe-Weimar—"delicate and not pretty"
Princess Alexandrine of Prussia—"not clever or pretty"
Princess Marie of Altenbourg—"shockingly dressed . . . always with her most disagreeable mother"

The patron saint of prostitutes, adopted in the Middle Ages, is Mary Magdalene (Sainte Marie l'Egyptienne).

The House of Commons in 1601 refused a second reading to an adultery bill on the equitable grounds that whereas the proposed law would not discomfit a poor man—whose wealth, being nonexistent, could not be confiscated—it acted harshly on impoverished women, whose future rights, in the form of dowry, were to be seized.

"A girl who flirts with her looks is not chaste; a scholar who flirts with his knowledge is not honest."

—Chinese proverb

The son of the Marquess of Queensbury—the elder Queensbury formulated the first boxing rules—was Lord Alfred Douglas, alleged homosexual lover of Oscar Wilde.

It was the old Marquess who brought Oscar to grief. In February 1895 he left a card for Wilde at the Albermarle Club inscribed, "To Oscar Wilde, Posing as a Somdomite!" Wilde was either incensed over the misspelling or the affront and determined to sue for libel. He later withdrew his suit, but Queensbury was hitting below the belt, using his influence to have Wilde tried twice under the amended acts for the suppression of white slavery. At the last trial, Wilde was convicted of gross indecency.

A ruinous change came over the aristocratic sons of England in the early eighteenth century. In droves they deserted prospects of marriage to heiresses and wedded themselves to the idea of romantic love, finding spouses dear to their hearts.

Even allowing for a constant 18-20 percent of noble bachelors, the proportion of sons marrying wealth fell steadily through the early nineteenth century from 80 percent to about 20 percent.

The trend was arrested and reversed in the late nineteenth century.

Charles Louis (Geneviéve) D'Eon (d. 1810) was banished from France a man and came back in 1777 by order of Louis XVI a woman. It was the only way to settle some sensitive points of honor between king and subject. Marie Antoinette helped Geneviéve choose her new wardrobe.

A concubine was called by the Romans a *semi-conjux,* half-married.

It is certain that Suzanne Valadon (aerialist, model, and painter) gave birth to Maurice Utrillo; the identity of the father is a long-standing art guessing game created by Valadon herself.

She professed it equally probable that Maurice was sired by Renoir or Degas (and left the door open to Puvis de Chavannes and Toulouse-Lautrec). This being an artistic and biological problem of some urgency, Valadon appealed to her acquaintances of Montmartre café society for a father. In the version according to Valadon—but Valadon is never to be trusted on the subject of Valadon—a congenial Spanish painter of small note, Miguel Utrillo, stepped forward averring that he "would be proud to sign his name to the work of either artist."

Ironically, stripped of its camouflage, the honor of paternity does in fact fall most probably to Utrillo.

"Handfasting" is not enough to constitute a marriage, or so ruled the courts of medieval England. Other insufficiences for a state of marriage to exist, besides clasping hands, included promises to "make her as good a woman as he was a man," to "do right by her" (*quod decet* in the thirteenth century), or to "do honor to a woman."

The wife of General Tom Thumb (Charles S. Stratton, 1838–83), forty-inch star of P. T. Barnum's Greatest Show on Earth, was Lavinia Warren. While courting his midget spouse Thumb competed for Lavinia's affections with Commodore Nutt, a famous performing English midget.

In 1918, with the Russian Revolution not yet a year old and the lines of governmental organization still unclear, the city of Vladimir passed an act to nationalize women.

This act, though soon superceded, provided that unmarried women over 18 must "register at the Free Love Office of the Commissariat of Welfare." They were to have a choice of, or be chosen by, single males aged 19 to 50. Children to become property of the Republic.

Of course, divorce throughout the early Soviet Union was quite easily accomplished: upon request the marriage registry office merely sent a form letter to the divorced spouse—who needn't have heard anything about it—announcing the end of the marriage.

The widely flaring breeches of fashionable men in the time of Elizabeth I could only be made to hold their shape by stuffing them with quantities of rags or feathers or whatever else would serve. Inasmuch as Elizabethan ladies were then dressing in vast hooped farthingales, the sexes were for a time virtually out of handholding range of each other.

Czar Ivan the Terrible (1530–84), nearly contemporary with Henry VIII (1491–1547), went Henry two better. Ivan was married eight times and, like Henry, resorted to quick expedients to rid himself of one or two.

Shoes are tied to a bridal conveyance in dim remembrance of an ancient custom (Ruth 4:7) regarding the transfer of land.

At the turn of the century in America, male sexual preference was indicated—or so the public believed—by wearing a red necktie.

The phrase used in print and in intelligent company at this time was "sexual invert" or just "invert."

About 1880 the first contraceptive ointment was marketed by an English chemist, W. J. Rendell. His preparation consisted chiefly of quinine and coco butter. Though it worked, marginally, quinine caused a large number of adverse reactions.

"No neurosis is possible with a normal sex life," stated Sigmund Freud. Even so, he gave up sex at the age of 42.

The average woman in present-day USSR has six to eight abortions in the course of her life; some women have as many as fifteen.

The Ape-Gentlewoman or the Character of an Exchange-Wench—title of an anonymous 1673 pamphlet spreading concern for the loosening of sexual behavior among nonprofessionals.

Brides in ancient Rome were lifted over the threshold, but not by the bridegroom. The purpose of this ritual was to prevent the bride from stumbling, which would have been a very bad omen.

When Kit Carson's second Indian wife, a Cheyenne, decided to divorce him, she did it in her tribe's traditional way: she threw all his belongings out of their tepee.

Johann Sebastian Bach was the father of twenty children, seven by his first wife and thirteen by his second.

The minimum age for marriage in ancient Rome was 12 for girls and 14 for boys.

Dante fell in love with Beatrice when she was 8 and he was 9. She died at 24. Dante made Beatrice the principal figure in his *Divine Comedy;* it is Beatrice who leads him to Paradise.

It was not unknown for women in colonial New England to get married in the nude—or in their undergarments. Ceremonies involving naked brides were usually performed at night or, if held during daylight hours, the bride might stand, naked, inside a closet next to her groom. The reason for this odd and un-Puritanical behavior was an old English tradition which held that if a woman got married "in her shift on the king's highway," her husband would not be held responsible for her premarriage debts.

After the forced abdication of Turkey's last sultan, Abdul-Hamid II, messages were sent around the empire in 1909 for relatives to come and claim the liberated members of the harem. Not all of the twelve hundred women found alternative living arrangements, and thus the fabled Seraglio grew into an old ladies' home.

While he was in Paris, Benjamin Franklin met that great prototype of the Latin lover, Giacomo Casanova. The two got along quite well: Franklin invited Casanova to a session of the French Academy.

Dolphins enjoy active, promiscuous sex lives. When making sexual advances, dolphins do not concern themselves with the size, age, sex, or relationship of their chosen partners. Nor do they always concern themselves with species: dolphins have been known to make advances to human beings—and to turtles.

Once inside her new home, a Roman bride would be handed a lighted torch. She would use the torch to light the hearth and would then toss the torch to her friends, who would scramble around trying to take possession of it—it was considered a lucky memento. The custom survives today in the bridesmaids' scrambling for the bride's bouquet.

The first woman to appear on the cover of *Playboy* magazine was Marilyn Monroe.

Knights never rode mares; it just wasn't chivalrous.

John Lennon's mother named him John Winston Lennon—he was born in 1940, and she named him after Churchill. In 1969 Lennon had his middle name legally changed to Ono, making him John Ono Lennon. His name thus echoed his wife's: Yoko Ono Lennon.

In *Sleeper* (1973) Woody Allen goes to sleep in 1973 and awakens 200 years later. One of the innovations he encounters is the beloved orgasmatron.

Gorillas beat their chests when they are **nervous**, not amorous.

Eagles mate in the air.

Little Wars: Sports

Coach Alonzo Stagg of the University of Chicago was first to number his football team's uniforms, in November 1913. The idea pleased fans but didn't catch on at other big schools for another ten years.

Leg slip, gully, silly mid off, square short leg, and backward point are a few of the possible positions a cricketer might play while fielding.

There is a system to these designations, of course. For example, the silly mid off is near the batsman (silly), at midfield (mid), and to the right of a righthanded batsman (off; opposites are leg or on).

There are 10 million volleyball players in China.

Bruce Lee (1940–73), star of martial arts movies and founder of an eclectic kung fu style, was the Hong Kong cha-cha champion of 1958. Though he supported himself for a brief time after his arrival in the US giving dance lessons, he quickly gravitated into the martial arts and finally into acting, when cast as Kato in the 1966 "Green Hornet" television series.

The Royal Blackheath, founded by James I in 1608, is the world's oldest golf club.

OLYMPIC GAMES

1896	Athens
1900	Paris
1904	St. Louis
1908	London
1912	Stockholm
1920	Antwerp
1924	Paris
1928	Amsterdam
1932	Los Angeles
1936	Berlin
1948	London
1952	Helsinki
1956	Melbourne
1960	Rome
1964	Tokyo
1968	Mexico City
1972	Munich
1976	Montreal
1980	Moscow
1984	Los Angeles

WINTER OLYMPICS

1924   Chamonix, France
1928   St. Moritz, Switzerland
1932   Lake Placid, USA
1936   Garmisch, Germany
1948   St. Moritz, Switzerland
1952   Oslo, Norway
1956   Cortina, Italy
1960   Squaw, Valley, USA
1964   Innsbruck, Austria
1968   Grenoble, France
1972   Sapporo, Japan
1976   Innsbruck, Austria
1980   Lake Placid, USA
1984   Sarajevo, Yugoslavia

Half an *Ave Maria* is the proper length of the horn note blown at hunt's end by the Master of Game.

A deliberate mutation of baseball is pesäpallo, introduced in 1922 after a decade of experimentation by the Finns. Bases in this game are progressively farther apart, constructed along a zigzag basepath. The sprint to home plate from third base is 147 feet as compared with only 66 feet going from home to first.

Since the devisers of the Finnish game wished to provide exercise to every participant, batters may elect to run without hitting the ball and, whether fair or foul, each batter receives no more than three pitches.

The game is still largely confined to Finland.

Winners of the America's Cup

1851   America
1870   Magic defeated Cambria, England, (1–0)
1871   Columbia (first three races) and Sappho (last two races) defeated Livonia, England (4–1)
1876   Madeline defeated Countess of Dufferin, Canada, (2–0)
1881   Mischief defeated Atalanta, Canada, (2–0)
1885   Puritan defeated Genesta, England, (2–0)
1886   Mayflower defeated Galatea, England (2–0)
1887   Volunteer defeated Thistle, Scotland, (2–0)
1893   Vigilant defeated Valkyrie II, England, (3–0)
1895   Defender defeated Valkyrie III, England, (3–0)
1899   Columbia defeated Shamrock, England, (3–0)
1901   Columbia defeated Shamrock II, England, (3–0)

1903	Reliance defeated Shamrock III, England, (3–0)
1920	Resolute defeated Shamrock IV, England, (3–2)
1930	Enterprise defeated Shamrock V, England, (4–0)
1934	Rainbow defeated Endeavour, England, (4–2)
1937	Ranger defeated Endeavour II, England, (4–0)
1958	Columbia defeated Sceptre, England, (4–0)
1962	Weatherly defeated Gretel, Australia, (4–1)
1964	Constellation defeated Sovereign, England, (4–0)
1967	Intrepid defeated Dame Pattie, Australia, (4–0)
1970	Intrepid defeated Gretel II, Australia, (4–1)
1974	Courageous defeated Southern Cross, Australia, (4–0)
1977	Courageous defeated Australia, Australia, (4–0)
1980	Freedom defeated Australia, Australia, (4–1)
1983	Australia II defeated Liberty, (4–3)

Anton Geesink (1934–), the first non-Japanese to win an international judo contest against Japanese opponents, was 6' 6" and 265 lbs. In 1961 this Dutchman won the world championship, defeating three famous Japanese judokas, all of them about 5' 9". This turned the judo world upside down, as oddsmakers had thought Geesink's size an insuperable handicap.

Two hundred eighty-four feet 6 inches is thought the longest hand-grenade throw—achieved by Alfred Blozis in 1944, not in combat, using a two-pound grenade.

The modern Olympic pentathlon was introduced in 1912. The five events—riding a horse through an obstacle course, fencing, firing a pistol at human-shaped moving targets, swimming, and running—were based on the skills required of a military courier during the Napoleonic wars. While carrying some vital message, such a courier often had to ride a horse over unfamiliar terrain; he might have to fence or shoot his way through enemy lines; eluding pursuers, he might be called upon to swim a river; and, finally, the courier would make a mad dash for the safety of a friendly encampment.

One of the popular ditties that helped elect Calvin Coolidge president in 1924 was "Keep Cool and Keep Coolidge." In 1927 the famed baseball player Babe Ruth adopted the slogan "Keep cool with cabbage." Ruth didn't eat cabbage—he wore it under his cap. The Sultan of Swat kept iced cabbage leaves in the water cooler in the Yankees' dugout. He would carefully select a leaf—a large one, for he had a large head—trim it, place it squarely on top of his head, and pull his cap down to conceal the vegetable from his fans. He replaced the leaves as needed during the course of a game (he found that one leaf kept him cool for about two innings). Ruth took care to remove the cabbage when going to bat. At least once, however, he forgot and belted a ball out of the park while still wearing his special coolant. The crowd cheered the "Babe" as he rounded the bases. When he reached home he bowed to the adoring spectators and doffed his cap, exposing two trimmed cabbage leaves (it was a hot, two-leaf day).

There has never been any such thing as a standard caber, the stripped tree trunk that Scotsmen toss in highland competitions. Hence, once a caber is tossed it may never be shortened or altered in any way—it remains of itself the only standard by which future tosses may be compared.

A large caber, 18–20 feet long, might weigh 120 pounds. Distance is not an aim in caber tossing; the object is to heave it through an end-to-end flip to a nearly straight-up landing.

The world's first public golf course was opened in 1896 in New York's Van Cortlandt Park.

The Duke of Wellington never said, "The battle of Waterloo was won on the playing fields of Eton." Wellington did attend Eton, for a very short time, but there were no organized team games while he was there.

Karate, judo, and kung fu are martial arts that were successfully exported from their countries of origin. Among the lesser known martial arts, some that have mostly stayed at home, are:

capoeira—Brazilian
cheena adi—Singalese
arnis—Philippine
bando—Burmese
pentjak-silat—Indonesian
gatka—Pakistani
kalari payat—Indian
krabi-krabong—Thai

The first Boston Marathon was run on April 19, 1897.

Squash and handball, played against walls and in a confined space, are descendants of "rackets," a game spawned in an eighteenth-century London debtors' prison. The game still exists, with all its original rules intact, but is rarely played today.

Hurling and shinty are both stick-and-ball games of ancient Gaelic descent, but evolved in slightly different ways. The Irish game, hurling or "hurleys" (the stick is called a hurley), encourages transporting and throwing the ball while it is balanced on the hurley's broad blade. Shinty, the Scottish variant, is the direct ancestor of field hockey and allows striking only with its narrower club, or camon.

Kentucky Derby Winners

Year	Winner	Jockey	Time
1909	Wintergreen	V. Powers	2:08.1
1910	Donau	F. Herbert	2:06.2
1911	Meridian	G. Archibald	2:05
1912	Worth	C. H. Shilling	2:09.2
1913	Donerail	R. Goose	2:04.4
1914	Old Rosebud	J. McCabe	2:03.2
1915	Regret	J. Notter	2:05.2
1916	George Smith	J. Loftus	2:04.3
1917	Omar Khayyam	C. Borel	2:04
1918	Exterminator	W. Knapp	2:10.4
1919	Sir Barton	J. Loftus	2:09.4
1920	Paul Jones	T. Rice	2:09
1921	Behave Yourself	C. Thompson	2:04.1
1922	Morvich	A. Johnson	2:04.3
1923	Zev	E. Sande	2:05.2
1924	Black Gold	J. D. Mooney	2:05.1
1925	Flying Ebony	E. Sande	2:07.3
1926	Bubbling Over	A. Johnson	2:03.4
1927	Whiskery	L. McAtee	2:06
1928	Reigh Count	C. Lang	2:10.2
1929	Clyde Van Dusen	L. McAtee	2:10.4
1930	Gallant Fox	E. Sande	2:07.3
1931	Twenty Grand	C. Kurtsigger	2:01.4
1932	Burgoo King	E. James	2:05.1
1933	Brokers Tip	D. Meade	2:06.4
1934	Cavalcade	M. Garner	2:04
1935	Omaha	W. Saunders	2:05
1936	Bold Venture	I. Hanford	2:03.3
1937	War Admiral	C. Kurtsinger	2:03.1
1938	Lawrin	E. Arcaro	2:04.4
1939	Johnstown	J. Stout	2:03.2
1940	Gallahadion	C. Bierman	2:05
1941	Whirlaway	E. Arcaro	2:01.2

1942	Shut Out	W. D. Wrigh*	2:04.2
1943	Count Fleet	J. Longden	2:04
1944	Pensive	C McCreary	2:04.1
1945	Hoop, Jr.	E. Arcaro	2:07
1946	Assault	W. Mehrtens	2:06.3
1947	Jet Pilot	E. Guerin	2:06.3
1948	Citation	E. Arcaro	2:05.2
1949	Ponder	S. Brooks	2:04.1
1950	Middleground	W. Boland	2:01.3
1951	Count Turf	C. McCreary	2:02.3
1952	Hill Gail	E. Arcaro	2:01.3
1953	Dark Star	H. Moreno	2:02
1954	Determine	R. York	2:03
1955	Swaps	W. Shoemaker	2:01.4
1956	Needles	D. Erb	2:03.2
1957	Iron Liege	W. Hartack	2:02.1
1958	Tim Tam	I. Valenzuela	2:05
1959	Tomy Lee	W. Shoemaker	2:02.1
1960	Venetian Way	W. Hartack	2:02.2
1961	Carry Back	J. Sellers	2:04
1962	Decidedly	W. Hartack	2:00.2
1963	Chateaugay	B. Baeza	2:01.4
1964	Northern Dancer	W. Hartack	2:00
1965	Lucky Debonair	W. Shoemaker	2:01.1
1966	Kauai King	D. Brumfield	2:02
1967	Proud Clarion	R. Ussery	2:00.3
1968	Dancer's Image	R. Ussery	2:02.1
1969	Majestic Prince	W. Hartack	2:01.4
1970	Dust Commander	M. Manganello	2:03.2
1971	Canonero II	G. Avila	2:03.1
1972	Riva Ridge	R. Turcotte	2:01.4
1973	Secretariat	R. Turcotte	1:59.2
1974	Connonade	A. Cordero	2:04
1975	Foolish Pleasure	J. Vasquez	2:02
1976	Bold Forbes	A. Cordero	2:01.3
1977	Seattle Slew	J. Cruquet	2:02.1
1978	Affirmed	S. Cauthan	2:01.1
1979	Spectacular Bid	R. Franklin	2:02.2
1980	Genuine Risk	J. Vasquez	2:02
1981	Pleasant Colony	J. Velasquez	2:02
1982	Gato del Sol	E. Delahoussaye	2:02.2
1983	Sunny's Halo	E. Delahoussaye	2:02.1

A cricket wicket consists of five pieces: three upright wooden rods driven into the ground, called the stumps, and two dowellike pieces sitting loosely in grooves atop them called the bails.

A "sticky wicket," however, is an unpredictable grass surface in front of the batsman. When the ball is "bowled," actually bounced once, to him on spongy turf or on a worn, pitted surface the batsman is in danger of misjudging its trajectory and being caught out (fly ball) or "stumped" (ball knocks the bails off the stump).

Billie Jean King was the first woman ever named "Athlete of the Year" by *Sports Illustrated*, in 1972.

It was Sir Arthur Conan Doyle who made skiing in Switzerland popular. Skis had long been used in Scandinavia, and their use was demonstrated in Switzerland during the 1880s, but it was not until Doyle published an article on the subject in 1894 that the notion caught on.

Super Bowl

Year	Winner	Loser	Site
1967	Green Bay Packers, 35	Kansas City Chiefs, 10	Los Angeles, Coliseum
1968	Green Bay Packers, 33	Oakland Raiders, 14	Orange Bowl, Miami
1969	New York Jets, 16	Baltimore Colts, 7	Orange Bowl, Miami
1970	Kansas City Chiefs, 23	Minnesota Vikings, 7	Tulane Stadium, New Orleans
1971	Baltimore Colts, 16	Dallas Cowboys, 13	Orange Bowl, Miami
1972	Dallas Cowboys, 24	Miami Dolphins, 3	Tulane Stadium, New Orleans
1973	Miami Dolphins, 14	Washington Redskins, 7	Los Angeles Coliseum
1974	Miami Dolphins, 24	Minnesota Vikings, 7	Rice Stadium, Houston
1975	Pittsburgh Steelers, 16	Minnesota Vikings, 6	Tulane Stadium, New Orleans
1976	Pittsburgh Steelers, 22	Dallas Cowboys, 17	Orange Bowl, Miami
1977	Oakland Raiders, 32	Minnesota Vikings, 14	Rose Bowl, Pasadena
1978	Dallas Cowboys, 27	Denver Broncos, 10	Superdome, New Orleans
1979	Pittsburgh Steelers, 35	Dallas Cowboys, 31	Orange Bowl, Miami
1980	Pittsburgh Steelers, 31	Los Angeles Rams, 19	Rose Bowl, Pasadena
1981	Oakland Raiders, 27	Philadelphia Eagles, 10	Superdome, New Orleans
1982	San Francisco 49ers, 26	Cincinnati Bengals, 21	Silverdome, Pontiac, Mich.
1983	Washington Redskins, 27	Miami Dolphins, 17	Rose Bowl, Pasadena

In the 1912 Olympics the US competitor in the pentathlon was George S. Patton, then a cavalry lieutenant and destined for greater fame during World War II. Patton finished fifth. (He was the first of six former US pentathletes to become generals.)

In sports running events it is always the first torso to cross the finish line that wins. Arms, legs, and head breaking the tape are of no account.

Turk Edwards (1907–73), the largest, heaviest tackle of his era and a Hall of Fame member, ended his eight-year football career with a knee injury sustained in a pre-game coin toss ceremony in 1944.

Blind man's bluff is an Americanism for blind man's buff—the "buffing," or buffeting, of the blinded one being the whole soul of the game.

Abroad, it is blind fly (Italy), blind buck (Scandinavia), or blind cow (Germany).

In the mid-nineteenth century Englishmen living in Australia grew weary of sending the hounds after kangaroo. Besides, kangaroo would occasionally take a dog in arms and run with it; they are not terribly sporting. So they imported foxes. These quickly became a numberless pest. The government of Victoria within a few years was paying a bounty on foxes, to the tune of over 20,000 "brushes" per year.

World Series Results, 1903–1983

1903	Boston AL 5, Pittsburgh NL 3
1904	No series
1905	New York NL 4, Philadelphia AL 1
1906	Chicago AL 4, Chicago NL 2
1907	Chicago NL 4, Detroit AL 0, 1 tie
1908	Chicago NL 4, Detroit AL 1
1909	Pittsburgh NL 4, Detroit AL 3
1910	Philadelphia AL 4, Chicago NL 1
1911	Philadelphia AL 4, New York NL 2
1912	Boston AL 4, New York NL 3, 1 tie
1913	Philadelphia AL 4, New York NL 1
1914	Boston NL 4, Philadelphia AL 0
1915	Boston AL 4, Philadelphia NL 1
1916	Boston AL 4, Brooklyn NL 1
1917	Chicago AL 4, New York NL 2
1918	Boston AL 4, Chicago NL 2
1919	Cincinnati NL 5, Chicago AL 3
1920	Cleveland AL 5, Brooklyn NL 2
1921	New York NL 5, New York AL 3
1922	New York NL 4, New York AL 0, 1 tie
1923	New York AL 4, New York NL 2
1924	Washington AL 4, New York NL 3
1925	Pittsburgh NL 4, Washington AL 3

1926	St. Louis NL 4, New York AL 3
1927	New York AL 4, Pittsburgh NL 0
1928	New York AL 4, St. Louis NL 0
1929	Philadelphia AL 4, Chicago NL 1
1930	Philadelphia AL 4, St. Louis NL 2
1931	St. Louis NL 4, Philadelphia AL 3
1932	New York AL 4, Chicago NL 0
1933	New York NL 4, Washington AL 1
1934	St. Louis NL 4, Detroit AL 3
1935	Detroit AL 4, Chicago NL2
1936	New York AL 4, New York NL 2
1937	New York AL 4, New York NL 1
1938	New York AL 4, Chicago NL 0
1939	New York AL 4, Cincinnati NL 0
1940	Cincinnati NL 4, Detroit AL 3
1941	New York AL 4, Brooklyn NL 1
1942	St. Louis NL 4, New York AL 1
1943	New York AL 4, St. Louis NL 1
1944	St. Louis NL 4, St. Louis Al 2
1945	Detroit AL 4, Chicago NL 3
1946	St. Louis NL 4, Boston AL 3
1947	New York AL 4, Brooklyn NL 3
1948	Cleveland AL 4, Boston NL 2
1949	New York AL 4, Brooklyn NL 1
1950	New York AL 4, Philadelphia NL 0
1951	New York AL 4, New York NL 2
1952	New York AL 4, Brooklyn NL 3
1953	New York AL 4, Brooklyn NL 2
1954	New York NL 4, Cleveland AL 0
1955	Brooklyn NL 4, New York AL 3
1956	New York AL 4, Brooklyn NL 3
1957	Milwaukee NL 4, New York AL 3
1958	New York AL 4, Milwaukee NL3
1959	Los Angeles NL 4, Chicago AL 2
1960	Pittsburgh NL 4, New York AL 3
1961	New York AL 4, Cincinnati NL 1
1962	New York AL 4, San Francisco AL 3
1963	Los Angeles NL 4, New York AL 0
1964	St. Louis NL 4, New York AL 3
1965	Los Angeles NL 4, Minnesota AL 3
1966	Baltimore AL 4, Los Angeles NL 0
1967	St. Louis NL 4, Boston AL 3
1968	Detroit AL 4, St. Louis NL 3
1969	New York NL 4, Baltimore AL 1
1970	Baltimore AL 4, Cincinnati NL 1

1971	Pittsburgh NL 4, Baltimore AL 3
1972	Oakland AL 4, Cincinnati NL 3
1973	Oakland AL 4, New York NL 3
1974	Oakland AL 4, Los Angeles NL 1
1975	Cincinnati NL 4, Boston AL 3
1976	Cincinnati NL 4, New York AL 0
1977	New York AL 4, Los Angeles NL 2
1978	New York AL 4, Los Angeles NL 2
1979	Pittsburgh NL 4, Baltimore AL 3
1980	Philadelphia NL 4, Kansas City AL 2
1981	Los Angeles NL 4, New York AL 2
1982	St. Louis NL 4, Milwaukee AL 3
1983	Baltimore AL 4, Philadelphia NL 1

World Series Television Announcers

1947: Bob Stanton, Bob Edge, Bill Slater

1948: Red Barber

1949: Jim Britt

1950: Jack Brickhouse and Jim Britt

1951: Jim Britt and Russ Hodges

1952: Mel Allen and Red Barber

1953: Mel Allen and Vin Scully

1954: Jack Brickhouse and Russ Hodges

1955: Mel Allen and Vin Scully

1956: Mel Allen and Vin Scully

1957: Mel Allen and Al Helfer

1958: Mel Allen and Curt Gowdy

1959: Jack Brickhouse and Vin Scully

1960: Mel Allen and Bob Prince

1961: Mel Allen and Vin Scully

1962: Mel Allen and Russ Hodges

1963: Mel Allen and Vin Scully

1964: Harry Caray, Curt Gowdy, Joe Garagiola, and Phil Rizzuto

1965: Vin Scully and Ray Scott

1966: Vin Scully and Curt Gowdy

1967: Curt Gowdy, Harry Caray, and Ken Coleman

1968: Curt Gowdy, Bill O'Donnell, and George Kell

1969: Curt Gowdy, Bill O'Donnell, and Lindsay Nelson

1970: Curt Gowdy, Tony Kubek, Jim McIntyre, and Chuck Thompson

1971: Curt Gowdy and Tony Kubek

1972: Curt Gowdy, Tony Kubek, Al Michaels, and Monty Moore

1973: Curt Gowdy, Tony Kubek, Monty Moore, and Lindsay Nelson

1974: Curt Gowdy, Vin Scully, Tony Kubek, and Monty Moore
1975: Curt Gowdy, Tony Kubek, Joe Garagiola, Dick Stockton, Ned Martin, and Marty Brennaman
1976. Joe Garagiola, Tony Kubek, Marty Brennaman, and Phil Rizzuto
1977: Keith Jackson, Howard Cosell, Tom Seaver, and Reggie Jackson
1978: Joe Garagiola, Tony Kubek, and Tom Seaver
1979: Keith Jackson, Howard Cosell, and Don Drysdale
1980: Joe Garagiola, Tony Kubek, Tom Seaver, Merle Harmon, and Ron Luciano
1981: Keith Jackson, Howard Cosell, and Al Michaels
1982: Joe Garagiola, Tony Kubek, and Dick Enberg
1983: Al Michaels, Howard Cosell, and Earl Weaver
1984: Vin Scully and Joe Garagiola

Tennis players calling "Love" are really saying "egg," or, more precisely, "zero." The word began in France, where tennis players had the habit of calling *"L'oeuf"* ("egg"). *L'oeuf* was the current slang for "zero," because of the resemblance of an egg to the number zero. In the process of being anglicized, egg became love.

Denied most forms of exercise by the severity of his illness, Napoleon in his last months on St. Helena had a counterweighted seesaw constructed in his billiard room. He believed his workouts had a beneficial effect.

A Roman boxing glove, or *caestus,* was weighted and bristled with spikes. Decisions were often by decease.

One of the more prominent of America's pre-Revolutionary figure skaters was expatriate painter Benjamin West. While in London in 1772 he performed on the frozen Serpentine a special movement called the Philadelphia Salute. The large crowds were delighted. Among those who appreciated West's performance was Colonel William Howe, later to lead British troops against West's countrymen.

Tracy Austin was quite a child prodigy. At the age of 4, she was on the cover of *World Tennis*. At 13, she was on the cover of *Sports Illustrated*.

The St. Louis, Missouri, Racket Club sponsored Charles Lindbergh's 1927 cross-Atlantic solo flight. Lindbergh honored his benefactors in the name of his plane: *The Spirit of St. Louis*.

The Ohio baseball team was the Cleveland Spiders before the name was changed to the Cleveland Indians in honor of Louis Sockolexis, a Maine Indian who was the first native American to play professional baseball.

Manalete (1917–47) and Islero dispatched each other August 29, 1947, in what was to have been the famous bullfighter's triumphal retirement corrida. Islero was a bull of the most dangerous Miura breed.

Cal Hubbard (1900–77) is the only man to have been elected both to the pro football Hall of Fame and to the baseball Hall of Fame. Eight years a tackle with several teams, he became after his retirement from football a most respected baseball umpire.

Inasmuch as knights were not encouraged to kill each other in the formal jousts of the thirteenth through fifteenth centuries, victory was awarded on points. Referees, or marshals as they were called, scored three points for unhorsing or disarming an opponent, one for breaking a lance on the helmet. Points were deducted for striking below the torso, hitting the saddle or the barrier, and for delivering a lance blow crosswise.
Jousters never galloped at each other but closed at a slow trot.

The first printed book devoted to exercise for health and wellbeing was *De Arte Gymnastica* (1573) by Hieronymus Mercurialis. The author recommended exercises for fun, fitness, and for treatment of specific complaints.

Sir Thomas Lipton, the man famous for his tea, was a yachtsman. He tried five times to wrest the America's Cup trophy from the United States.

Carousels did not begin as merry-go-rounds. The carousel can be traced back to the twelfth-century tournaments in which Arabs and Turks fought on horseback. European knights came home from the Crusades with their own version of the carousel. In the late fifteenth century, the Italians called their tournaments *caroselle*, from *garosello*, meaning "little war." In these, knights rode a circular course trying to spear a target ring—or one another. The French mechanized carousels in 1680, the English added steam power, and German cabinetmakers brought them to this country in the 1800s. The little ring still appears on some, a faint reminder of the carousel's warlike past.

Eight Drunken Fairies: Success and Failure

Gustavus III, king of Sweden, was convinced that coffee was poisonous. Not all of his subjects agreed, so Gustavus devised a little experiment to prove his theory. He took two criminals, both condemned to death, and sentenced one to drink coffee every day—he expected the unfortunate fellow to die quickly. He gave the other criminal a sort of pardon—he ordered him to drink tea every day, thus providing a comparison. Two doctors were given the chore of overseeing this experiment. The doctors were the first to die. When Gustavus died, in 1792, the two criminals were still sipping at their commuted punishments. The two men lived long lives. The first to die lived 83 years—he was the tea drinker.

One remarkable idea never tried in World War II was that of Geoffrey Pike to build giant aircraft carriers of ice frozen to shape. The massive ice hulls were to be toughened with an admixture of wood pulp. For ships equipped with enough refrigeration capacity, hulls would be virtually self-renewing, an obvious advantage in dealing with torpedo and bomb damage.

Pike served as an adviser to senior British commanders during the war and proved his plan in principle. It has never been tried.

Columbus didn't make it back to Spain with all three of his ships (and only the *Nina* was destined to make a second voyage to America). On Christmas Eve, 1492, as he and his men were preparing to return to Spain with their exciting news of the New World, the helm of the *Santa Maria* was entrusted to a cabin boy. The ship foundered on a coral reef on the north coast of Hispaniola. Columbus had the ship torn apart: the lumber was used to construct the first European settlement in the New World, a fort in which Columbus left behind forty volunteers. The name of the fort was *La Navidad* ("Christmas").

When Columbus returned to *La Navidad* on his second voyage, he found the forty men dead. The local Indians explained that immediately after his departure, the men had taken to stealing from the Indians and raping their women. The Indians had found it necessary to kill them.

Emma Goldman (1869–1940), a fiery anarchist chiefly remembered for her association with the attempt to assassinate Henry C. Frick, was imprisoned in 1916 for publicly advocating birth control.

Not everyone believed the stories Marco Polo told about what he had seen during his journeys in the east. Many people dismissed his reports as hyperbole; he was nicknamed *Milione* ("million") because it was said that he always talked in millions. He died in 1324. While he was on his deathbed, a priest implored him to repent for all the "lies" he had told about his travels. Polo's last words were a response to the priest: "I have not told half of what I saw."

The Pilgrims landed, of course, at Plymouth Rock (December 14, 1620) but not before landing at a number of other places along the coast. It was not until after a month of desperate exploration and worsening winter seas that the group decided it could not do better than disembark at Plymouth (as they named it, after the last land they had touched in England).

Today he is forgotten, but in his time Joaquin Miller was known to a select few as "the Byron of the West" and "the Kit Carson of Poetry." He was born—in a covered wagon rolling west, or so he claimed—Cincinnatus Heine Miller, sometime around 1841. After working in Oregon as a newspaper editor, lawyer, miner, Indian fighter (he later claimed to have fought with the Indians against the whites), and judge, he turned his hand to poetry. One of his first efforts was a strident defense of the Mexican bandit Joaquin Murietta; the inspired bard later changed his name from Cincinnatus to Joaquin Miller (the name under which he can rarely be found in anthologies of American poetry). Miller drifted into San Francisco, eager to try his luck in that city's literary circles, during the late 1860s. The San Franciscans recognized him as harmless and let him pass through their midst unnoticed. Seeking the recognition he knew he deserved, Miller then went to London. The British intellectuals embraced Miller as an authentic American genius, a true "frontier poet." They were particularly impressed by his floppy sombrero and cowhide boots. The rough-hewn American found kindred spirits among London's Pre-Raphaelite Brotherhood. It was in London that Miller heard himself described as "the Byron of the West," etc. Miller foolishly chose to leave London. He returned to San Francisco, where his poems and special persona still failed to cause excitement.

Miller's poems, collected in such works as *Songs of the Sierras, Fallen Leaves,* and *By the Sun-Down Seas,* were considered bombastic and imitative. He wrote his sentimental doggerel when the spirit moved him and rarely found it neccessary to rephrase a single line. He is perhaps best remembered for his unusual home in Oakland, California. He claimed he couldn't write without the sound of rain on the roof, so he had water pipes installed over the house to sprinkle water on his shingles during those awkward moments when he lacked inspiration.

NOBEL PRIZES

Year	Peace	Chemistry	Physics
1901	J. H. Dunant Frédéric Passy	J. H. van't Hoff	W. C. Roentgen
1902	Elie Ducommun C. A. Gobat	Emil Fischer	H. A. Lorentz Pieter Zeeman
1903	Sir William R. Cremer	S. A. Arrhenius	A. H. Becquerel Marie S. Curie Pierre Curie
1904	Institute of International Law	Sir William Ramsay	J. W. S. Rayleigh
1905	Baroness Bertha von Suttner	Adolf von Baeyer	Philipp Lenard
1906	Theodore Roosevelt	Henri Moissan	Sir Joseph Thomson
1907	E. T. Moneta Louis Renault	Eduard Buchner	A. A. Michelson
1908	K. P. Arnoldson Fredrik Bajer	Sir Ernest Rutherford	Gabriel Lippman
1909	Auguste Beernaert P. H. B. Estournelles de Constant	Wilhelm Ostwald	Guglielmo Marconi C. F. Braun
1910	International Peace Bureau	Otto Wallach	J. D. van der Waals
1911	T. M. C. Asser A. H. Fried	Marie S. Curie	Wilhelm Wien
1912	Elihu Root	Victor Grignard Paul Sabatier	N. G. Dalen
1913	Henri La Fontaine	Alfred Werner	Heike Kamerlingh Onnes
1914		T. W. Richards	Max von Laue
1915		Richard Willstätter	Sir William H. Bragg Sir William L. Bragg
1916			
1917	International Red Cross		C. G. Barkla
1918		Fritz Haber	Max Planck
1919	Woodrow Wilson		Johannes Stark
1920	Léon Bourgeois	Walther Nernst	C. E. Guillaume
1921	Hjalmat Branting C. L. Lange	Frederick Soddy	Albert Einstein

Physiology or Medicine	Literature
E. A. von Behring	R. F. A. Sully-Prudhomme
Sir Ronald Ross	Theodor Mommsen
N. R. Finsen	Bjørnstjerne Bjørnson
Ivan P. Pavlov	Frédéric Mistral
	José Echegaray
Robert Koch	Henryk Sienkiewicz
Camillo Golgi	Giosué Carducci
S. Ramón y Cajal	
C. L. A. Laveran	Rudyard Kipling
Paul Ehrlich	R. C. Eucken
Elie Metchnikoff	
Emil T. Kocher	Selma Lagerlöf
Albrecht Kossel	Paul Heyse
Allvar Gullstrand	Maurice Maeterlinck
Alexis Carrel	Gerhart Hauptmann
C. R. Richet	Sir Rabindranath Tagore
Robert Barany	
	Romain Rolland
	Verner von Heidenstam
	K. A. Gjellerup
	Henrik Pontoppidan
Jules Bordet	C. F. G. Spitteler
S. A. S. Krogh	Knut Hamsun
	Anatole France

Year	Peace	Chemistry	Physics
1922	Fridtjof Nansen	F. W. Aston	N. H. D. Bohr
1923		Fritz Pregl	Robert A. Mullikan
1924			K. M. G. Siegbahn
1925	Sir Austen Chamberlain Charles G. Dawes	Richard Zsigmondy	James Franck Gustav Hertz
1926	Aristide Briand Gustav Stresemann	Theodor Svedberg	J. B. Perrin
1927	F. É. Buisson Ludwig Quidde	Heinrich Wieland	A. H. Compton C. T. R. Wilson
1928		Adolf Windaus	Sir Owen W. Richardson
1929	Frank B. Kellogg	Sir Arthur Harden Hans von Euler- Chelpin	L. V. de Broglie
1930	Nathan Soderblom	Hans Fischer	Sir Chandrasekhara V. Raman
1931	Jane Addams Nicholas Murray Butler	Carl Bosch Friedrich Bergius	
1932		Irving Langmuir	Werner Heisenberg
1933	Sir Norman Angell		P. A. M. Dirac Erwin Schrödinger
1934	Arthur Henderson	Harold C. Urey	
1935	Carl von Ossietzky	Frédéric Joliot-Curie Irène Joliot-Curie	Sir James Chadwick
1936	Carlos Saavedra Lamas	P. J. W. Debye	C. D. Anderson V. F. Hess
1937	E. A. R. Cecil, Viscount Cecil of Chelwood	Sir Walter N. Haworth Paul Karrer	C. J. Davisson Sir George P. Thomson
1938	Nansen International Office for Refugees		Enrico Fermi

Physiology or Medicine	Literature
A. V. Hill	Jacinto Benavente y
Otto Meyerhof	Martinez
Sir Frederick G.	W. B. Yeats
Banting	
J. J. R. Macleod	
Willem Einthoven	W. S. Reymont
	G. B. Shaw
Johannes Fibiger	Grazia Deledda
Julius Wagner-	Henri Bergson
Jauregg	
C. J. H. Nicolle	Sigrid Undset
Christian Eijkman	Thomas Mann
Sir Frederick G.	
Hopkins	
Karl Landsteiner	Sinclair Lewis
Otto H. Warburg	E. A. Karlfeldt
E. D. Adrian	John Galsworthy
Sir Charles	
Sherrington	
Thomas H. Morgan	I. A. Bunin
G. H. Whipple	Luigi Pirandello
G. R. Minot	
W. P. Murphy	
Hans Spemann	
Sir Henry H. Dale	Eugene O'Neill
Otto Loewi	
Albert von Szent-	Roger Martin du
Gyorgyi	Gard
Corneille Heymans	Pearl S. Buck

Year	Peace	Chemistry	Physics
1939		Adolf Butenandt Leopold Ruzicka	E. O. Lawrence
1940–1942		No prizes awarded.	
1943		Georg von Hevesy	Otto Stern
1944	International Red Cross	Otto Hahn	I. I. Rabi
1945	Cordell Hull	A. I. Virtanen	Wolfgang Pauli
1946	J. R. Mott Emily G. Balch	J. B. Sumner J. H. Northrop W. M. Stanley	P. W. Bridgman
1947	American Friends Service Committee and Friends Service Council	Sir Robert Robinson	Sir Edward V. Appleton
1948		Arne Tiselius	P. M. S. Blackett
1949	John Boyd Orr, Baron Boyd-Orr	W. F. Giauque	Yukawa Hideki
1950	Ralph J. Bunche	Otto Diels Kurt Alder	C. F. Powell
1951	Léon Jouhaux	Edwin M. McMillan Glenn T. Seaborg	Sir John D. Cockroft Ernest T. S. Walton
1952	Albert Schweitzer	A. J. P. Martin R. L. M. Synge	Felix Bloch E. M. Purcell
1953	George C. Marshall	Hermann Staudinger	Frits Zernike
1954	Office of the United Nations High Commissioner for Refugees	Linus C. Pauling	Max Born Walther Bothe
1955		Vincent du Vigneaud	Willis E. Lamb, Jr. Polykarp Kusch
1956		Sir Cyril N. Hinshelwood Nikolai N. Semenov	W. B. Shockley W. H. Brattain John Bardeen
1957	Lester B. Pearson	Sir Alexander R. Todd	Tsung-Dao Lee Chen Ning Yang

Physiology or Medicine	Literature
Gerhard Domagk	F. E. Sillanpää
E. A. Doisy	
Henrik Dam	
Joseph Erlanger	J. V. Jensen
H. S. Gasser	
Sir Alexander Fleming	Gabriela Mistral
E. B. Chain	
Sir Howard W. Florey	
H. J. Muller	Hermann Hesse
C. F. Cori	André Gide
Gerty T. Cori	
B. A. Houssay	
Paul H. Mueller	T. S. Eliot
W. R. Hess	William Faulkner
Egas Moniz	
Philip S. Hench	Bertrand Russell,
Edward C. Kendall	Earl Russell
Tadeus Reichstein	
Max Theiler	Pär F. Lagerkvist
S. A. Waksman	François Mauriac
F. A. Lipmann	Sir Winston L. S.
Sir Hans A. Krebs	Churchill
J. F. Enders	Ernest Hemingway
F. C. Robbins	
T. H. Weller	
A. H. T. Theorell	Halldór K. Laxness
D. W. Richards, Jr.	Juan Ramón
A. F. Cournand	Jiménez
Werner Forssmann	
Daniel Bovet	Albert Camus

Year	Peace	Chemistry	Physics
1958	Georges Henri Pire	Frederick Sanger	P. A. Cherenkov Igor Y. Tamm Ilya M. Frank
1959	Philip J. Noel-Baker	Jaroslav Heyrovsky	Emilio Segrè Owen Chamberlain
1960	Albert J. Luthuli	W. F. Libby	D. A. Glaser
1961	Dag Hammarskjöld	Melvin Calvin	Robert Hofstadter R. L. Moessbauer
1962	Linus C. Pauling	M. F. Perutz J. C. Kendrew	L. D. Landau
1963	International Committee of the Red Cross League of Red Cross Societies	Giulio Natta Karl Ziegler	Eugene Paul Wigner Maria Goeppert Mayer J. Hans D. Jensen
1964	Martin Luther King, Jr.	Dorothy Mary Crowfoot Hodgkin	Charles Hard Townes Nikolai Gennadiyevich Basov Alexander Mikhailovich Prokhorov
1965	United Nations International Children's Emergency Fund	Robert Burns Woodward	Richard Phillips Feynman Tomonaga Shinichiro Julian Seymour Schwinger
1966		Robert S. Milliken	Alfred Kastler
1967		Manfred Eigen Ronald George Wreyford Norrish George Porter	Hans Albrecht Bethe
1968	René Cassin	Lars Onsager	Luis W. Alvarez
1969	International Labor Organization	Derek H. R. Barton Odd Hassel	Murray Gell-Mann

Physiology or Medicine	Literature
Joshua Lederberg	Boris L. Pasternak
G. W. Beadle	
E. L. Tatum	
Severo Ochoa	Salvatore
Arthur Kornberg	Quasimodo
Sir Macfarlane Burnet	Alexis St.-L. Léger
P. B. Medawar	
Georg von Bekesy	Ivo Andrić
J. D. Watson	John Steinbeck
F. H. C. Crick	
M. H. F. Wilkins	
Sir John Carew Eccles	George Seferis
Alan Lloyd Hodgkin	
Andrew Fielding Huxley	
Konrad E. Bloch	Jean Paul Sartre
Feodor Lynen	
François Jacob	M. A. Sholokhov
André Lwoff	
Jacques Monod	
Francis Peyton Rous	S. Y. Agnon
Charles Brenton Huggins	Nelly Sachs
Ragnar Granit	Miguel Angel
Haldan Keffer Hartline	Asturias
George Wald	
Robert W. Holley	Kawabata Yasunari
H. Gobind Khorana	
Marshall W. Nirenberg	
Max Delbrück	Samuel Beckett
Alfred D. Hershey	
Salvador E. Luria	

Year	Peace	Chemistry	Physics
1970	Norman E. Borlaug	Luis Federico Leloir	Louis Eugéné Neel Hans Olof Alfven
1971	Willy Brandt	Gerhard Herzberg	Dennis Gabor
1972		Stanford Moore William Howard Stein Christian B. Anfinsen	John Bardeen Leon N. Cooper John Robert Schreiffer
1973	Henry A. Kissinger Le Duc Tho	Ernst Otto Fischer Geoffrey Wilkinson	Leo Esaki Ivar Giaever Brian D. Josephson
1974	Sean MacBride Sato Eisaku	Paul J. Flory	Martin Ryle Antony Hewish
1975	Andrei D. Sakharov	John Warcup Cornforth Vladimir Prelog	Aage N. Bohr Ben Roy Mottelson James Rainwater
1976	Mairead Corrigan Betty Williams	William Nunn Lipscomb	Burton Richter Samuel Chao Chung Ting
1977	Amnesty International	Ilya Prigogine	Philip W. Anderson Sir Nevill F. Mott John H. Van Vleck
1978	Menachem Begin Anwar al-Sadat	Peter Mitchell	Peter Kapitza Arno A. Penzias Robert W. Wilson
1979	Mother Teresa	Herbert C. Brown Georg Wittig	Steven Weinberg Sheldon L. Glashow Abdus Salam
1980	Adolfo Pérez Esquivel	Paul Berg Walter Gilbert Frederick Sanger	James W. Cronin Val L. Fitch
1981	Office of the United Nations High Commissioner for Refugees	Kenichi Fukui Roald Hoffman	Nicolaas Bloembergen Arthur Schawlow Kai M. Siegbahn
1982	Alfonso Garcia Robles Alva Mydral	Aaron Klug	Kenneth G. Wilson
1983	Lech Walesa	Henry Taube	Subrahmanyan, Chandrasekhar, William A. Fowler

Physiology or Medicine	Literature
Julius Axelrod	Alexandr I.
Bernard Katz	Solzhenitsyn
Ulf von Euler	
Earl W. Sutherland	Pablo Neruda
Gerald M. Edelman	Heinrich Böll
Rodney R. Porter	
Konrad Lorenz	Patrick White
Nikolaas Tinbergen	
Karl von Frisch	
Albert Claude	Eyvind Johnson
George Emil Palade	Harry Martinson
Christian de Duve	
David Baltimore	Eugenio Montale
Renato Dulbecco	
Howard M. Temin	
Baruch Samuel	Saul Bellow
Blumberg	
Daniel Carleton	
Gajdusek	
Rosalyn S. Yalow	Vicente Aleixandre
Roger C. L.	
Guillemin	
Andrew V. Schally	
Werner Arber	Isaac Bashevis
Daniel Nathans	Singer
Hamilton O. Smith	
Allan MacLeod	Odysseus Elytis
Cormack	
Godfrey Newbold	
Hounsfield	
Baruj Benacerraf	Czesław Miłosz
George D. Snell	
Jean Dausset	
Roger W. Sperry	Elias Canetti
David H. Hubel	
Torsten N. Wiesel	
Sune K. Bergström	Gabriel Garcia
Bengt J. Samuelsson	Màrquez
John R. Vane	
Barbara	William Golding
McClintock	

Butch Cassidy and the Sundance Kid have long been two of the Old West's most famous folk heroes, and the 1969 movie about them, *Butch Cassidy and the Sundance Kid,* directed by George Roy Hill, did nothing to diminish their fame. According to both the film and popular legend, the two affable outlaws died in a shootout with the Bolivian army in 1919 in San Vicente. Fans of Butch and Sundance will be pleased to learn that the South American "death trap" was probably just one more hoax devised by the wily pair to throw the law off their tracks.

There is no evidence that Butch and Sundance died in South America, and the families of both men insist that the two gringos departed Bolivia in good health and returned to the United States. The Sundance Kid supposedly married his longtime girlfriend, Etta Place, and lived with her in Wyoming until his death in 1957. The stories about Butch's later life are more varied. He was reportedly spotted in Alaska, prospecting for gold with Wyatt Earp; his former girlfriends all claimed that he paid them friendly visits during the 1920s; and his own sister maintained that she saw him, alive and well (he had put on weight), in 1925.

According to some accounts, Butch moved to Spokane, Washington, where he died of pneumonia in the late 1930s; according to others, he went to live in an eastern city, worked for the railroad, and fathered two daughters. The strongest evidence suggests that he made it back to the United States and opened a business making adding machines—a suitable profession for a onetime holdup man.

Montezuma's revenge is a well-known complaint of travelers; Santa Anna's revenge would seem to be chewing gum. The Mexican leader, spared by Sam Houston in 1836 and several times exiled from Mexico, showed up in New York in 1846, where he interested a local inventor in the uses of chicle.

Actually, no uses were discovered. It was through observing the Generalissimo, Presidente, and Perpetual Dictator chewing on the rubbery enigma during brain-storming sessions that its real purpose was divined.

Modern chewing gum is made from a base of polyvinyl acetate, just like record discs.

The color theories of M. E. Chevreul (1786–1889) and Ogden Nicholas Rood (1831–1902) were influential among Post-Impressionist painters, particularly with Georges Seurat. Rood, a New Englander and a weekend painter, on one occasion viewed some modern works at the Durand-Ruel gallery. His opinion then, as expressed to his son, was that perhaps it were better he hadn't written *Modern Chromatics*.

Somewhat later he came to the more forgiving view that his writings had been gratuitously misinterpreted.

During World War II the Germans were for a time prompted to believe the Allies possessed an infrared detector with precision enough to locate U-boats. Acting on this information German scientists developed an ingenious and effective anti-infrared paint. It didn't cut their U-boat losses, since high-resolution radar was the real Allied secret, but ranks as a considerable technological feat nonetheless.

The Atmospheric Railway operated in 1847 along the coast of Devonshire from Exeter to Newton Abbot. Designed by the famous Isambard Kingdom Brunel (1806–59), its motive power was supplied by stationary vacuum pumps that pulled a piston along a continuous slotted fifteen-inch tube running beside the rails.

Although speeds of 68 mph were attained, mid-eighteenth- century materials were not up to visionary designs. Leather flaps that sealed the slot (to maintain vacuum pressure) behind and ahead of the traveling piston stiffened or were eaten by rats.

Current interest in "Star Wars" technology, beams that intercept and destroy satellites, missiles, aircraft, etc., is a revival—though at a higher technological level—of the thinking that produced radar. R. M. Watson-Watt, the inventor of radar, was actually approached by the British Air Ministry to determine the feasibility in 1934 of melting an aircraft with as yet unknown beam weapons. He rejected the concept but announced detection, at least, might be possible.

In those days the Air Ministry was also shopping around for death rays and posted a £1000 reward for the first such contraption to kill a sheep at 100 yards.

Pravda ("Truth"), now the official daily newspaper of the Soviet Union, is descended in name from a revolutionary publication of the 1880s. This first *Pravda,* published in Geneva, was in reality a project of the Czar's secret police, the Okhrana, to discredit Russian radicals by adopting the most extremist views and schemes.

Okhrana agents distinguished themselves at important editorial positions in the Bolshevist press right up to the revolution, an embarrassing success.

The first man to fly was also the first man to die in a flying accident. On November 21, 1783, Pilatre de Rozier flew over the city of Paris in a balloon. His next attempted flight ended in disaster when the hydrogen in his balloon caught fire.

That the English language allows two spellings of dispatch (despatch) is purely the fault of Samuel Johnson. When listing the word for his dictionary he merely misspelled it. The erroneous listing escaped his proofreading.

Civil War artillery underwent a strange transformation in its design. Beginning with the Dahlgren gun, tough because it was smoothly shaped and hence evenly cooled, artillery became almost reliable—it didn't blow up nearly so many gun crews.

The Dahlgren gun became a Rodman gun if it were cooled after casting from inside its bore, making the interior barrel surface strongest. An even more "reliable" gun.

The final development was to turn the Rodman gun into a Parrot gun, i.e., to shrink fit red-hot wrought-iron hoops around the breech for even greater strength and range. But the hot iron often destroyed the carefully achieved effects of Dalhgren shaping and Rodman cooling, and once again, now throwing a heavier shell farther, artillery was blowing up gun crews.

No fewer than thirteen American presidents have served who were elected by less than a majority of the popular vote. The smallest percentage was garnered by John Quincy Adams in 1824, 32 percent. (Woodrow Wilson was elected to *both* of his terms by less than 50 percent of the popular vote.)

Official tallies, of course, are of electoral college ballots and not by the popular count.

Within the long, many-branched history of Chinese martial arts, several kung fu styles are considered a little esoteric even by Chinese standards. The Tibetan hop-gar school, also called mui-fa-jeong, is the plum-stump style. Students and masters practice atop large stakes ("plum stumps") driven into the ground, moving and menacing airily around an array of five to seven slender pedestals.

Adherents of the Eight Drunken Fairies style feign a calculated drunkenness, dealing mayhem from tipsy and collapsed postures.

And a practitioner of kung-li-ch'uan, or sa-kung-li ("stupid kung fu"), may spend half a lifetime dealing himself crippling blows to develop his toughness.

324

See You Next
Purple: Time

According to the Bible, Methuselah lived 969 years. His name-sake, a bristlecone pine in northern California, has outdone him: the tree has a confirmed age of 4600 years and is believed to be the oldest living thing on Earth. The largest living thing on Earth is also a tree, a sequoia named General Sherman in California's Sequoia National Park. It stands 270 feet tall.

There are two dates on the flag of Bulgaria: 681, the year in which the Bulgars settled the area they now inhabit, and 1944, the year in which Bulgaria was liberated from Nazi rule.

Of the nineteenth century Mark Twain said, "It's two most interesting characters were Helen Keller and Napoleon."

In all medieval rituals for attaining invisibility, the thing cannot be done in less than nine days beginning, always, on Wednesday. Hence, no one can become invisible before Thursday.

Not all insects have fleeting lifespans. Queen termites may survive for more than fifty years. Queen ants can live up to fifteen years; worker ants live about seven. A queen bee may live up to six years; a worker bee has an expected lifespan of six months.

The Spanish-American War lasted 112 days; World War II lasted 2194. The so-called Hundred Years War lasted 116 years.

Swans live up to seventy years.

Greenwich, England, wasn't officially named the world's prime meridian until October 13, 1884, when the decision was put to a vote at an international conference in Washington, D.C. Not all of the delegates were in favor of Greenwich. Some thought Jerusalem made a more sensible choice; others opted for Egypt's Great Pyramid. The French obstinately insisted on Paris. They finally said they would adopt Greenwich only if the British would adopt the metric system. France didn't adjust to Greenwich until 1911, when it gave up Paris Mean Time (which was one-fifth of a second off Greenwich Mean Time).

Bulova Watch had the honor of broadcasting the first commercial television advertisement, on July 1, 1941. The twenty-second ad cost $9.

The gestation period of an elephant is about two years.

The name of London's famous Big Ben does not refer to the tower. Nor does it refer to the tower's clock. Big Ben is the largest of the clock's bells; it weighs thirteen tons. The bell is named for Sir Benjamin Hall, commissioner of works when it was installed.

Dates of the solstices, corresponding to the longest and shortest days of the year, are not the times of maximum or minimum Earth distance from the sun. These are (perihelion) January 2 and (aphelion) July 4.

The time zones established in the United States are the invention of Charles Ferdinand Dowd, principal of Temple Grove Ladies Seminary in Saratoga Springs, New York. Until Dowd came up with the idea of dividing the country into zones, in 1870, almost every county, city, and even hamlet kept its own local time (called sun time). For example, when it was 12:15 PM in Portland, Maine, it was noon in New York City and 11:40 in Buffalo, New York. US railroads had more than eighty different standards of time, and a traveler crossing the country by rail had to reset his watch twenty times. Dowd did away with the local time variations by dividing the country by meridians into zones that were one hour—15 degrees—apart. The zones—Eastern, Central, Mountain, and Pacific—were marked off from Greenwich, England. In 1872 the US railroads proposed adoption of so-called railroad time—using the four time zones—and the federal government agreed in 1883. At noon on November 18, 1883, the railroads and most of the nation adjusted their clocks to the new system.

Geese are the longest-lived domesticated birds: some live twenty-five years.

One of the first clocks made in America—and it may well have been the very first—was a wooden clock assembled by Benjamin Banneker, a free black living in Baltimore, Maryland. He built the clock in 1753, and it kept perfect time until the day, in October of 1806, that Banneker was buried: while his funeral was in progress, his home was destroyed by fire.

The common housefly has a lifespan of between nineteen and thirty days.

327

September 2, 1751, was immediately followed by September 14, 1751, in England and her colonies. This was the year England finally abandoned the Julian calendar for the Gregorian, last of the European nations to do so.

In addition to making up those eleven days in September, New Year's Day was moved from March 25 to January 1, commencing officially as of January 1, 1752. Nothing can have happened in English or American history on January 1, 1751, through March 24, 1751, as these dates never existed.

Thus, when inattentive historians or unaware readers calculate an interval as between, say, January 25, 1748, and March 25, 1749—which is only two months—they may erroneously add an extra year.

In the year 2000, the average American will be 36 years old.

Of all the hobo symbols inscribed on bridges, water tanks, and railroad stations around the country, the most easily recognized are merely Arabic numerals. The single digit "6," for example, states with eloquent brevity that six months in jail is the usual lot of hoboes here.

Even in the dirty and dangerous big cities they love to call home, and even with their tiny size, sparrows, hardy birds, live as long as twenty years.

DERIVATION OF DAYS AND MONTHS

Day/Month	Named after
Sunday	the Sun
Monday	the Moon
Tuesday	Tiu, Norse god of war
Wednesday	Woden, Anglo-Saxon chief of gods
Thursday	Thor, Norse god of thunder
Friday	Frigg, Norse goddess
Saturday	Saturn, Roman god of harvests
January	Janus, Roman god of doors and gates
February	Februa, Roman period of purification
March	Mars, Roman god of war
April	aperire, Latin 'to open'
May	Maia, Roman goddess of spring and growth

June	Juno, Roman goddess of marriage
July	Julius Caesar
August	Augustus, first emperor of Rome
September	septem, Latin 'seven'
October	octo, Latin 'eight'
November	novem, Latin 'nine'
December	decem, Latin 'ten'

Although the Gregorian calendar is in use officially throughout most of the world, sometimes sharing the year with Buddhist or Moslem calendars, these nine nations prefer to do without Gregorian dating altogether: Iran, Jordan, Kuwait, Libya, Oman, Saudi Arabia, and Yemen use various Islamic calendars; Bhutan adheres strictly to its Buddhist calendar; and Nepal has a system all of its own, starting its twelve-month year in mid-April.

At the end of the year 1 BC our calendar begins immediately with AD 1. There is no year "0."

Blue jays live up to fourteen years in the wild, cardinals have been known to live twice as long.

The French revolutionary calendar was in use for just over twelve years, from October 5, 1793, to January 1, 1806, but it seems a little longer since the beginning of time was literally backdated to September 23, 1792, for official record keeping.

Fabre d'Eglantine (1750–94), who named the new thirty-day months, was the first to have this privilege since the Caesars. His choices:

Vendémaire (Sept. 23–Oct. 21)—wine month
Brumaire (Oct. 22–Nov. 20)—foggy month
Frimaire (Nov. 21–Dec. 20)—frosty month
Nivôse (Dec. 21–Jan. 19)—snowy month
Pluviôse (Jan. 20–Feb. 18)—rainy month
Ventôse (Feb. 19–Mar. 20)—windy month
Germinal (Mar. 21–Apr. 19)—budding month
Floréal (Apr. 20–May 19)—flowering month
Prairial (May 20–June 18)—meadow month
Messidor (June 19–July 18)—reaping month
Thermidor (July 19–Aug. 17)—hot month

Fructidor (Aug. 18–Sept. 17)—fruit month

The five days left over each year—six in a leap year—were made national holidays.

TRADITIONAL ANNIVERSARY GIFTS

BIRTHSTONES

Year	Gift	Month	Hebrew (Biblical)	Present day
1	paper	January	garnet	garnet
2	cotton	February	amethyst	amethyst
3	leather	March	jasper	aquamarine
4	fruit, flowers			bloodstone
5	wood	April	sapphire	diamond
6	iron, sugar	May	chalcedony	emerald
7	wool, copper		carnelian	chrysoprase
8	bronze		agate	
9	pottery	June	emerald	pearl
10	tin, aluminur			moonstone
11	steel			alexandrite
12	silk, fine line	July	onyx	ruby
13	lace			carnelian
14	ivory	August	carnelian	peridot
15	crystal			sardonyx
20	china	September	chrysolite	sapphire
25	silver			lapis lazuli
30	pearl	October	aquamarine	opal
35	coral		beryl	tourmaline
40	ruby	November	topaz	topaz
45	sapphire	December	ruby	turquoise
50	golden			zircon
55	emerald			
60	diamond			
75	diamond			

The average lifespan of a (wild) turkey is six years.

The human being is the longest-lived mammal.

The smallest of the world's time zones is that just east of the International Date Line. It comprises only the west coast of Alaska, the Aleutian Islands, and a few Pacific archipelagos. Time here is an hour earlier than Hawaii, six hours earlier than New York, and twenty-four hours earlier than easternmost Siberia, which is just fifty miles away across the Bering Strait.

Certainly the least populous time zone is that of Greenland, three hours east of New York. Because of its barrenness, no one has chosen officially a time zone for the interior of Greenland. Only along the sparsely settled coasts is there a correct time of day.

Cockroaches have a lifespan of about forty days.

Easter can fall on any date between March 22 and April 25. It is always the first Sunday after the full moon on or next after March 21.

The last time Easter fell on April 25 was in 1943. It will not happen again this century. Easter on March 22 last occurred in 1818; this will not happen at all in the twentieth century.

The seventeen-year cicada, or locust, requires seventeen years of underground feeding to mature in the north, but only thirteen years in the southern United States.

Domestic cats have lifespans of about fifteen years; some live twice that long.

To the critcal ear, it seems, the tempo of a Beethoven symphony is always too fast or too slow. Conductors have especially strong views on the subject: the slowest major recording of Beethoven's Ninth Symphony is Wilhelm Furtwangler's, seventy-three minutes and fifty seconds; Arturo Toscanini, the fastest, did it in sixty-three minutes and twenty-five seconds—a great improvement, or a travesty, depending on your viewpoint.

During October–December 1929 the Soviet Union adopted a calendar with only a five-day week. Days of the week had no names but were called yellow, orange, red, purple, and green. (Everyone had one color-coded day off per week.)

Although this attempt at suppression of the weekend, and its religious significance, was quickly abandoned, efforts continued until 1940 to implement a popularly acceptable five-day week with number names for the days.

Whangdoodles and Gandy Dancers: Transportation

John Denver wrote "Leaving on a Jet Plane," made famous by Peter, Paul and Mary.

American author James Agee died in a taxicab.

Northwest Orient Airlines in 1959 installed a Lowery organ on its New York to Minneapolis-St. Paul route. A cadre of six organists rotated flight shifts.

Wheeled toys have been found in Mexican tombs that date to the first century AD. However, the wheel was not used for transportation in the Americas until after the arrival of the Spanish.

Man's first unmoored balloon ascent occurred in November 1783 (Pilatre de Rozier and the Marquis d'Arlandes). It required only fifteen years more to devise the first aerial stunt, when Testu Brissy took a specially trained horse up with him.

During the heyday of the 1920s, Zelda and F. Scott Fitzgerald amused themselves by taking rides around New York on the rooftops of taxicabs.

Both Isaac Asimov and Ray Bradbury—two of the greatest prophets of space travel—refuse to travel by airplane. Bradbury also doesn't drive a car, although he will consent to be a passenger.

Henry Ford sold his first car to a dentist from Chicago named Pfennig on July 15, 1903.

It was believed at the time of her launching in 1936 that the *Queen Mary* was too large to roll in high seas. Thus, not until months and multiple injuries later was she fitted out with handrails.

On January 7, 1784, Dr. John Jeffries and Jean-Pierre Blanchard took part in the first balloon flight across the English Channel. Born in Boston, Dr. Jeffries had been a Loyalist during the American Revolution and had moved to England; Blanchard was an enthusiastic French aeronaut. The two men took off from Dover, headed for France. They carried food and drink, thirty-four books, and a letter. (This was the first air-mail letter. It was from William Franklin, illegitimate son of Benjamin Franklin, to Temple Franklin, William's illegitimate son.) The balloon did not achieve the desired altitude. In fact, during most of the Channel crossing it bobbed just over the waves and threatened to land itself on the water. Trying to lighten the craft, the two men began throwing things overboard. They took off most of their clothing and, in a final effort to do away with unneeded weight, they emptied their bladders over the side. They succeeded in keeping the balloon aloft and ultimately landed in France in the forest of Guines.

The *Great Eastern,* oceangoing paddlewheeler, was the largest iron ship of her day. Christened *Leviathan*—but the name never took— she required three months to launch, November 1857 to January 1858, as the largest hydraulic rams available exploded while pushing her inches at a time into the Thames.

Her sails were almost never raised, though she carried six masts, called Monday, Tuesday, Wednesday, Thursday, Friday, and Saturday. "There is no Sunday at sea," one wag said.

Although the helicopter was not perfected until the twentieth century, toy helicopters were made as far back as the fourteenth.

The world's first rail fatality was a Member of Parliament, William Huskisson (1770–1830), killed by the famous *Rocket* while he was officially opening the Manchester-Liverpool line.

Sometime during April of 1925 a film was shown during an Imperial Airways flight from Britain to the Continent. It was the first time a film had been shown on an airplane. The film shown, *The Lost World,* was an Arthur Conan Doyle adventure yarn remarkable for its special effects, which recreate prehistoric animals encountered on a scientific journey to a deserted island. The film was made in 1925 and was, of course, silent.

The shortest covered railroad bridge in the world is a ninety-foot span at Wolcott, Vermont, built by the St. Johnsbury & Lamoille County Railroad.

Boston was the first US city to have a subway. The first branch of the Boston subway, the Boylston Street line running between the Public Gardens and Park Street, opened on September 1, 1897.

An unexpected benefit of the Panama passage to oceangoing vessels is the trip across Gatun Lake—its fresh water kills barnacles accumulated on hulls.

The military vehicles known as tanks got their name somewhat indirectly. The first tanks were developed in England during World War I. The experimental models had to be moved from place to place during the final tests, and the committee in charge of the new weapon was given the responsibility of keeping the work secret. It was a difficult task: the large, canvas-covered objects being shipped around the countryside were attracting attention. One member of the committee suggested calling the mysterious packages "water carriers." He thought they could claim the "water carriers" were for use in the Sinai desert. This notion did not please another of the committee's members. "We call everything by initials." he said. "I will not stand for being on anything called the W. C. Committee." After further discussion, the word *tank* was suggested. It stuck.

The name of William "Captain" Kidd's ship was the *Adventure Galley*.

The Sears Tower in Chicago has the world's fastest passenger elevator. It is capable of traveling at twenty miles per hour as it moves up and down the 1452-foot building.

The Central Pacific and Union Pacific railroads, which met each other May 10, 1869, at Promontory Point, Utah, to complete America's first transcontinental rail route, were subsidized by the government at from $16,000 to $48,000 per mile of track, depending on terrain.

Richard Wagner was inspired to write the opera *Der Fliegende Hollander* ("The Flying Dutchman") by the legend of one particular Dutch ship. The Dutch East Indiaman captained by Hendrik Vanderdecken sailed from Amsterdam in 1680 bound for the Dutch East Indies settlement at Batavia. The ship never made it, but beginning in 1680 there were numerous reported sightings of it. The last duly reported sighting of the doomed *Flying Dutchman* was in October 1959 by officers of a Dutch freighter. Earlier sightings include one entered into his diary by King George V of England in July 1881.

Sir Isaac Newton once calculated the tonnage of Noah's Ark: taking the cubit to be 20½ inches, Ark length therefore 515 feet and beam 86 feet, he obtained a displacement of 18,231 tons.

When it commenced in 1869 the transcontinental rail service from Omaha to Sacramento offered three fares: first class ($100), coach ($75), and immigrant ($40).

The word *mush,* used as a command to the huskies pulling a sled, is from the Canadian French *mouche!* ("run!"), which in turn is from *moucher,* "to fly," from the French *mouche,* meaning the insect fly.

Though its etymology is still a mystery, and the word has not found its way into the *Oxford English Dictionary,* writers of the early nineteenth century called the recently improved machine lathe a "go-cart."

The first airplane passenger was Charles W. Furnas, the Wright brothers' mechanic. On May 14, 1908, Wilbur took him for a twenty-nine-second, 1968-foot flight.

In 1837 steerage passage for German immigrants leaving the port of Bremen for the United States cost $16.

The lowest toll ever paid transiting the Panama Canal was 36 cents. It was paid by author Richard Haliburton, who swam the locks over the course of several days. He was charged, as with any vessel, by cargo tonnage—in this case 140 lbs.

The first commercial airline was KLM of the Netherlands, which made its first run from Amsterdam to London on May 17, 1920.

The Washington Monument's first elevator, steam-powered, was considered so dangerous that it was open only to men. Women and children had to climb the much safer 897 steps to the top.

Many railroading terms are a familiar part of the language, e.g., caboose, main-line, highball; some do not show their railroad origins, like gangbuster, for a labor agitator, or "riding high," for riding atop a freight car. Some fanciful words that didn't find their way into the vernacular are whiffletree, for a coupling; whangdoodle, a telephone along the line; nixie, for a dead letter; pifflicated, drunk; and gandy dancer, a laborer (from a tool manufacturer, the Gandy Co. of Chicago).

That most ubiquitous of all tools, the doohickey, existed in the railroader's vocabulary, too. Within this trade it was a handle or rod to assist in setting a brake.

Debutante Slouch:
Upward Mobility

The first American Indian admitted to West Point was David Moniac of the Creek tribe. He rose to the rank of major and was killed in the Battle of Wahoo Swamp in 1836 while fighting against the Seminole Indians in Florida.

Both Millard Fillmore and Andrew Johnson were indentured servants in their youth. Johnson was indentured to a tailor, Fillmore to a clothmaker.

The history of the word *snob* is that of a word moving up in the world. Its original late-eighteenth-century meaning was cobbler or cobbler's apprentice. Soon it was broadened to include the whole lower, laboring classes. By 1840 it meant vulgar, and by 1850 it signified the vulgar imitators of wealth and refinement.

And by 1910 this social-climbing word described attitudes of the genuinely wealthy and refined.

In 1892 the minimum age for marriage of Italian girls was raised to 12.

Only 36 of the roughly 900 hereditary titles of Great Britain are descended in lineages that originate before the year 1500.

Several famous men served as volunteer ambulance drivers during World War I, among them Malcolm Cowley, e. e. cummings, Dashiell Hammett, Ernest Hemingway, John Howard Lawson, John Dos Passos, and Robert Service.

Marie Dolores Eliza Rosanna Gilbert was born in Limerick, Ireland, in 1818. She shucked off most of this weighty baptismal inheritance when still a young girl. She wanted to dance and, more precisely, she wanted to be a Spanish dancer. From Dolores she made Lola; for a surname she invented Montez.

At 19, the dark-eyed beauty eloped with a British army officer. The marriage soon ended in divorce, and Montez moved to her adopted homeland, Spain, to study dancing. Her studies did her little harm and little good: when she debuted on the English stage in 1843, she was a dismal failure. But Montez's beauty, charm, and unflagging courage won her a fascinating life. Having bombed in Britain, she went to the Continent, where she soon became famous for her affairs with notable men, among them Franz Liszt and Alexandre Dumas pere. In 1846 she became the mistress of King Ludwig I of Bavaria; he made her countess of Lansfeld.

Montez's dabbling in politics and the outlandish sums Ludwig lavished on her did not please the local populace and helped provoke the Revolution of 1848. Banished from Bavaria, she toured Spain, Italy, and Greece with a new husband. Audiences failed to respond to her special style, so she left both her husband and Europe and set sail for New York in 1851. When no one on the East Coast threw roses at her feet, she went to San Francisco, arriving there in 1853. Known by now as "the countess," she finally found the success she sought.

Her act in San Francisco began with a play she had written, *Lola Montez in Bavaria,* in which she played herself with unabashed exactitude. The play did not make her famous, however. Her fame in San Francisco was due to a special dance she had perfected, a version of the tarantella called the Spider Dance. Montez would pretend to be attacked by spiders and would leap around the stage trying to free herself. This leaping involved much lifting of skirts (shy miners would avert their eyes). Or she would pretend to be attacked by just one spider hidden somewhere on her luscious body. She would delight the audiences by exploring for that pest. Sometimes she took the role of the spider (although how she did so is no longer clear).

When audiences tired of her Spider Dance, Montez married a third time and tried to settle down in Grass Valley, Nevada, where she had a cute little villa and passed the time playing with her pets, which included dogs, parrots, and a small bear. In 1855 she decided to make a comeback on the distant stages of Australia; she was back in San Francisco in 1856. Although she no longer performed the Spider Dance, she still showed signs of her enthusiastic approach to life: she auctioned off her jewelery to help support the children of a man who jumped ship on the return voyage from Australia. No one out west was interested in Montez's dancing, however. She left San Francisco in October 1856 and went to New York. She died in 1861 in a room on West 17th Street.

Nathan Bedford Forrest was named the first Grand Wizard of the Ku Klux Klan in 1867.

American naval hero John Paul Jones was born just John Paul. In 1773, while Jones was in command of a ship called *Betsy* off the coast of Tobago, members of his crew mutinied, and he killed one of the sailors, probably in self-defense. He decided not to wait around for a trial, however, and fled. It was then, in an attempt to throw the law off his tracks, that he added "Jones" to his name.

The first professor of Italian at Columbia University was Lorenzo Da Ponte, the Italian adventurer, poet, and librettist—he wrote the librettos of three of Mozart's operas. When he arrived in the United States in 1805, all he had to his name was a box of violin strings.

Rumors that cockroaches will take over the earth in the event of nuclear catastrophe are not without foundation. An average cockroach can take 60,000 roentgen of radiation; humans can absorb no more than a few hundred.

The only rhinoceros to be elected to public office was Cacareco, voted into the Sao Paulo, Brazil, city council in October 1959. She was not allowed by the authorities to claim her seat.

Milwaukee's Pabst beer won a blue ribbon at the 1893 Chicago's World's Fair, becoming Pabst Blue Ribbon.

Wyatt Earp, famous lawman and dubious hero of the gunfight at the OK Corral, lived long enough to see the heyday of the Old West recreated on film. He spent his last years in Los Angeles, hanging around movie lots hoping to be asked for advice. When he died, in January 1929, William S. Hart and Tom Mix served among his pall-bearers.

Issei are first generation Japanese immigrants, people born in Japan; Nisei are second generation, born in the United States; Sansei are the children of Nisei, and Yonsei are the children of Sansei.

On June 16, 1884, La Marcus Thompson, who made his fortune by inventing seamless hosiery, opened the first American roller coaster, the Switchback Railway on West 10th Street in Coney Island.

"I only regret that I have but one life to give for my country," exclaimed Nathan Hale on that sunny morning of September 22, 1776, when he was hanged by the British for spying. Hale's executioner was a 15-year-old black named Bill Richmond. Richmond was a Tory, and he later went to England, where he gained fame as the national heavy-weight boxing champion.

Ho Chi Minh left his homeland, Vietnam, when he was 21 and went to London, where he worked in the kitchen of the Carlton Hotel under the tutelage of French chef Escoffier.

The future Duke of Wellington had to leave Eton when he was 15 because his parents no longer had the money to keep him there.

John Fitzgerald Kennedy was not the youngest president in US history: he was the youngest person ever elected to the office, however. Kennedy was 43 when he was inaugurated; Theodore Roosevelt was 42 when he took over the presidency following the assassination of McKinley.

News from Jamaica, October 6, 1751: "There is advice that one Dobbins, in a sloop at Parker's Bay had turned pirate, robbed a sloop off Blackwater, and cut the master's nose off and had also attempted to take two or three canoes off Whitehouse."

US dramatist Eugene O'Neill spent his last days in a Boston hotel. His last words, spoken minutes before he died, were, "I knew it, I knew it! Born in a hotel room—goddamn it!—and dying in a hotel room!"

Hannibal Hamlin occupies a small space in that bleak region of anonymity that is home to most American vice-presidents. However, Hamlin, who was Lincoln's first vice-president, performed at least two noteworthy acts during his term of office. A teetotaler, he banned the sale of alcoholic beverages in the Senate chambers, incurring the indignant wrath of that hard-drinking crew. And, during the summer of 1864, Hamlin enlisted as a private in the Maine Coast Guards. During his two months' service, the 55-year-old vice-president did guard duty and worked as a cook. Hamlin was the highest elected official ever to serve in so low a military rank while still in office.

We are familiar with the "debutante slouch," that affectation of graceful world-weariness greatly admired by blasé youth of the 1920s and 1930s, but proper posturing in the 1870s required an "Alexandra limp."

Fashionable English ladies adopted the disability that had befallen Crown Princess Alexandra (1844–1925) after a bout of rheumatic fever in February 1867. Those in the know limped on the right. No one feigned, however, the increasing deafness of Alexandra, also a result of her illness.

Brilliant Boots:
Vanity

James Joyce's last words were "Does nobody understand?"

The motto of Harry Houdini, American magician and escape artist, was "Secure knots secure not Houdini."

Grace Kelly is, thus far, the only movie star to appear on a postage stamp. Monaco printed stamps commemorating her marriage to Prince Rainier IV in 1956.

The largest architectural dome in the world is that of St. Peter's, Rome. The second largest is atop the state capitol building in Providence, Rhode Island.

Limelight, introduced around 1830, was indeed the light from lime heated to incandescence, but the amounts of gas required made this kind of illumination both expensive and temperamental.

Jacques Offenbach (1819–80), composer of operettas (the cancan is taken from one), was not a handsome person; he attracted insults. Of him the Goncourt brothers wrote: "a skeleton in pince-nez who looks as if he is raping a double-bass."

Among members of German university dueling societies the precaution was often taken of placing a hair within and along the length of a facial wound. This was to insure infection and thus a highly visible scar when the cut healed. Salt was another expedient.

Castes in India were thought to have a universal existence. Even cobras must have castes, reasoned the Hindus, the Brahmans among them having the deadliest bite.

Colonial New Jersey had a law on its books that provided: "all women, of whatever rank, profession or degree, whether virgins, maids, or widows, who shall after this act impose upon, seduce, or betray into matrimony any of his Majesty's subjects, by virtue of scents, cosmetics, washes, paints, artificial teeth, false hair, or high-heeled shoes, shall incur the penalty of the law now in force against witchcraft and like misdemeanors."

One day, gentleman farmer James Fenimore Cooper was reading an English romance aloud to his wife. When he reached the end of the book, the exasperated Cooper exclaimed, "Pshaw! I can write a better novel than that." His wife challenged him to try. The result was *Precaution* (1820), Cooper's first novel. It was not a great success, but it inspired Cooper to relinquish the quiet life of the country gentleman and become a novelist.

The flag that Columbus had with him on his first expedition to the New World was white with two green letters, *F* (Ferdinand) and *Y* (Isabella), divided by a green cross. Over each letter was a gold crown.

The earliest surviving dentures are a set of calves' teeth bound with gold wire found in an Etruscan cave.

Theodore Roosevelt was a man of boundless energy. He also delighted in being the center of attention. It was said of him that, "When he attends a wedding, he wants to be the bride, and when he attends a funeral, he wants to be the corpse."

Miss America Winners

1921	Margaret Gorman, Washington, D.C.
1922–23	Mary Campbell, Columbus, Ohio
1924	Ruth Malcolmson, Philadelphia, Pennsylvania
1925	Fay Lamphier, Oakland, California
1926	Norma Smallwood, Tulsa, Oklahoma
1927	Lois Delaner, Joliet, Illinois
1933	Marion Bergeron, West Haven, Connecticut
1935	Henrietta Leaver, Pittsburgh, Pennsylvania
1936	Rose Coyle, Philadelphia, Pennsylvania
1937	Bette Cooper, Bertrand Island, New Jersey
1938	Marilyn Meseka, Marion, Ohio
1939	Patricia Donnelly, Detroit, Michigan
1940	Frances Marie Burke, Philadelphia, Pennsylvania
1941	Rosemary LaPlanche, Los Angeles, California
1942	Jo-Carroll Dennison, Tyler, Texas
1943	Jean Bartel, Los Angeles, California
1944	Venus Ramey, Washington, D.C.

1945	Bess Myerson, New York City, N.Y.
1946	Marilyn Buferd, Los Angeles, California
1947	Barbara Walker, Memphis, Tennessee
1948	BeBe Shopp, Hopkins, Minnesota
1949	Jacque Mercer, Litchfield, Arizona
1951	Yolande Betbeze, Mobile, Alabama
1952	Coleen Kay Hutchins, Salt Lake City, Utah
1953	Neva Jane Langley, Macon, Georgia
1954	Evelyn Margaret Ay, Ephrata, Pennsylvania
1955	Lee Merriwether, San Francisco, California
1956	Sharon Ritchie, Denver, Colorado
1957	Marian McKnight, Manning, South Carolina
1958	Marilyn Van Derbur, Denver, Colorado
1959	Mary Ann Mobley, Brandon, Mississippi
1960	Lynda Lee Mead, Natchez, Mississippi
1961	Nancy Fleming, Montague, Michigan
1962	Maria Fletcher, Asheville, North Carolina
1963	Jacquelyn Mayer, Sandusky, Ohio
1964	Donna Axum, El Dorado, Arkansas
1965	Vonda Kay Van Dyke, Phoenix, Arizona
1966	Deborah Irene Bryant, Overland Park, Kansas
1967	Jane Anne Jayroe, Laverne, Oklahoma
1968	Debra Dene Barnes, Moran, Kansas
1969	Judith Anne Ford, Belvidere, Illinois
1970	Pamela Anne Eldred, Birmingham, Michigan
1971	Phyllis Anne George, Denton, Texas
1972	Laurie Lea Schaefer, Columbus, Ohio
1973	Terry Anne Meeuwsen, DePere, Wisconsin
1974	Rebecca Ann King, Denver, Colorado
1975	Shirley Cothran, Fort Worth, Texas
1976	Tawney Elaine Godin, Yonkers, N.Y.
1977	Dorothy Kathleen Benham, Edina, Minnesota
1978	Susan Perkins, Columbus, Ohio
1979	Kylene Baker, Galax, Virginia
1980	Cheryl Prawitt, Ackerman, Mississippi
1981	Susan Powell, Elk City, Oklahoma
1982	Elizabeth Ward, Russellville, Arkansas
1983	Debra Maffett, Anaheim, California

Herbert Spencer was only one of nine children born to his parents—but he was the only one to survive to adult life. Spencer later made a name for himself as a philosopher. Along with Charles Darwin and Thomas Huxley, he helped establish the theory of evolution. Spencer was particularly vocal on the subject of "survival of the fittest."

Grace Slick of the Jefferson Airplane named her daughter god. Explaining the lowercase *g*, she said, "We've got to be humble about this."

Benjamin Franklin whitened his teeth with a preparation of powdered charcoal and honey.

A few pieces of toppled marble columns are all that remain of the temple of Artemis (Diana) at Ephesus, one of the Seven Wonders of the Ancient World. The temple was destroyed by fire in 356 BC. The fire was the result of arson, and it wasn't difficult for the outraged Ephesians to find the culprit. He proudly came forward and announced that he had destroyed the temple deliberately in order that his name might live forever. The man was executed, and the citizens of Ephesus methodically expunged every record of his name from their rolls. They also made it unlawful to mention his name. Had they not gone to such great lengths, the man's name might have been forgotten. But it has remained: Herostratus. The villain got his wish.

Louis Vuitton began branding his initials on his canvas luggage in 1898.

Michelangelo signed only one of his sculptures, the *Pietà*.

Stumping for his congressional campaign of 1829, Davy Crockett concluded a speech, saying:
"Friends, fellow-citizens, brothers and sisters: they accuse me of adultery; it's a lie—I never ran away with any man's wife, that was not willing, in my life. They accuse me of gambling, it's a lie—for I always plunk down the cash.
"Friends, fellow-citizens, brothers and sisters: they accuse me of being a drunkard, it's a d——d eternal lie—for whiskey can't make me drunk."

Throughout the history of Western art aristocrats had their portraits painted more frequently than any other group until 1860 when, for the first time, bourgeois faces outnumbered them. By 1875 the countenances of intellectuals also exceeded the noble total.

Sir Walter Raleigh, one of history's great fashion plates (but only the second nattiest of Elizabeth I's courtiers; the Duke of Buckingham outshone him), appeared on state occasions in jeweled shoes worth in the neighborhood of $100,000.

Although Elizabeth criticized Raleigh and others for such ostentation, she herself left a wardrobe with over 3000 changes of dress.

Worried that his penis was abnormally small, F. Scott Fitzgerald asked Ernest Hemingway into a closet, exposed himself, and asked his fellow author for his honest opinion. Hemingway assured Fitzgerald that his penis was perfectly normal and then, to prove his point, took him to a nearby museum to examine the nude statues.

The blond Celtic hordes encountered by Julius Caesar were often enough not naturals. Bleaching the hair was a fashion among the Gauls.

The Admiral of the Ocean Sea, as Christopher Columbus was created by Ferdinand and Isabella, was known more popularly toward the end of his life as the Admiral of Mosquitoes.

In the brief imprisonment of 1500 that was his final humiliation, Columbus developed a curious pride in the manacles he wore and asked to be buried with them.

"Please let me have the formula for shoe-polish—a brilliant head demands brilliant boots, too."

—Ludwig von Beethoven

Dirty, Vulgar, Debasing: Vice

In 1825 President John Quincy Adams got himself in trouble when he tried to spend $61 of his presidential furniture budget on a pool table. The public outcry was so loud that he finally paid for the table with his own money.

Among the eighteen kinds of games foresworn by Buddha (in the *Pali Discourses*) are plowing with toy plows, turning somersaults, guessing a playfellow's thoughts, and mimicking deformities.

Even after undergoing thirty-six operations for cancer of the jaw, Sigmund Freud continued to smoke cigars.

George Armstrong Custer wrote letters every night to his wife—one was eighty pages long.

In 1973 vodka outsold whiskey in the United States for the first time.

The most popular hobby in the world is stamp collecting.

To gyp someone is to cheat or swindle them. The word comes from gypsy.

The first natives that Columbus's men saw smoking were on the island of Colba, later known as Cuba and later famous for its tobacco.

Vlad IV, fifteenth-century prince of Wallachia (now part of Romania), was known in his time as Vlad the Impaler because of his fondness for impaling people on wooden stakes. During the six years of his rule, he found reasons to impale 40,000 people. The stakes he preferred were long and rather blunt: his victims died excruciating deaths. Vlad IV's father, another nonbenevolent ruler, was known in his day as Vlad Dracul ("Vlad the Devil"); Vlad IV was therefore also called Draculea ("son of the Devil"). Bram Stoker used stories of Vlad IV as the basis for his 1897 novel *Dracula*.

Sears and Roebuck's 94-cent "White Star Secret Liquor Cure" could be administered by wives "in tea, coffee, or food without the consent of the unfortunate victim of the drink habit."

The company claimed it contained such things as cayenne, valerian, ipecac, gold chloride, ammonium muriate, saccharin, scutellaria,

352

and, oh, yes, erythroxylon coca. That is to say, a small dose of cocaine. In addition, though not listed on the label, small amounts of morphine went into the bottle. The Pure Food and Drug Act of 1906 was the first to require that narcotic ingredients be named on the label. Sale of narcotics was unregulated in the United States until 1914.

Though it sounded too good to be true, the Sears product delivered. Drinkers surreptitiously given the "cure" developed an inexplicable new allegiance to coffee.

Among the perquisites of members of the English House of Commons is free snuff. It is dispensed from a box near the chamber entrance to aid in keeping the members awake.

Trying to stave off federal censorship the American film industry adopted its own *Production Code* in 1930. (Two earlier industry attempts, the 1924 *Formula* and the 1927 *Don'ts and Be Carefuls,* hadn't worked well.)

Forbidden under the original Code's profanity clause were *cripes, lousy, nuts,* and the Bronx cheer. Women were not to be referred to as *alley cats, bats, broads, tarts, chippies, sluts,* or *Madam* (in the professional sense).

Damn and *hell* had their own paragraph.

It was against the law in the Massachusetts Bay Colony to celebrate Christmas. In 1659 a fine of five shillings was levied against anyone caught refraining from work or feasting on Christmas Day.

The McDonald's restaurant chain withdrew a plastic coffee stirrer when it was learned that the stirrer was being used as a cocaine spoon.

Charles Fey invented the slot machine.

The Eighteenth Amendment to the Constitution—prohibition— was rejected only by Rhode Island.

Twenty billion bottles of Budweiser beer are made each year.

American poet Amy Lowell smoked cigars.

U. S. Grant ate cucumbers for breakfast.

353

"Whoop," from which is derived "whoopee," is listed in *English Interjections of the Fifteenth Century* as a call to sheep. Walter Winchell believed himself responsible for making a noun of it.

Cigarettes were a byproduct of wartime privations in Spain during the Napoleonic campaigns. Spaniards took to wrapping a little tobacco in a small paper, a *papelito*. Because the new smoke was instantly a fashion among French youth, it is the French name that has stuck.

Alferd E. Packer, who really did spell his first name Alferd, is believed to be the only convicted cannibal in the history of the United States. For that reason, he has become a folk hero to many Americans, particularly in the state of Colorado, where he ate his way to fame.

After service in the Union Army during the Civil War, Packer went west and worked as a guide. In 1874 he led a group of gold-seeking prospectors across Colorado's San Juan mountains. It was winter, and the journey came to an end when the group was trapped in a mountain pass by a mighty blizzard. Only one man walked down from the snowy mountains—Alferd E. Packer. He appeared at the Lake City Indian agency, where he offered no explanations, showed no interest in food, but had a great thirst for whiskey.

When spring thaws melted the mountain snows, the skeletons of five men were found, the head of each split by an ax. Packer was arrested, but he escaped. He was recaptured in 1883 and confessed to killing and eating his five companions. The judge at his trial was furious with Packer; his anger was more political than moral, however. Delivering his sentence, the judge declared, "Stand up, Alferd Packer, you voracious, man-eating son-of-a-bitch. There were seven Democrats in Hinsdale county, and you ate five of them. I sentence you to hang until you are dead, dead, dead as a warning against reducing the Democratic population of the state."

Everything was made ready for the hanging—printed invitations were sent out. But Packer was saved by a legal loophole and escaped the noose. He was sentenced instead to forty years in prison. He served only eighteen: in 1901 he was released following a campaign led by the *Denver Post*. The freed cannibal settled near Denver, where he was popular with local kids. He handed out candy and told amusing tales.

Today, Packer enjoys great fame. Each April, Packer societies in thirteen states have special dinners in his honor (steak tartare is the usual main dish). The University of Colorado is fiercely proud of its Alferd E. Packer Memorial Grille, and Packer Day at the university is celebrated with rib-eating and meat-tossing contests. A bust of Packer was placed in the state capitol, and a plaque was erected on "Cannibal Plateau" in memory of the five men Packer devoured. The political nature of Packer's misdeeds has not been forgotten. In 1952 the Republican legislators of Colorado tried to have a plaque honoring Packer put up in the state capitol, but they were rebuffed by angry Democrats. Republicans still outnumber Democrats in the state.

Phalarus (r. ca. 570–ca. 554 BC), tyrant of Sicily, dined on the flesh of infant children. For nearly sixteen years he terrorized his corner of the island. He is most infamous for a large, hollow brass bull in which he roasted those who in some way displeased him. The victims were placed in the bull, and the bull was set over a roaring fire. Thanks to the bull's cunning design, the cries of the unfortunate victims issued from the bull with a sound like the bellowing of a real bull. This delighted Phalarus. He selected as his first victim Perillus, the smith who had constructed the terrible torture device. It was said of Phalarus that this was the only just act he ever committed.

Among those physiological mysteries to which a great deal of research is not being devoted is the passing of gas (flatus). The weighty *Merck Manual* notes that a complete explanation for the production of intestinal gas is not available.

The *Merck* offers, however, guidance in classifying the symptom and some benchmark performances—141 passages in a single day (70 within one four-hour period) is the highest reported count.

Without pretending to have exhausted the subject, the manual recommends a nomenclature that includes three principle species: the "slidder," also known as the "crowded elevator variety"; the open-sphincter, or "pooh," type; and the staccato percussive sort.

In rare individuals, emission can be willed. One artiste, styling himself Petomane (French *peter,* "to fart"), performed dependably at the Parisian Moulin Rouge.

Federal courts, because of the wording of 18 U.S.C. 1461, have been called upon to make narrow definitions of the words obscene, lewd, lascivious, filthy, and indecent.

Generally speaking the courts have arrived at the following distinctions:

obscene—tends to deprave or corrupt morals; offensive to chastity and modesty.

lewd—tends to excite lustful thoughts; licentious.

lascivious—dissolute, unchaste; relates to sexual impurity; synonym for lewd.

filthy—dirty, vulgar, morally debasing; not as strong as lewd and obscene.

indecent—offending common propriety, delicacy; grossly vulgar; immodest, impure.

Deadly Beat:
Violence

The first Burma Shave signs were installed by Allan Odell, inventor of the idea, near Lakeville, Minnesota, on US Highway 65 in September 1926. Not yet a fully evolved concept, the first five-part ad read: "Cheer Up/ Face/ The War/ Is/ Over."

Custer was the strongest man in his class at West Point.

When the revolutionary mob stormed the Bastille, July 14, 1789, that aged bastion of repressive monarchy, symbol of injustice, contained just seven inmates: four forgers, two lunatics, and one young man of flagrant tastes and doubtful morals detained at his family's behest.

The largest battleships ever built were the *Yamato* and the *Musashi,* Japanese ships constructed just before World War II. Each of the monster ships displaced 72,800 tons, and both were armed with eighteen-inch guns. It took nineteen torpedoes and nineteen bombs to sink the *Musashi* during the Battle of Leyte Gulf; five torpedoes and countless bombs finally sent the *Yamato* under during the Battle of the East China Sea.

At the age of 15, while practicing his fast-draw technique, Nelson Rockefeller shot himself in the leg with an air pistol.

Esarhaddon, an Assyrian king, wanted his vassals to do right by his son, Ashurbanipal, when the time for a succession arrived. In 672 BC, therefore, he required them all to swear it in the names of twenty-two deities and on pain of sixty-two curses. The most imaginative of them provide for transgressors that their families shall change color like chameleons, that they shall never meet other than murderous women, that their clothes shall be made of duckweed, that they be caught in bronze traps, and that they nevermore have any privacy.

When he was 15, Jimmy Carter shot his sister in the rear end with a BB gun.

The destructive power of the test bombs dropped on Bikini atoll in the summer of 1946 inspired a French fashion reporter: he applied the name of the atoll to a new, devastating fashion in women's swimwear: the bikini.

In 1477 Edward IV decided it was time to get rid of his factious younger brother, George, Duke of Clarence. Edward had George locked away in the Tower of London. Since George's favorite drink was malmsey wine (the sweetest variety of Madeira), Edward had him drowned in a large cask of it.

During his first day in the New World, October 12, 1492, Christopher Columbus decided to test the local natives. He drew his sword and extended it, blade first, toward a nearby native. The man reached out and took hold of the sword. The native showed surprise when the sharp blade cut his hand; Columbus was pleased. Columbus took the native's failure to recognize his European weapon as proof that the natives were friendly and peaceful. Two days later Columbus wrote about the natives—the Arawak Indians—in a letter to Queen Isabella in his journal. "When Your Highness so commands," he wrote, "they could be carried off to Castile or be held captive on the island itself because with fifty men they could all be subjugated and compelled to do anything one wishes."

What the Arawaks did was perish. They were wiped out, leaving only one word: *hammock*. The hammock and its name were introduced to Europeans by Columbus. Hammocks were soon being used on ships crossing the Atlantic and exploring other oceans and seas.

Ezra Pound mastered the martial art of jiujitsu. He once grabbed hold of Robert Frost in a restaurant and tossed him over his shoulder.

During a visit to New York City in 1931, Winston Churchill forgot that Americans drive on the other side of the road. He looked the wrong way while crossing a street and was knocked flat by a taxicab.

American poet Vachel Lindsay killed himself by drinking disinfectant.

In 1916 George S. Patton wounded himself in the thigh when he stamped his foot and his Colt .45 fired in its holster. The experience turned Patton against the Colt .45, and although he was fond of packing a pistol, he never packed a Colt .45.

Strafe, meaning to fire from an aircraft at targets on the ground or just to rake targets at close range, comes from the slogan of the Germans in World War I: *Gott strafe England,* "God punish England."

While touring Europe with Buffalo Bill's Wild West show, Annie ("Little Sure Shot") Oakley shot a cigar out of the mouth of Germany's Kaiser Wilhelm.

A single popular song, *Gloomy Sunday,* played over the radio, is credited with raising the Hungarian suicide rate in 1956.

The expression "hoist with his own petard," for which we are indebted to Shakespeare, means literally to be lifted or blown up by one's own bomb.

HISTORIC ASSASSINATIONS

Victim	Details of assassination	D
Philip II, king of Macedonia	Pausanias, young noble with a grudge	33
Julius Caesar, Roman dictator	Stabbed by Brutus, Cassius *et al.* in Senate	4
St. Thomas à Becket, English archbishop	Slain by four knights in cathedral	12/29/1
James I of Scotland	Plot: Sir Robert Graham *et al.*	2/21/1
Henry III of France	Stabbed by fanatic monk (Jacques Clément)	8/2/1
Henry IV of France (de Navarre)	Stabbed by fanatic (François Ravailliac)	5/14/1
Albrecht von Wallenstein, Austrian general	Irish and Scottish officers	2/25/1
Gustavus III of Sweden	Plot: shot by Johan Ankarström	3/29/1
Jean Marat, French revolutionary	Stabbed in bath by Charlotte Corday	7/13/1
Abraham Lincoln, US president	Shot by actor, J. Wilkes Booth, in theatre	4/14/1
Alexander II, emperor of Russia	Nihilist bomb	3/13/1
James Garfield, US president	Shot at station by Charles Guiteau	7/2/1
William McKinley, US president	Shot by anarchist, Leon Czolgosz, at Buffalo	9/6/1
Francis Ferdinand, archduke of Austria	Alleged Serbian plot: shot in car by Gavrilo Princip at Sarajevo (sparked World War I)	6/28/1
Rasputin, powerful Russian monk	By Russian noblemen	12/31/1
Pancho Villa, former Mexican bandit/rebel	Ambushed in car	7/20/1
Anton Cermak, mayor of Chicago	By anarchist Joseph Zangara, with bullet intended for president-elect F D Roosevelt	2/15/1
Engelbert Dollfuss, Austrian chancellor	Shot by Nazis in chancellery	7/25/1
Huey Long, corrupt American politician	By Dr. Carl Austin Weiss	9/8/1
Leon Trotsky, exiled Russian communist leader	Axed in Mexico by Ramon del Rio	8/21/1
Mahatma Gandhi, Indian nationalist leader	Shot by Hindu fanatic, Nathuran Godse	1/30/1
Abdullah ibn Hussein, king of Jordan	In Jerusalem mosque	7/20/1
Anastasio Somoza, Nicaraguan president	Shot by Rigoberto López Pérez, in León	9/21/1
Ngo Dinh Diem, S. Vietnamese president	By generals in coup	11/21/1
John F. Kennedy, US president	Shot in car, in Dallas, Texas	11/22/1
Malcolm X (Little), US Black Muslim leader	Shot at rally	2/21/1
Sir Abubakar Tafawa Balewa, Nigerian premier	Army coup	1/15/1
Rev. Martin Luther King Jr. US Civil Rights leader	Shot on hotel balcony by James Earl Ray in Memphis, Tennessee	4/4/1
Robert F. Kennedy, US senator	Shot by Arab immigrant, Sirhan Sirhan, in Los Angeles (Hotel Ambassador)	6/15/1

Aldo Moro, president of Italy's Christian Democrats and five times prime minister of Italy	Kidnapped by 'Red Brigade' terrorists and later found dead	5/9/1978
Lord Mountbatten, uncle of Duke of Edinburgh	Explosion in sailing boat off coast of Ireland; IRA	8/27/1979
John Lennon, musician/songwriter and ex-Beatle	Shot in street in New York by Mark David Chapman	12/15/1980
Anwar el Sadat, president of Egypt	Shot by rebel soldiers while reviewing military parade	10/6/1981

The Colt .45 was adopted by the US Army in 1911. The army wanted a handgun for use in battles against mounted enemies; they wanted a gun powerful enough to knock over a horse, the theory being that if you got rid of the horse, you got rid of the rider, too.

The famed outlaw Jesse James was a terrible shot—he suffered from conjunctivitis.

Tortures of the Spanish Inquisition were chiefly three:

potro—a table with cords that were tightened gradually around the body by twisting their ends.
toca—water slowly dripped into the mouth by way of a linen cloth forced into the mouth and down the throat.
garrucha—suspension from the ceiling by the wrists, bound behind the back, with weights added to the feet.

The Renaissance noblewoman was well accoutered with her poison-dispensing ring, but in Japan the discreet lethal object was a *kanzashi*, a hairpin often tipped with poison.

When the English biographer, critic, and unabashed homosexual Lytton Strachey was called up for military service in 1916, he gave the officers interviewing him a hard time. "What would you do," asked one of the officers, "if you saw a German soldier attempting to rape your sister?" "I should try," replied Strachey, "to interpose my own body."

Kiaijutsu is the Japanese martial art of martial sound. When the voice is cultivated for its fighting edge, sources agree, it is the vocal quality, not volume, that counts. The highest achievement, which is to kill with the unaided voice, is reputed not to have been accomplished in Japan for over a century.

Use of the kiai is not confined to combat; the voice may be studied for its healing power, too.

Similarly, in Chinese kung fu many schools practice a healing touch. The reverse is dim mak, a touch vibrating with hidden energy, or perhaps aimed at a secret anatomical weakness, that kills its victims weeks or even months after contact.

The great Neapolitan tenor Enrico Caruso was once arrested for pinching a lady's derriere in New York City's Central Park.

Of 1050 mute swans discovered dead in Great Britain in 1966, 65 percent had died in collisions. Because the swan is nearsighted, and because its mass makes its flight control somewhat sluggish, overhead wires are an especial hazard, but they are known to have flown into the cliffs of Dover, airplanes, and bridges.

Occasionally they land on wet roads, apparently mistaking them for rivers, and one of this actuarial group was sat on by a cow.

Sir Hiram Stevens (1840–1916) invented the Maxim machine gun; his son, Hiram Percy Maxim, invented the silencer.

A Chinese recipe for gunpowder of the eleventh century:

1 chin 14 ounces sulphur
2.5 chin saltpeter
5 ounces charcoal
2.5 ounces pitch
2.5 ounces dried varnish
2 ounces dry vegetable matter
5 ounces tung oil
2.5 ounces wax

But by the fourteenth century a European formulation was simply:

1 pound sulphur
2 pounds charcoal
6 pounds saltpeter

German U-boat activity in World War I, which led to America's entering the conflict, involved a total of 360 U-boats, of which 198 were lost. No more than 61 were ever at sea at one time.

Gat is underworld slang for a gun, specifically a revolver. The word is a shortened form of Gatling gun. During the days when guns were called Gats, a holdup man was commonly called a Gat goose, a gat-toter was a gunman, and a holdup was referred to as a gat-up.

The traveler in Italy cannot help but encounter numerous paintings of a seminude man pierced by an alarming number of arrows. The subject of these paintings is Saint Sebastian, a Christian martyr who was very popular with Renaissance painters. The pictures tell only part of Sebastian's tale. A Christian when Christians were being fed to lions, Sebastian joined the Roman army in order to comfort persecuted Christian soldiers. He eventually became an officer in the imperial guard. When it was discovered that Sebastian was a Christian, the emperor Diocletian sentenced him to be a living target for his archers. Although difficult to believe—judging by all the well-placed arrows piercing his body in paintings—Sebastian survived the ordeal. His wounds were healed by Irene, widow of Saint Castulus, another martyr. When Diocletian heard that Sebastian was still alive, he ordered that he be beaten to death with cudgels. Sebastian did not survive the battering.

"Big Berthas," the terrifying howitzers with which the Germans laid siege to the Belgian forts in 1914, were named for Bertha Krupp von Bohlen und Halbach, daughter of Friedrich Alfred Krupp and proprietress of the Krupp Iron Works, where the cannons were made. (The Germans, who knew what Bertha Krupp looked like, called the guns *dicke Bertha*—"fat Bertha.")

Flak, meaning antiaircraft guns or the bursting shells from such weapons, is an acronym from the German *Flieger Abwehr Kannonen,* meaning "antiaircraft guns."

Between 1946 and 1958, Bikini atoll in the Marshall Islands was the site of twenty-three US atomic and hydrogen bomb tests. The first bomb dropped on the area, in July 1946, was adorned with a picture torn from a *Life* magazine—a pinup shot of Rita Hayworth.

A set of artists' paint brushes are practiced as weapons in the obscure kung-fu art of *ban-gwan-pi* (translates: justice brush).

"Brown Bess," nickname for the British issue musket carried by redcoats into the Revolutionary War, was capable of hitting a foot square target at forty yards every time; at 100 yards hits were only 24 out of 42 tries—archers could do about 30 percent better.

Eighteenth- and nineteenth-century kings of Dahomey, who were unusually successful in repelling the incursions of their neighbors and Europeans, maintained an elite guard of several thousand women armed with muskets and cutlasses.

It is said of the "Paris Gun," the special Krupp artillery piece that shelled Paris from eighty miles away during March-April 1918, that its 130-foot barrel vibrated for two minutes after each firing. Barrels of such large weapons must be slung frequently to correct for droop and either the barrel or its liner tube replaced every 50-60 firings. In the case of the Paris Gun, unique girderlike bracing controlled droop, and shells were provided in sets numbered 1-60, each fractionally fatter than the last to compensate for barrel-liner wear.

This was not the largest gun ever built, however, a distinction that belongs to "Gustav" and "Dora," 80 cm (31.5 in) rail guns of World War II. Each was served by two complete antiaircraft regiments.

"Every man has a right to utter what he thinks truth, and every other man has a right to knock him down for it."

—Samuel Johnson (1709–84)

Jean Baptiste Lully, court musician to Louis XIV, was first to impose upon happily anarchic stringplayers the *coup d'archet,* the unified rising and falling of bows. When conducting he beat the time heavily with a staff—and died of the resultant infection when his downbeat jabbed a carbuncle in his foot.

Where Three Roads Meet:
Words and Phrases

A "potwalloper" was more than just a "pot boiler," the word's actual meaning, it referred to voters hurried into an English borough before an election, just in time to meet archaic residency requirements. Before the Reform Act of 1832, such a requirement might entail nothing more than to have "boiled water" at a certain address for a specified length of time.

Alexander J. Ellis (of the Philological Society of Great Britain) in 1879 and subsequent investigators demonstrated the rather mysterious fact that Yorkshiremen counting their sheep, Massachusetts children reciting hide-and-seek formulas, and Maine Indians trading with settlers all used close variants on the names of Celtic, particularly Welsh, numerals.

Also traceable to the Welsh is "eeny, meeney, miney, moe" (one, two, three, four) and "hickory, dickory, dock" (eight, nine, ten).

Double Irish Chain, Courthouse Steps, Kansas Troubles, Lemon Star, True Sunburst, and Virginia Lily are all names of traditional American patchwork quilt designs.

The oldest letter in the alphabet is O.

Blind folios are pages, as at the beginning of a book or separating chapters, that bear no page number though they are counted in assigning the page numbers following them.

There is no word for rat in Latin, or in classical Greek, for that matter. That's because the Romans and Greeks hadn't seen any. When the first rat hordes invaded Europe—like the Mongols they seem to have come from Asia—the best that chroniclers could do was to refer to the *mus major*, "the big mouse." In 1910 *rattus* replaced *mus* in the formal lexicon, though this is merely a latinization of an eleventh-century Anglo-Saxon word.

Dates of the black rat's arrival are not known precisely; estimates hover between the sixth and eighth century AD. But the brown rat arrived in Europe around 1716. Its style of travel was also that of a barbarian army: reports mention waves of these rats descending on towns and massed crossings of the Volga.

The appearance of brown rats in England, around 1728, coincided with the arrival of George II. The unpopularity of the new monarch suggested a name for the new pest: Hanoverian rat. This name might have stuck had a naturalist named John Berkenout not heard a rumor that the rat had actually arrived in England aboard a ship from Norway. With scientific precision, Berkenout nailed the rumor to some made-up Latin and came up with *Rattus norvegicus,* the name that has lasted.

It wasn't until 1775 that the brown, or Norway, rat reached the New World, adding yet another burden to the oppressed colonies.

"Tell it to the Marines" is in the United States a directive to lodge a complaint elsewhere, but in Great Britain, where the expression originated, it is used to indicate skepticism.

The esperanto alphabet, devised by Dr. L. I. Zamenhof, has twenty-eight numbers, all of them Roman but lacking *q, w, x,* and *y.* Splitting *c, j, g, h, s,* and *u* each into two sounds accounts for the balance.

The derisive term *mick,* sometimes used offensively of Irishmen, comes from the common Irish given name Michael. Another common Irish name, Patrick, became paddy, as in paddy wagon. The common Spanish name Diego led to the disparaging term *dago.* The offensive term *kike,* used for Jews, probably originated as *kiki,* a repetition of *-ki,* the common ending of names of Jews from Slavic countries. *Spic,* the offensive word for Latin Americans, supposedly comes from the phrase "no *speek* English."

The word *robot* comes from the Czech word for "slave," *robotnik.* The word was coined by Czech playwright Karel Capek in a play called *R.U.R. (Rossum's Universal Robots),* which was a big success on the New York stage in 1923.

A hangnail doesn't hang, it hurts. The word comes from an Old English word *angnaegl,* "painful prick in the flesh."

Orange, it is often said, has no rhyme in English. Or maybe that's not the problem at all:

> What is the rhyme for porringer
> What is the rhyme for porringer
> The king he had a daughter faire
> And the Prince of Orange her.
>
> —Jacobite song (ca. 1689)

"*A, e, i, o,* and *u* are the vowels and sometimes *y* and sometimes *w*," elementary teachers used to say. But the *w* is only a pure vowel in Welsh, and the only borrowed word still encountered in this spelling is *crwth*, signifying a shallow-bodied stringed instrument of Celtic origin.

Of course, *w* often acts as *u* when it follows another vowel.

The "D" in D-day stands for "day" in the same way that the "H" in H-hour stands for "hour": the repetition is used for emphasis.

John Paul Jones named his ship *Bonhomme Richard* after the Richard in Benjamin Franklin's *Poor Richard's Almanack.*

Italic type was invented by the Venetian printer Aldus Manutius (Aldo Manuzio) in 1500. Manutius devoted himself to publishing Greek and Roman classics, and to save space in Latin texts he had a type designed after the Italian cursive script (said to be the script of Petrarch). He used it in a 1501 edition of Virgil, which he dedicated to Italy. Because of the dedication, the type came to be called Italic.

A very curious word is "colonel" which, in English, is sounded in Spanish and spelled in French. Probably derived from Latin *columna,* for column, or perhaps *corona,* for crown, the English pronunciation comes from the Spanish form, *coronel.*

The phrase *gung ho* came into use during World War II. It was popularized by Evans F. Carlson, a US Marine officer who had served as an observer with the Chinese Army in 1937—*gung-ho* was a Chinese Army motto meaning "work together," and Carlson made it the password of his marines.

British radio operators used "Ack" for the letter *A*, hence ack-ack ("A-A") for antiaircraft fire.

A "turn-shoe" is one that is made inside out and put right side out when finished. This was the chief method of assembly until the mid-nineteenth century, but is now used only for certain specialized and athletic shoes.

Nanook is the Eskimo word for polar bear.

The word *honcho,* used in the United States for "boss," is from the Japanese word *hancho,* meaning "squad leader" (*han,* "squad"; *cho,* "leader").

The vowel sounds of English have changed a great deal since Elizabethan days. Shakespeare rhymed *please* with *knees* and *grace* and rhymed *grapes* with *mishaps.*

When it served the world's writing needs, *abortive* parchment was considered the finest, that is, parchment made from the skins of aborted lamb fetuses.

Military radio and telephone communications require a phonetic alphabet for words that have to be spelled out clearly. During World War II, the alphabet used by American radio operators was Able, Baker, Charlie, Dog, Easy, Fox, George, How, Item, Jig, King, Love, Mike, Nan, Oboe, Peter, Queen, Roger, Sugar, Tare, Uncle, Victor, William, X-ray, Yoke, and Zebra.

The sinking of the *Maine* on February 15, 1898, did much to push the United States into war with Spain. The popular phrase "Remember the *Maine"* is well remembered; the phrase's refrain—"To hell with Spain!"—has been forgotten.

The arcane language of the computer world has given us at least one acronym with an old-fashioned moral: GIGO, which stands for "*garbage in, garbage out*" (if you put garbled information into a computer, you'll get garbled output). To some, GIGO is but a simplistic rewording of Saint Paul's stern warning to the Galatians (6:7), which begins, "Whatsoever a man soweth . . ."

During World War I US Army colonel J. T. Thompson devised a compact machine gun. He dubbed his new weapon the "trench broom." The war ended before Thompson's machine gun could be put into production.

Nicknamed "tommy gun" in Thompson's honor, the gun later found civilian uses in the streets and back alleys of America's urban centers.

In 1859 an army of French and Sardinians won a decisive victory over an army of Austrians near the Lombardy town of Magenta. The very bloody battle provided the name for a newly developed purplish-red dye: magenta.

Tennis was invented in 1873 by Major W. C. Wingfield, an Englishman looking for something new to do at garden parties. To create the game Wingfield combined aspects of squash racquets, court tennis, and badminton. He didn't call the game tennis: he fancied *Sphairistike,* Greek for "ball playing."

People meeting in public squares often exchange unimportant news and gossip. In ancient Rome, as in most contemporary cities, such squares were located where roads crossed. The Latin word for a place where three roads meet is *trivium,* a natural collecting place of information and gossip from many parts —and the origin of the word *trivia*.